MENZIES

The Forgotten Speeches

MENZIES

The Forgotten Speeches

David Furse-Roberts
Editor

Jeparit Press

Published by Jeparit Press, 2017

Jeparit Press was established in 2017 as an imprint of Connor Court Publishing Pty Ltd, in association with the Menzies Research Centre, dedicated to publishing enduring works of Australian political philosophy and history. The imprint is edited by Nick Cater.

Connor Court Publishing Pty Ltd

PO Box 7257

Redland Bay QLD 4165

sales@connorcourt.com

www.connorcourt.com

ISBN: 9781925501506

Cover design by Branded Graphics

Front cover photograph of Sir Robert Menzies © News Limited

Back cover photograph of Sir Robert Menzies giving a victory salute c. 1954 © Fairfax Media

CONTENTS

FOREWORD

If there is bright side to four decades of indifference towards Sir Robert Menzies it is this: new generations can delight in discovering his wisdom and wit for the first time.

Few if any of these speeches have been published before and only a handful of them have been available in digital form. Most have been preserved in typewritten manuscripts in the basement of the National Library on the shores of Lake Burley Griffin. Like the discovery of Tutankhamun's tomb, the treasures retrieved by David Furse-Roberts from the vault beg a question: what next?

The Menzies Research Centre's twin tasks – promoting sound public policy and celebrating Sir Robert's legacy – are inextricably linked. This volume is much more than a record of our history; it is a guide to the present that charts a path to the future. It is an important step towards rejuvenating the philosophy that empowered Australians to strive and prosper in the decades of reconstruction after World War II.

Sir Robert's singular ability to capture the essence of his liberal philosophy in a memorable turn of phrase provides the grip needed to traverse the shifting sands of today's political landscape. They provide an antidote to the divisive politics of identity, illiberalism and irrationalism that bedevil us today.

Menzies: The Forgotten Speeches demonstrates the persuasive power of the English language. It is a reminder that forceful arguments are crafted, not spun; that potent expressions are worked on, not workshopped; and that focus groups are no substitute for a focused mind.

Nick Cater
Executive Director
Menzies Research Centre
March, 2017

PREFACE

Robert Gordon Menzies served as Australia's prime minister for longer than anybody before or after. He served in peace and war, the wars being as far apart as the Second World War and the Vietnam War. He presided over an era of unprecedented wellbeing for the typical family, and he initiated the nation's switch of focus – away from Europe and towards Asia. His nineteen years as prime minister formed a surprisingly long period, because Australia, unlike nearly every other western democracy, compelled its national leader to face re-election every three years. He won eight federal elections.[1]

One reason for his triumphs in Canberra was his ability to explain and above all to persuade. As a speech maker, whether in parliaments or town halls or private dinners, he was, at times, breath-taking. His voice, melodious, was pleasing to the ears, except those of his opponents. He possessed the skills of an actor without appearing to be one. At crowded public meetings when he heard the loud remarks of a hostile interjector he must have inwardly rejoiced, knowing how easily he would exploit the interruption. "His capacity to think on his feet was exceptional", recalled James Killen, another parliamentary orator. Sir Robert Menzies, he added, "appealed to the mind, not to the heart". He could speak simply, even about complex things.

Adversity helped to secure his political longevity. His first period in power had ended in August 1941 when various politicians in his own party and the heads of the big-city media (especially the Fairfax and Murdoch newspapers and the now defunct Melbourne *Argus*) turned against him. He was not defeated: he chose to resign. During the following eight years in opposition he created and consolidated a new political party, the Liberal Party of Australia. Nowadays seen as essentially a conservative he had radical ideas; and the new Liberals – more perhaps than any previous party in the democratic world – allowed women to wield equal power behind the scenes.

---

1 Robert Menzies won the Federal elections of 1940, 1949, 1951, 1954, 1955, 1958, 1961 and 1963.

Back in the 1940s, the political, economic and military crises were more severe and frequent than they are today, but Menzies used them as building blocks on which to construct a distinctive ideology. When the welfare state was expanding quickly under John Curtin and Ben Chifley during those Labor years, 'Bob' Menzies welcomed social security but saw its long-term dangers. He more or less predicted Canberra's recurring dilemma: how to find a balance between a state that rightly protects its people but also weakens them as individuals by making them depend too much on governments. As early as 1943 he predicted that a high level of social security could lead to huge national debts and a decline in individual enterprise and vigour. "Show me a nation in which everybody lives on the government", he told a crowd in a suburban hall, "and I will unhesitatingly declare it a nation whose decline and fall are at hand." In Canberra in 1952, he insisted that a leader had to show "a willingness to accept unpopularity" if his policy was crucial for the nation's future.

A federalist, he admired the common sense and political acumen of those who in the 1890s shaped the Commonwealth constitution. But half a century later he believed that education, primarily a state responsibility, was so important that the Commonwealth must "fundamentally" be the pilot rather than just the wealthy paying-passenger. As prime minister he was to lead the centralising trend whereby universities and then secondary schools were heavily financed by Canberra. At the same time he and his Coalition colleague, Sir Earle Page, guided the federal government into the expensive field of health, while refusing to follow Britain's national health scheme with its limitations on the patients' freedom of choice. All in all, he was rather more a centralist than is now realised.

Thanks to David Furse-Roberts, we can read this collection of "forgotten speeches". He selected and edited these speeches, tackled the hard task of transcribing and punctuating those which existed only in the sound archives, and annotated and introduced them. Many readers will come to appreciate his work, for it helps to bring Menzies alive again.

Professor Geoffrey Blainey AC
Melbourne, January 2017

INTRODUCTION

From the Funeral Oration of Pericles in 431 BC to Winston Churchill's "Finest Hour" speech of 1940, the reputation of great leaders has been forged by their power at the podium. Long after the policy blunders or personal foibles of princes, presidents and prime ministers have been forgotten; it has often been their defining speeches that have earned them an immortal place in the history books. Australia's greatest Prime Minister, Sir Robert Menzies, appreciated that the three statesmen he greatly admired, Edmund Burke, Abraham Lincoln and Winston Churchill, were each distinguished by his command of the language. There is little doubt that Menzies desired to be similarly remembered for mastering the art of speech-making. Speech "remains the most potent instrument for spiritual, social and political progress,"[1] he said in 1963. "Its practitioners are numerous, for it is attractive. Its masters are few, for its difficulties are great."

The purpose of this volume is to showcase what have arguably become the "forgotten speeches". They are forgotten for the reason that they have never been published; few Australians could be aware of the riches that flowed from Menzies' pen that lie dormant in the archives. Themes as diverse as communism, Christianity, democracy, the Cold War, the role of government, the place of women, citizenship and Australian national identity were explored with alacrity and rigour. The project of compiling these speeches of Menzies into a publishable volume arose from my abiding admiration of Australia's longest serving prime minister and my firm belief that his Liberal vision of "civic unselfishness" is of enduring value to our national life. My fascination with Menzies was piqued during my teenage years when I read the story of his steely determination and irrepressible optimism to overcome the seemingly impossible. After his inglorious departure from the prime ministership in 1941, Billy Hughes famously quipped that Menzies was "as helpless as a beetle

---

1 Robert Menzies, "Speech and Speakers", *The George Adlington Syme Oration*, University of Melbourne, 28 May 1963.

on its back", yet, less than a decade later, he returned triumphantly as Prime Minister to lead his country from 1949 to 1966. Already struck by Menzies' stately bearing and appearance, I tuned into some old film clips and was even more enamoured by his richly cultivated elocution and supreme command of the "King's English". To me, his baritone voice captured the "best of British" oratory with an authentic Australian touch that could appeal to governors and gardeners alike. While urbane and erudite, he was the master of simplicity in his clarity and directness of speech.

Since joining the Menzies Research Centre in January 2016, my personal interest in Menzies only intensified as I delved through files of his speeches in the National Library to appreciate not only his style but his substance. In my research for *The Forgotten Speeches*, I uncovered not a dusty old "museum piece" at home with the Morphy-Richards toaster and AWA radiogram, but a prescient and forward-looking statesman whose ideas on freedom, foreign policy, education and immigration gave inspiration and shape to modern Australia. The speeches compiled for this volume revealed that Menzies was both a policy pragmatist and an idealist. As well as making routine pronouncements on a range of policy areas, Menzies also found suitable occasions to probe the deeper philosophical questions beyond the mundane realm of day-to-day politics. The liberal philosophy he espoused, in Margaret Thatcher's words, reflected "a warm and deep understanding of human nature". At the same time as encouraging every individual to be their best self and make that best "even better", he also reminded men and women that they were all "members of one another" and their "brother's keeper".

The 51 speeches in this volume cover a chronological expanse of Menzies' public life from his time as a young Victorian minister in the late 1920s to his days as a distinguished elder statesman in the mid-1970s. This collection of speeches includes a mixture of radio broadcasts, messages, addresses, orations, lectures and treatises. The speeches of Menzies were delivered in a range of locations from the floor of the House of Representatives to town halls, school assembly halls, churches, lecture theatres and studios. The occasions attending these speeches ranged from the solemn to the celebratory. Whether it was his 1947 Pleasant Sunday Afternoon address on the perils of the resurgent, all-powerful state, a citizenship ceremony in 1963 to welcome new Australians, or a dinner in 1973 to toast Australia's links to Scotland, Menzies was at hand to deliver a fitting speech.

What came first: the speaker or the politician? Menzies had cultivated the art of public speaking long before entering the public fray. His extra-curricula participation in debating contests, addresses to the Historical Society and the fulfilment of his duties as president of the Students' Representative Council at the University of Melbourne gave Menzies a taste of public speaking. The training in mooting and courtroom advocacy that Menzies received through his legal studies furthered his cultivation of the forensic art.[2] His rapid advancement in the legal profession was in no small part attributable to his recognised public speaking prowess as an advocate. Throughout his career, Menzies cared greatly about the art of speaking, whether in Parliament, to international gatherings or to more homely audiences, like those of the Pleasant Sunday Afternoons in Melbourne's Wesley Church.

Menzies was eagerly sought after as a speaker to open new buildings, factories, hydro-electric works, lakes, fetes, shows, hospitals, schools, colleges and sporting events, and was in constant demand as an after dinner speaker. Menzies was a master of what he thought of as the science of government, but he also saw politics as an art, and talked of speaking as the acme of that art.[3] Frederick Shedden, the Defence Department Secretary who worked closely with Menzies in both of his administrations and accompanied him to England in 1941, was one who saw lucidity as the secret of Menzies' success as a speaker in all settings:

> His crystal-clear mind and beautiful English explain difficult things that worry the ordinary citizen, in such a manner that he [the citizen] feels they are the very things he has been feeling but unable to express himself.[4]

2 Allan W Martin, "Speech is of Time", *The Sir Robert Menzies Lecture* (Melbourne: 1994).
3 Ibid.
4 Frederick Shedden quoted by Martin, "Speech is of Time".

A young Geoffrey Blainey was another who deeply admired the public speaking abilities of Menzies. Recalling his days as a pupil at Melbourne's Wesley College, the Australian historian offered this assessment of Menzies when he observed him speak at his *Alma Mater*:

> He was the finest speaker I had heard – such eloquence, such timing, such a sense of the majesty of words, such a feeling for the occasion. There was a stately courtesy, which sometimes he even used when criticising opponents, though he was also capable of strong words delivered with mighty force. He had wit and a sense of fun: he could mock himself when the occasion called for it.[5]

Like Burke, Lincoln and Churchill, Menzies viewed public speaking as a critical tool to mastering the art of politics. For Menzies, the power of speech could not only communicate ideas but inspire the minds and hearts of people in a democracy. For speakers to effectively connect and engage with their constituencies, Menzies saw the authenticity of speech as paramount. For this reason, he tended to shun the modern practice of outsourcing speech-preparation to professional speech-writers. Instead, he preferred his words to flow directly from his own mouth and to formulate his speeches spontaneously from the podium using only minimal notes. The object of the speaker was to move and persuade. The speaker must project his or her personality in words which at least appeared to come fresh from their mind and lips. The interest of the audience was piqued not by reading verbatim from a transcript but by the power and passion in the natural elocution of a speech.[6]

As a keen student of history, Menzies also appreciated that it was the self-made speeches which would stand the test of time by virtue of both their oratorical quality and authenticity. Citing the example of Abraham Lincoln, he observed that if the President "had not, on the way to Gettysburg, discarded the prepared speech and resorted to his own language, what he had to say would never have rung around the

---

5 Geoffrey Blainey, "Reflections on the Current State of the Nation", *The Sir Robert Menzies Lecture* (Melbourne: 1991).
6 Robert Menzies, *The Measure of the Years* (London: Cassell & Co, 1970), p 10.

world or achieved immortality". It was speeches, such as the Gettysburg Address, which would allow the future historian to perceive a past figure whom they had neither known nor heard, through their own words. If the speech, however, was drafted by an anonymous speechwriter and not the statesman, "the historian's light on the statesman becomes a little dim".[7] The historian would still be able to grasp the message and basic ideas in the speech written for the historical figure, but the important nuances of meaning and expressions of emotion would not be so apparent. In his self-made speeches such as his *Forgotten People* address, the memorable turns of phrase and personalised style of Menzies was there for future historians to appreciate. As the product of an individual's own mind and voice, a person's style of speech can be regarded as unique as their own fingerprints. Menzies, of course, was no exception with his speeches exhibiting a distinctive structure and pattern. Combining whimsicality with gravitas, they would typically begin with a few light-hearted remarks and anecdotes before delving into the substance of his message with a few humorous quips along the way.

....

The project of publishing the speeches of Menzies is an important and timely one given the somewhat limited coverage they have received in the existing literature. Menzies' memoirs, *Afternoon Light* (1967) and *The Measure of the Years* (1970), gave readers a feel for the pattern and style of Menzies' language. The memoirs revealed his candid outlook on significant issues, his reaction to events such as Britain's entry into the Common Market. They did more than that, however; they did justice to shedding light on the interests and preoccupations of a very public yet reserved figure, not least on his twin pastimes of cricket and the law.

Authentic as they were, however, the memoirs differ from his speeches in two important respects. First, they were by definition retrospective while the speeches were contemporaneous. While they discussed some contemporary developments of the period in which they were written, they were largely a reflective account of his past experiences and achievements in public office. The included pen

---

7 Menzies, op. cit., p 10.

portraits of the statesmen he had met and recapitulations of the policy initiatives his government had introduced. Unlike the speeches he made at the podium, these memoirs did not necessarily capture the occasion as it unfolded before his very eyes. As such, they lacked the impromptu delivery and instantaneous quality that his speeches typically offered.

Second, the memoirs represented a different style of writing from that of his speeches. The speeches exhibited a distinctive structure, pattern and prose, imbued, for the most part, with a natural cadence and rhythm. By frequently beginning his sentences with conjunctions such as "and" or "but", it may appear Menzies was flouting the rules of modern grammar but, in truth, he was merely following the speech-pattern typical of great literature such as the King James Bible. Indeed, it is noteworthy that other great speech-makers from John F Kennedy to Barack Obama have similarly transgressed these "rules". Menzies' speeches were extemporised rather than composed. He neither employed a speechwriter to write his scripts nor composed his own, apart from a few set occasions. Rather, he would scribble down notes from which he would develop his lines as he spoke to his audience. This collection of his speeches from the podium therefore presents all of Menzies' trademark anecdotes, witticisms and turns of phrase that were largely absent from the memoirs penned at his desk.

Readers turning to the biographical studies of Menzies, which might have been expected to offer snippets of Menzies' speeches, will find the offerings somewhat limited. In writing *Menzies: Last of the Queen's Men* (1968), Kevin Perkins drew upon raw materials, such as newspaper files, parliamentary and public library records in conjunction with the personal recollections of others, to produce one of the first biographies of Menzies since his retirement. Perkin's biography offered some interesting insights into both Menzies' public and private life but there was scant evidence that the author engaged directly with Menzies' speeches. Cameron Hazlehurst in *Menzies Observed* (1979) undertook the somewhat similar task of producing a portrait of both Menzies "the politician" and Menzies "the man". To a far greater extent than Perkins, Hazlehurst incorporated excerpts from Menzies' own speeches and correspondence into his narrative. While these provided readers with some welcome glimpses of Menzies' speech-making, they were confined to a limited number of public occasions at which he spoke. As part of Hazlehurst's aim to provide a well-rounded portrait of the statesman, these fragments of Menzies were also mixed with large numbers of extracts from journalists, parliamentary colleagues and other public figures. Like Hazlehurst's work, Marjorie Jackson's *The Menzies Era 1949-1966* (1987) reproduced a wide range of documentary sources, including some welcome excerpts from Menzies' parliamentary speeches on bank nationalisation and communism. The selection, again, however, was limited with Jackson's study primarily focused on exploring the issues and themes of the Menzies era rather than on the actual speeches of the Prime Minister himself.

As to the modern biographies and studies of Menzies, the most ambitious and comprehensive is A W Martin's *Robert Menzies: A Life* (Vol I, 1993) and (Vol 2, 1999). In this two volume work, Martin drew on a vast array of primary and secondary source material, including the Menzies Family Papers, to produce a scholarly, authoritative account of Menzies' personal and public life. In what is still arguably the flagship biography of the former Prime Minister, Martin continued the tradition of using original sources to illuminate the finer contours of Menzies' life but surprisingly few of these were public speeches that Menzies had given either before, during or after his prime ministership. In the meantime, Scott Prasser, J R Nethercote and John Warhurst produced *The Menzies Era: A Reappraisal of Government, Politics and Policy* (1995). The study examined several public policy facets of Menzies and his government but featured few references to his speeches. Desiring to chronicle the politics and events of the post-war period presided over by Menzies, the former Australian Prime Minister, John Howard, published *The Menzies Era: The Years that Shaped Modern Australia* (2014). In this comprehensive volume, Howard provided a sympathetic yet erudite account of the preoccupations and policy achievements of the Menzies years. While Howard's *Menzies Era* meticulously engaged with the relevant historical documentation, there were only limited instances where it drew directly on the speeches of Menzies. Most recently, John Nethercote's edited volume, *Menzies: the Shaping of Modern Australia*

(2016) provided a critical analysis of Menzies' prime ministership and policy achievements but did not seek to showcase any of his speeches.

Only two compendiums of Menzies' speeches have being released to date. In 1958, the London-based publisher, Cassell & Company, released *Speech is of Time*, a collection of sixteen speeches and articles chosen by Menzies himself. The title was suitably inspired by the maxim of the Scottish writer Thomas Carlyle who wrote that "Speech is of Time, Silence is of Eternity". In a brief preface, the Prime Minister revealed that he had made his selection of speeches from "many hundreds" for the benefit of "future students of what is now recent or contemporary history". He anticipated that his selection of speeches would "be of some help to those who fear that the dramatic impact of modern science and technology may distort our sense of social values and further depress those human studies which remain the greatest hope of true civilisation". His purpose of publishing these speeches was therefore to convey his own worldview and set of principles to future generations who may validly question why the Prime Minister spoke and acted as he did on the great domestic and foreign policy issues of his time.

Menzies' choice of published speeches in 1958 was no doubt influenced by the international climate of the time and the prevailing course of events in Australia and the world. With Menzies conceiving the Cold War as not only a geopolitical standoff between the United States and the Soviet Union, but as virtually a cosmic battle for the soul of human civilisation, he believed it was more pressing than ever to reaffirm the moral precepts he regarded as critical to the flourishing of Western civilisation and modern democracy. Accordingly, Menzies included his headland speeches, *Freedom in Modern Society* (1936) and *Democracy and Management* (1958), as timely apologetics for democracy and its merits. With the intensifying space race between the two superpowers driving a huge investment in science and technology, Menzies was anxious to ensure that these rapid Cold War advances in machinery, transportation and weaponry would not come at the expense of human understanding, peace and goodwill as they had done so earlier in the century with two horrific world wars. In his 1958 address on "Modern Science and Civilisation" to the Australasian Medical Congress, Menzies reminded his audience that science as an instrument could only accomplish good if the human mind and spirit behind it was also good.

In addition to the spectre of the Cold War, the changing place of Britain in the post-war order was another development that weighed heavily on the mind of Menzies who still saw Australia's interests as intimately intertwined with those of the "old country". As Britain's prestige as a world power continued to wane in the post-war years, with the Suez Crisis of 1956 representing a seminal crisis of confidence for Britain and its Commonwealth, the Prime Minister chose to devote a large portion of his volume to speeches addressing this theme. These speeches served the purpose of highlighting Menzies' abiding faith in the English tradition, his affection for the fraternity of the Commonwealth as a beacon for freedom and civilisation, his admiration for Winston Churchill, Stanley Baldwin and other leading statesmen, his immediate support for Britain's stand against President Nasser of Egypt during the Suez Crisis; and his circumspect attitude towards the bold internationalism of the United Nations.

Almost six decades later, Menzies' *Speech is of Time* stands as an invaluable resource, furnishing students of history and politics with rich first-hand insights into both the mindset and the distinctive speaking-style of Australia's longest serving Prime Minister. The pivotal role of Britain in world affairs and the defence of civilised human virtues were two of Menzies' enduring preoccupations that this historic volume continues to illuminate for contemporary readers. Yet it represents a long-outdated and incomplete canon of Menzies' speeches that fails to do sufficient justice to the sheer breadth of subjects and themes on which he spoke with eloquence and insight. Following his retirement from office in 1966, there would have been the opportunity to publish a successive volume of fresh speeches and writings but this project was never undertaken. Thus, to this day, his headland speeches from 1959 onwards remain unpublished and largely forgotten.

Since Menzies' own *Speech is of Time*, the Victorian Division of the Liberal Party in 2011 edited and republished *Robert Menzies' The Forgotten People and Other Studies in Democracy*. With a thoughtful introductory essay by Dr David Kemp and a foreword by Menzies' daughter, Heather Henderson, this volume represented the first posthumous publication of Menzies' recorded 1942 speeches. Whilst Menzies published his original edition in 1943, it had long since been out of print and the republication of this volume in 2011 brought many of Menzies' most historic speeches within the reach of a new generation to study and appreciate. Broadcast from radio studios during his "wilderness years" of the early 1940s, the *Forgotten People* speeches are of singular historical importance, aiding our understanding of the political philosophy that became the central core of the Liberal Party founded two years later.

While the Liberal philosophy espoused by Menzies in 1942 stemmed largely from the immediate concerns of the people his new party would seek to represent, it stood within the broad stream of liberalism embodied by such figures as Edmund Burke, Alexis de Tocqueville and John Stuart Mill. Even years before Friedrich Hayek penned his *The Road to Serfdom* in 1944, Menzies understood the need for free people to safeguard the liberal democratic tradition from the challenge of statist ideologies, whether fascist or communist. In his 1936 speech, *Freedom in Modern Society*, the future Prime Minister remarked that "the chief end of totalitarianism is to glorify power and enjoy it forever, while the chief end of democracy is the achievement and development of individual freedom". As Nick Cater observed in *Quadrant* (September 2016), "it is a mark of Menzies' intellectual capacity that he foreshadows Hayek by warning that tyranny is the inevitable consequence of centrally planned state economic intervention". With overreaching State control, "the abandonment of classical liberal principles leads to a loss of freedom, stagnancy and weakening of moral fibre".

As *Speech is of Time* would to later, *Robert Menzies' The Forgotten People* performed the critical task of showcasing Menzies' own words to a wider readership, introducing not only liberalism and democracy, but also topics as diverse as women in war, post-war planning, the

Statute of Westminster, education, compulsory unionism and even "the importance of cheerfulness". Most importantly, the volume succeeded in capturing the liberal philosophy of Menzies in what proved to be an eminently formative phase of his career in which he publicly articulated and developed the political creed he would go on to champion as Prime Minister for over sixteen years. For all the invaluable insights it offered into Menzies' original thought, however, *The Forgotten People* captured only a narrow chronological span of Menzies' speeches from just the year 1942. In the speeches of that year, the themes of the war effort and the defence of the free world from totalitarian conquest predominated. But as important as these preoccupations were for Menzies, there were numerous other salient events and subjects that commanded his attention in both the years before and after. These included the ongoing flourishing of liberal democracy, the eventual formation of the Liberal Party in 1944, the challenge of communism both in Australia and abroad, the onset of the Cold War after 1945, the great post-war policy questions of social security, health, education and immigration, the coronation of Queen Elizabeth in 1953, Australia's developing relations with its South East Asian neighbours, Australia's evolving national identity, the rich and enduring legacy of the Judeo-Christian tradition, and not least, the importance of good character and speech.

....

This volume can be seen as a series of snapshots of Menzies' thoughts spanning almost half a century of public life. They are arranged thematically rather than chronologically, allowing readers to appreciate each distinctive limb of Menzies' political outlook. The first chapter takes "Liberalism and Free Enterprise" as the opening theme to cover the speeches where Menzies had set out to further define and develop his guiding philosophy of Australian liberalism. While his *Forgotten People* speeches of 1942 formed the primary blueprint of his political creed, Menzies used subsequent forums to restate and elaborate his liberal principles. Most importantly, he used such occasions to explain how he and his new liberal movement would apply these principles to

11

the public policy issues of the day, including post-war reconstruction, education and social security. This chapter includes keynote speeches at two historic moments for the Liberal Party of Australia: the Albury Conference of December 1944 in which the party was inaugurated, and the Sydney Rally of August 1945, where the party made its official public debut.

In chapter two, "Freedom and Democracy," Menzies expounds the basic human impulses that make societies, such as Australia, truly democratic. Typically lengthier in nature than many of his routine policy speeches, these addresses resembled philosophical treatises in which Menzies would take time to reflect on the ethics and practices that individual men and women needed to cultivate in order to build a strong and free society for all.

In chapter three, "Politics, Parliament and Government", Menzies discusses the great themes, traditions, institutions and personalities of the political world he inhabited. These included the menacing presence of communism both during and after the Second World War, the challenge of post-war reconstruction, the choice confronting Australians between the liberal democratic pathway and the democratic socialism offered by Labor, the proper responsibilities and limits of government, the practicalities of Australian federalism, and the relationship of politics to other professions, including medicine, the law and the media.

Menzies' consciousness of Australia's place in the world had both a contemporaneous and an historical dimension. Accordingly the fourth chapter, "Australia and the World", catalogues speeches where Menzies spoke of Australia's international links in each of these two senses. As Prime Minister, Menzies was no isolationist as he recognised that Australia, as a global contributor, had a consequential part to play in the Second World War and a cause to defend in the Cold War. As Australia engaged closely with its allies and neighbours in the prevailing world order, Menzies also appreciated the importance of Australia's historical ties with Britain and argued that these should never be allowed to diminish, even as Britain and Australia became more enmeshed in their own respective regions.

The fifth chapter, "National Identity and Citizenship", contains speeches which reveal that Menzies envisioned an Australia that was enterprising and ruggedly individualist yet, at the same time, a warm and friendly community of citizens. To be sure, he took great pride in the fact that many of Australia's core institutions and values were inherited from Britain but believed that Australia had cultivated its own unique qualities. In a citizenship ceremony, he contrasted Australia's openness and relative lack of class-consciousness with the "snobberies of class" found in the "older countries of the world".

Turning to Menzies' chief policy preoccupations during his time in office, chapter six canvases some of the keynote speeches Menzies made on education, an abiding interest of his since young adulthood. Imbued with a love of learning from his Scots heritage, Menzies regarded the provision of quality education, and university education especially, as a priority for Australian governments to invest in for not only the academic enrichment of the young but also for the future health of human civilisation. With so much of the 20th century disfigured by war and human barbarism, Menzies saw education, particularly in the humanities disciplines, as fundamental to advancing human understanding, peace and goodwill.

Together with education, social security was another policy pre-occupation for Menzies. Chapter seven features speeches by the Liberal Party founder on how government in the post-war era could help guarantee the social welfare and security of Australians. The first two speeches in this section reveal how Menzies desired to recalibrate Australia's social welfare system according to the principle of "contribution". With welfare recipients making a contribution under a proposed scheme of "social insurance", they would gain a sense of healthy self-respect and dignity. Echoing the words of the British economist, Sir William Beveridge, Menzies aspired to deliver a social welfare system that would not stifle "incentive, opportunity and responsibility". With Menzies always envisioning a critical role for private enterprises in the welfare sector, his third speech in this chapter pays tribute to the work of charities such as Legacy for the indispensable niche they fulfill in providing personalised care and attention to those in need.

While Menzies is understandably remembered for his long and illustrious reign in politics, it was preceded by a very distinguished legal career at the Victorian Bar. His interest in, and love for, the law remained a constant. Chapter eight, "The Law and the Constitution", includes two of his speeches by that bookended his public life. The first was made while serving as a junior minister in 1928; the last was made in 1974, during his twilight years. Despite the four decades which separate these speeches, a definite unifying theme emerges which was Menzies' profound esteem for the law, and the Australian Constitution especially, for its role in safeguarding the personal rights and liberties of all individuals.

The worldview of conviction politicians such as Menzies cannot fully be understood without considering their spiritual principles or religious faith. Chapter nine, "Faith and Religion", includes speeches where Menzies freely spoke his mind on matters of spiritual significance. While he was certainly not given to ostentatious, public displays of his religiosity, his Scots Presbyterian faith was real and he did not conceal the fact that his views on politics, culture and ethics were informed by Judeo-Christian precepts. As the speeches in this section reveal, his anti-communism was largely driven by the hostility of the ideology towards religion and Christianity; his warm rapport with Australia's Jewish community was based upon his profound respect for the Hebrew tradition and its contribution to Western civilisation; and, finally, the sacred text of the Bible for him represented "the repository of our faith and inspiration".

With Menzies frequently typecast as the symbol of the old Australia, along with its conservative attitudes on gender, it may come as a surprise to some readers that Menzies took an early interest in advancing the status and wellbeing of women. This tenth chapter, "Status and Role of Women", includes two speeches by Menzies where he spoke of his vision to see women not only play a greater part within his Liberal Party, but also to see their participation in higher education and the professions increase over time. To be sure, his conception of a woman's role within the family remained fairly traditional but he did not believe that this was

14

necessarily at odds with advancing the status of women in public and professional life.

It is fitting that a collection of speeches should conclude with a chapter on rhetoric and oratory. In "Speech, Language and Character", it becomes clear that Menzies not only practised but preached the art of fine speech-making. His favoured forum at which to impress the importance of good speech and language was the school assembly hall, where he saw the rising generation as tomorrow's torchbearers of his beloved English tongue. For Menzies, the practice of polished speaking and writing went hand-in-hand with the cultivation of good moral character. From his speeches, it is evident that he envisioned the model citizen as somebody who could not only speak and write well, but as somebody who possessed inner reserves of courage, honesty and courtesy. As a classic democrat, he believed that the flourishing of freedom in society ultimately depended upon the character of its citizens.

In showcasing this diverse collection of Menzies' speeches on a broad range of themes, this volume undertakes to familiarise readers with Menzies' original thoughts on the politics, policies and ideas that helped define modern Australia. In addition, this collection serves to acquaint readers with Menzies' unique and memorable style of speech. In an age when the great art of oratory is less esteemed and seldom practised, when politicians are inclined to read, usually verbatim, from scripts prepared by others, this volume will give readers a feel for how real speeches can be crafted in the hands of master.

1

LIBERALISM AND FREE ENTERPRISE

A Liberal Revival, Broadcast, Melbourne (29 October 1943)

As Menzies succeeded in 1944 to weld fourteen disparate non-Labor movements into a new cohesive political force to supersede the moribund United Australia Party, he decided to take the name "Liberal" for his new Party. Much of the inspiration for adopting this new name can be found in this speech where he called for an Australian "revival" of liberal thought. For all his denunciation of Labor socialism, he was at pains to emphasise that the alternative he was seeking was not a return to a *laissez-faire*-style "reactionary capitalism" but an enlightened liberal philosophy that fostered individual initiative and enterprise with an eye to realising social justice for every citizen. Menzies had understood Australia's political tradition to be basically liberal, but with the wartime challenges of communism and fascism from abroad, together with the ascendency of the Labor Party domestically, liberalism was a tradition he was keen to revive for the present and future. For it to flourish, it needed to be sustained by principles and policies that made it more possible for every man and woman to lead a free, full and dignified life. Far from desiring to promote a selfish capitalism, however, Menzies' creed of liberalism held that the rights of individuals to seek profit and reward for themselves must be subordinate to their public and private responsibilities to their neighbour.

....

Australia is undoubtedly at the beginning of a revival of liberal political thought. It will no doubt be one of my functions in the coming months to speak and write about various aspects of this matter. But there will be involved many conferences, much thought and work, a great stirring of minds, before any widespread Australian campaign can begin.

My purpose tonight is therefore to give you some preliminary material about which you may weave your own ideas. A good deal has been said recently in the press about the desirability of changing the name of the United Australia Party and many suggestions have been made as to what new name it should adopt. Few people will, I think, not agree that the name "United Australia Party" has lost a good deal of the significance which attached to it at the time of its creation, when Mr Lyons[8] and his followers, in association with the then "National party", took part in a new grouping of political forces to which the name United Australia Party was given.

But the first thing that we should establish in our own minds is that we don't solve any political problem merely by changing a name. To have true significance and validity, a new name should describe a new movement; and a new movement in politics should not be content merely with an election programme. It should have a political philosophy, or as I prefer to put it, a political religion. Great movements are never purely a matter of organisation, tremendously important though organisation is. Nor can they be produced manually by artificial means. To have a really great movement, one worthwhile, you must have great ideas. That there are great ideas inherent in what we call the "liberal" approach to politics nobody can doubt, and my colleagues and I will hope to play an active part in formulating and expressing them.

But our task is rendered more difficult by a good deal of the devastatingly clever propaganda put forward in Australia by those opposed to the liberal tradition and the liberal conception. The communists, for example, who have lived and grown on capitalising grievances and whose approach to social and political institutions is a destructive one, have for many years tried to persuade people that in the modern world you must be either a Fascist or a Communist, that is, a supporter of right-wing or left-wing dictatorship. This sort of argument did not make very much headway until relatively recently, but the Australian Communist has had such a boost from the efforts and success

---

8 Joseph Aloysius ('Joe') Lyons (1879-1939) was Menzies' predecessor as Australian Prime Minister from 1932 to 1939 and leader of the former United Australia Party (UAP).

of Russian soldiers that the space they now obtain through almost every medium of publicity is out of all proportion to their deserts. In their eyes – or, at least, in their mouths – to be against communism is to be for fascism.

What nonsense this is to preach in a country which is essentially liberal and which distrusts all fascism, brown or black or red. To take another example of current propaganda, Labour journals and advocates set out always to tar their opponents with the brush of "big business", as if our choice was between socialism and reactionary capitalism with uncontrolled competition and an economic law of the jungle as the alternative to complete State ownership and management. This argument has about it that kind of bogus logic which may easily deceive people unless they are awake. The fault in the logic is of course that in this world the choice is not between dead black and clear white or between bright red and bright blue. Sensible people may very well prefer a blend of colour and indeed we know that the harmonies of nature (which are no bad example for us, after all) are the production not of a harsh choice between extremes but of almost infinite compromise and variety.

The choice is not between extremes. The choice in practical truth is between communism or fascism on the one hand and an enlightened Liberal system on the other, which has no desire whatsoever to go back to unrestricted and ruthless competition, but which does see in the system of individual initiative, a driving quality, a motive power, an instrument of progress which is of such great value to mankind that to destroy it would be to inflict almost untold hardships upon future generations.

The precise formulation of this liberal viewpoint is a matter to which, as I have said, many of us are directing much attention. It is a matter which involves a choice of political means. Perhaps we do not sufficiently realise that almost all political parties have political ends very much in common. For example, if you were to say to a Liberal politician: "What is your test of government?" he must inevitably reply: "Whether it ensures human happiness and security for the individual and develops all the possibilities which reside in him". If you were to say to him: "What are the natural rights of a citizen?" He would reply, as I do, that provided he is a capable and willing citizen he is entitled to employment, to a sufficient family income, to adequate family medical services, to a healthy family home, the means of education for himself and his children, to the right to select his own means of living and to make his own career.

The Socialist and Communist will both retort that these things can be obtained only by substituting government action and mastery for private ownership and private profit.

This is where they make their great error. It is easy to talk about private profit as if there was something disreputable about making it. Yet the vast majority of men are profoundly influenced by the prospect of obtaining it. Whether the profit is on the sale of goods or the investment of money or the doing of work for something above the statutory wage there can be no doubt that it does spur men to greater efforts.

The old metaphorical expression about the "government stroke", while it does an injustice to many people who are fine servants of the people, really does contain at least this truth – that except in rare cases great energies and great skill will be put forward more readily when there is a hope of special reward.

The real thing to perceive is that if the desire for profit or award is put in its proper place as the servant of human progress we avoid both the extremes of socialism and a purely selfish capitalism.

The happiness of our people depends not only upon security but upon progress, for security without progress will simply mean in the long run falling living standards. Social action may be the best guarantor of security but a willingness to take risks for reward is the greatest guarantor of progress. We must keep both. The two things are essentially reconcilable once we understand quite distinctly that any modern conception of a proper social order must include the view that our rights to make profits or get rewards for ourselves must be secondary to that discharge of our public and private responsibilities upon which the security of our neighbours will depend.

Speech at Conclusion of Albury Conference to Inaugurate the Liberal Party (16 December 1944)

At the conclusion of the Albury Conference to inaugurate the Liberal Party of Australia in December 1944, Menzies rose to give this headland speech to elaborate on the core principles that his new Party stood for. The Albury Conference (14-16 December) followed on from the earlier Canberra Conference (13-16 October), both of which had been convened in response to a letter Menzies had circulated to all of Australia's non-Labor groupings calling for the formation a new political force. Menzies told the party faithful that there could not have been a more opportune time in the history of Australia to establish a new party to advance liberal causes and ideals. Working in close concert with the existing Country Party, Menzies pledged that his Liberal Party would protect the interests of farmers, business people and war veterans. In his vision for a flourishing liberal democracy, Menzies affirmed that his party would seek always to elevate the dignity of the individual.

....

...This has been the most important conference, as indeed the Canberra conference was. I have felt since the beginning that it was of the first significance that it should succeed, that under no circumstances, having set our hands to this plough, should we turn back.

That spirit existing in every delegate to this conference is the real thing that has brought us success. It has been my honour to preside and do what I could in relation to these problems. I appreciate more than I can say your appreciation. There could have been no success at Canberra or at Albury without a genuine cooperative effort, and the nature of that effort is best understood if one recalls that only a few months ago there were many organisations in existence, that occasionally there was conflict and friction.

Such things are seized upon by our political opponents, and frequently magnified by them. Now, as a result of our coming together, of utterly frank discussion and utterly honest decision – a fine combination – we have been able to evolve a machinery that will inevitably bring into existence in the fullest sense a party of an Australia-wide character.

There can never have been a time in the history of Australia when such a party was more needed.

We all realise that not only must we have a machine which we have produced but we must learn to use it with promptness and skill and enthusiasm in order that we may influence public thinking in Australia, not only in this generation but also in the next ...

In the first place, we have brought into existence for the first time in the history of Australia the Liberal Party of Australia. As I said in Canberra we have existed for too many years as a series of separate State organisations. This is the first occasion on which those of, broadly speaking, our political way of thought have established themselves on an Australian footing.

That is a tremendous step. It is a vital step, because I do not believe that with the growing importance of national politics anything short of an Australian political organisation is fit to give expression to the ideas and inmost thoughts of hundreds of thousands of Australian citizens.

There is a second feature of what we have done. In the past there has been no real or effective liaison between Parliamentary leaders who propound policy and those in the organisations who organise in support of it. In this case we have taken steps to provide in both the Commonwealth and the States a policy committee which I hope will be a very active and permanent feature of the set-up. It will enable Parliamentary leaders and their colleagues to be brought directly into contact with the ideas of outside members of their organisations, so that policies may not become too remote from life, or Parliamentarians become too cynical.

Parliamentarians will be enlivened by ideas from outside, and outside ideas maybe a little tempered by political considerations.

Members and policy: The members of the Liberal Party of Australia, who I hope will number scores of thousands before a year has gone, will, through their sub-branches, state councils, the Federal executive, and those who represent them on policy committees, have an effective voice in the shaping of policy. As you know, we have two aspects of our policy. One consists in the formulation of our objectives. We formulated them at Canberra, and we have reaffirmed them here.

Those objectives constitute a real human charter for the people of Australia. They are among the provisions of the Constitution which can be moulded from time to time by the council. Therefore, by democratic process, every member of the Party, through their executive representatives, will have an opportunity in influencing the shaping of those objectives. Meetings will be held. It is of the essence of a Liberal party in Australia that Australian citizens should at all times know substantially where that Party stands on great public questions.

The second aspect of policy is that in Parliament we have aimed with some success at associating ourselves with certain matters of political principle. No party serves the imagination of the people unless the people know the party stands for certain things and will fight for those things until the bell rings.

I anticipate that as a result of the existence of an active standing committee on policy we will be able to put before the people in print, by speech, by broadcasting, precise statements of our policy. Our members, through elected representatives on State and Federal councils, will be able to exercise due influence upon the form and content of those statements of policy.

Women's Place in Organisation: A third thing that arises is that men and women will side-by-side be members of this organisation. I would like to express the hope on behalf of the men represented here that as a result of this joint and equal partnership with this great movement we will find on councils and executives an adequate representation of women (Hear, hear!).

Women are unquestionably destined to exercise more and more influence upon practical politics in Australia. There was a time when they were thought to stand side [sic], exercising only passive influence. That has gone. In the education of the electorate in liberal ideas they have for many years been an effective force. Now we have an organisation in which all distinctions have gone, and with men and women working equally for the one body the resultant education value of our movement is going to be extremely increased.

Mr E K White said that if you looked at the results of our work, the Constitution we have drafted, you will find a machine. Might I offer this warning? One of the great diseases of modern democracy is that too many people have thought that once you achieved the machine your interest had come to an end. Far too few of us have realised that democracy is not an end in itself. As an end in itself it means nothing. It is a means to an end, it is a means to living on the part of men and women. If there has been any failure in democracy it is due to the fact that too many people said the struggle for freedom is over when we have achieved institutions.

If we stand for anything as Liberals we stand for the inescapable responsibility of the individual, his dignity, his significance, his responsibility for every other individual. In that sense we are an individualist movement, not in the bad sense of saying, "Each for himself and the devil take the hindmost", but in the good sense of saying that every man is his brother's keeper (Hear, hear!). That is the essence of liberal democracy and we shall fail in our purpose if we think that having got a machine to give expression to it our task is over.

On the contrary, our task now begins. We are, I believe, in a technical sense equipped for it, but it is upon our spirit and our willingness to work that its success will turn.

Liberal Party Rally, Assembly Hall, Sydney (31 August 1945)

While Menzies initially brought the Liberal Party into being at the Canberra and Albury conferences of 1944, the official launch of his new political movement took place at a Sydney Rally in August 1945 only days after the Second World War had ended. In his address, he reaffirmed the liberal principles of private enterprise, reward for effort, individual dignity and cooperation between government and citizen. With a glimpse of what he proposed to do in policy terms if returned to power, he applied the principles of his party to the "concrete" issues of employment, taxation, social security, rehabilitation, housing, primary industries, education and international affairs. As an intellectual yet practical-minded leader, Menzies made it plain that his new party was about making liberal principles deliver practical policy results. He and the Liberal Party were not so much preoccupied with a doctrinaire philosophy for its own sake as with harnessing the right ideas to positively impact the lives of ordinary men and women.

....

Preliminary:

My purpose is to put before you the broad views of the Liberal Party of Australia upon some of the more important questions now arising. We expect over the next few months, as a result of consultation between parliamentary members and members of the party Council, assisted by the work and suggestions of many thousands of members of the organisation, to develop our views not only upon these but upon a wide range of subjects.

Before dealing with specific problems, however, there are some preliminary matters to be stated:

There is a good deal of confusion, some of it deliberately created, about the Liberal approach to "private enterprise". The expression is unfortunate since to some minds it appears to suggest that private interests are being preferred to public benefit. If the expression connotes "each for himself", with no provision against depressions, with big monopolies running free, with an absence of proper government controls, then it is something which liberalism cannot support.

But when we Liberals speak of "private enterprise" or "free enterprise" or the like we are laying emphasis upon the element of initiative for reward which we believe to be the great dynamic of progress. We believe in security, but we believe also in progress; in rising living standards; in full and better lives for every citizen; in better houses and schools and furniture and food and clothing.

None of these things can be attained unless we have increased, cheaper, and more effective production. And this in turn depends, we believe, upon the encouragement, recognition and reward of extra skill and extra effort, whether it be that of employer or employee.

We do not stand for some mutual hostility between the government and the private citizen in business. We believe in the cooperation of government and citizen, the former formulating and enforcing social and industrial obligations, preserving true and fair competition by a strict control of monopolies, cooperating with business in long-range planning, while business itself supplies the drive and ambition and progress without which security will become a delusion and living standards will fall.

In a few words, liberalism proposes to march down the middle of the road. Its watchwords will be –

A fair deal and a good opportunity for every human being; no privilege, if by privilege we mean advantage, except for the industrious and skilful; a sound and appropriate education for every child, whatever the economic position of the parents; general provision for the citizen against the chances and disasters of life; high pay for high endeavour.

To us, Australia is not seven million people to be thought about and ordered about and legislated about as a mere mass. To us, Australia is seven million individuals, the progress of each of whom is a priceless asset to Australia, and the honest contribution of each of whom is the essential foundation of all good community life. It is therefore to the preserving of the freedom of the citizen, his mind, his body, his spirit, that liberalism dedicates itself. Only from genuinely free, progressive, diligent and encouraged individuals can a really powerful nation be built. I now turn to a necessarily brief statement of how the Liberal Party applies these broad principles to some of the concrete questions of the moment:

Employment:

This is the greatest of our domestic problems. The depression has left an ineradicable mark upon the mind and conscience of this generation. Our first resolve must be and is that never, while we have a brain to plan or two hands to fight or work with, must such a depression occur again. How then are we to secure that constant employment at good and rising wages which represents the antithesis of depression?

- Employment for all in a free society.
- The coordination of government activity and individual initiative to encourage the fullest development of long-term employment, whether commercial, industrial, or rural. We stand for long-term jobs, not short-term jobs. That is why, as a first line of attack upon the employment problem, we turn to the commercial, industrial and rural businesses of the country, rather than to short-term, and perhaps dead-end, employment in government works.
- To give small business, which employs such a huge total, its chance, we shall protect and foster it.
- Increasing production as the basis of increases in living standards and social security. A slowing down of production will damage the worker immeasurably. Increasing production demands increasing markets. Increasing markets cannot be won easily unless we produce commodities that are both good and cheap. Cheap production depends upon effort and efficiency, not upon wage slashing. We believe that high wages and high production are natural and inevitable allies.
- The full development of the power resources of Australia.
- The constant improvement of working conditions.

27

- The development of new industries especially for export, and of the need for scientific research.

- The preparation of public works carefully selected in type and place, planned to the last detail, and available to be put into operation for the development of national production at the first sign of any recession in general business conditions.

- A taxation policy which is designed to encourage production by encouraging employees to earn higher wages, employers to develop their businesses and establish liquid reserves, and investors to take risks with their Capital.

- Freedom of business enterprise to establish itself and to expand.

- Social Security, which is dealt with elsewhere, but which is of itself a great stabiliser of business and therefore of employment.

Social Security:

The purpose of all measures of social security is not only to provide citizens with some reasonable protection against misfortune but to reconcile that provision with their proud independence and dignity as democratic citizens. The time has gone when social justice should even appear to take the form of social charity. Therefore, the Liberal Party will vigorously pursue a policy on these lines:

- Generous provision for superannuation, incapacity, sick pay, medical and the like expenses, unemployment and widowhood.

- No means test. The means test is the inevitable consequence of non-contributory social services, but it is the complete embodiment of the substitution of benevolence for justice.

- Contribution by all persons in receipt of income.

- The encouragement, over and above government schemes, of supplementary voluntary schemes.

I emphasise, to avoid misunderstanding, that the adoption of the contributory scheme will not prejudice any accrued rights to free benefits, or deprive of future benefit those not able for economic reasons to make contributions.

Rehabilitation:

This great subject reminds us of one of the greatest of our obligations. We must discharge it in no niggling spirit. We must honour our obligations with pride and generosity. On what principles should rehabilitation proceed? We submit a few of these principles as follows:

- Servicemen and women who are not incapacitated shall not suffer economic disadvantage as a result of their absence from civilian life.

- Servicemen and women who are incapacitated shall enjoy generous pensions and receive efficient and free medical attention with suitable supplementary pensions for their dependents.

- Having regard to the fact that there is an economic disadvantage which arises from absence from civilian life, provisions of re-establishment should apply to all who have been members of the Services.

- As part of the general policy of employment for all, and recognising that even in a state of full employment there will still be competition for individual jobs, there must be really effective preference in employment to ex-service men and women.

- Preference to ex-servicemen in the obtaining of homes.

- The rehabilitation and re-establishment of discharged service personnel should be brought under one fully coordinated Commonwealth ministry, staffed by those who, from their own experience, understand and sympathise with the problem of the ex-servicemen.

- Side-by-side with a centralisation of Commonwealth

rehabilitation authority there should be the highest possible degree of decentralisation by means of local or industrial committees. The Liberal Party, thinking always in terms of the individual, regards the problem of rehabilitating servicemen as essentially an individual problem which will require a high degree of special individual human treatment.

Housing:

We recognise that the present grave shortage of houses not only in the metropolitan areas but in the country represents a condition of National emergency. It demands and has demanded for some time past the formulation and instant carrying out of a policy and programme not based upon some unworkable centralisation or making insufficient use of existing and experienced bodies, but depending essentially upon the cooperation of Commonwealth, State and local authorities.

The policy should be:

- to ensure at once, without red tape or circumlocution, that sufficient manpower is made available to produce building materials and erect homes;

- to permit no public works other than those of an urgent nature or those which are themselves related to housing, to be undertaken to the detriment of the housing program;

- to establish priorities prohibiting luxury homes until the basic requirements of the people are satisfied. We should concentrate primarily upon lower income requirements, though all citizens should be permitted to erect homes commensurate with their reasonable living standards;

- in collaboration with the Central Bank, to ensure the necessary finance for both government and private building;

- to provide for extended activities by the state governments in homebuilding, primarily aimed at slum abolition;

- to proceed promptly with the building of War Service Homes;

- to encourage and assist building by private enterprise as the quickest, cheapest and most effective means. The small builder is of immense importance;

- to avoid the creation of a serious future problem by establishing and rigorously enforcing proper standards of house construction and incidental services;

- to provide for the abolition of Sales Tax on building materials;

- to remember at all times that one of the greatest things to be done for the citizens of the country is to encourage their ownership of their homes and the things that go with them. We should therefore encourage building for home ownership, and with this in view we should use and generously extend the credit foncier[9] system;

- to control the prices of materials, home equipment and building sites during the inevitable period in which the demand will far exceed the supply. The keeping down of the cost of building homes is absolutely vital since inflated costs will be reflected for many years in higher interest bills and higher rentals.

In the whole of this problem the Liberal Party of Australia points out to the people that cheap and satisfactory housing is possible only when all elements are employed in the production of homes and the use of building materials and services operate at their highest level of efficiency, and for adequate pay or other reward. The real standard of the cost of the homes to be built in the next few years will depend upon the skills and honesty of the work put into them by employer and employee, manufacturer and merchant alike.

---

9 A "credit foncier" is a company licensed for the purpose of carrying out improvements, by means of loans and advances upon real securities.

Taxation:

- There must be an all-round reduction of the taxation burden. There is every reason why this should be made at once, for there can be little doubt that even substantially reduced rates of tax would hardly affect the total tax yield during the next few years when civil production will be enormously increased and, with it, civil earnings.

- Special consideration should be given to the problem of the family taxpayer, particularly with reference to allowances for children, medical and the like expenses, and education.

- Those allowances which now take the form of rebates should be re-converted into deductions, to the great benefit of the taxpayer.

- A special examination should be made into the working of "Pay-As-You-Go" taxation, with a view to eliminating any injustices which have arisen. We have particularly in mind the fact that many persons, e.g. wage earners, maybe in the result overcharged, and become entitled to refunds which are received long after the overpayment.

- There should be a re-examination by some competent authority such as the States Grants Commission, of the rebates payable to the States under the Uniform Taxation laws.

Primary industries:

- Stabilisation schemes based upon guaranteed prices to be ascertained annually by competent, impartial tribunals on the model of the Tariff Board.

- Such schemes not to discriminate between persons engaged in the one industry.

- Good wages and conditions for rural workers.

- The amenities of rural life to be developed to standards comparable with those of the cities. E.g. better country housing; bigger and bolder schemes of water conservation and distribution; electric light and power; refrigeration;

good roads and transport; first class schools; the establishment of a few first-class universities in provincial centres.

- The resources of science to be made available to the man on the land not in the mass but to each farmer as an individual.
- A national attack upon destructive elements such as bush fires and wind and water erosion.
- Adequate provision for cooperation with Great Britain which is our best customer for most of our primary products.

Education:

The Liberal Party supports the motion submitted by me at Canberra on July 26th. In brief, we stand for:

- A revised and extended education system.
- Increased facilities for secondary, rural, technical and university training, and adult education.
- A searching revision of the problem of the qualifications, status and remuneration of teachers.
- The acceptance of Commonwealth responsibilities for the provision of generous financial aid to the States.
- The ascertainment of the purposes for which such aid should be granted by a qualified commission set up by the Commonwealth and the States in cooperation.

We believe that there must be no such thing as privilege in education. It is vital to the community that the qualities and abilities of each individual child should be fully developed.

We are not advocating a dull uniformity of educational method from one end of Australia to the other. There will and should continue to be great variations. In the same way we are not advocating the same type of education for all children, since the ultimate purpose of education differs in so many cases. But we believe that our educational system will fail unless it produces not only a measure of literacy and some minimum of skill, but a desire to learn, a real community sense and spirit, and proper standards of values.

International Affairs:

- The prevention of war in the future is one of the greatest tasks of mankind. Australia must play its part in such prevention. We therefore support Australian participation in the world security organisation now under ratification.

- Australian participation involves duties as well as rights, actions as well as resolutions. We must therefore at all times maintain a defence policy, including all necessary measures of training and equipment, which will make our participation in world security both active and real.

- We desire increasingly close collaboration between Australia, Great Britain and the other British countries, not as something inconsistent with the World Charter, but as a first vital practical contribution to its success.

We should recall that world security is as yet on paper. The bargain contained in the paper will suffer many stresses and strains in future years. The Association of the British peoples is not primarily on paper; it is primarily in the blood and its strength has been toughened by many a trial in the past.

The Liberal Party deplores the practice recently adopted by Ministers of raising publicly and arguing through the columns of the Press differences between Australia and Great Britain. The strength of the British Empire with all its undoubted influence for peace and justice is more than the sum of the strengths of its individual parts. It is foolish and dangerous to forget this fact.

Ethics of Business and Commerce, Speech to the Associated Chamber of Commerce, Menzies Hotel, Sydney (22 November 1954)

With free enterprise lying at the heart of Menzies' Liberal philosophy, the Prime Minister used this address to the Chamber of Commerce as an opportunity to explain the positive moral impulses behind business and commerce. While Menzies was mindful of the potential for unscrupulous people to abuse commerce and exploit it for greedy, selfish ends, he reminded his audience that commerce could be a tremendous force for good to both the individual and the community if it was honestly conducted. As well as giving the individual a sense of self-worth and purpose, commerce provided a forum for cooperation between the seller and the buyer which forced the individual to look beyond their own self-interest. In its capacity to produce new goods and services, together with the creation of fresh employment opportunities, commercial activity was of immense benefit to the community. For these reasons, Menzies made the support and promotion of free enterprises a core part of his policy agenda.

....

This, Sir, is the Chamber of Commerce. Although I am, of all politicians, perhaps, in this country, the greatest believer in the individual, his rights and his destiny, I merely want to remind you that commerce is something mutual. No man conducts commerce by himself. He can't be at the one and same time his own seller and his own buyer, unless he is one of those glorious optimists who stand for parliament occasionally and lose their deposits. Therefore, when I talk to you about commerce, I talk about something that has mutuality in it. Not one of you here tonight could live by himself or to himself. Therefore, commerce involves cooperation and cooperation, although it is a word that has been put into rather debased usage from time to time, is something which involves mutual understanding, mutual tolerance, a willingness to learn, a willingness to understand that the interests of the total body are greater than the interests of the individual. The fact that I am an individualist, the fact I believe in the individual doesn't prevent me from knowing that the individual does the best service when he realises that all his efforts as an individual are to be put forward in the long run on behalf of the total body corporate. Indeed, the whole difference between my political philosophy and the political philosophy of my opponents, or some of them, is this; that I believe in the individual, in what he can do for the nation, whereas they believe in the nation and what it can do for the individual.

Then, Sir, that means this, doesn't it – that every one of you here tonight is properly and naturally to say "I have a business. This is my business. This is what I want to do for my business". It is eminently proper that you should want your business to be the business, to expand it, to increase its usefulness, to increase its profit. An awful lot of nonsense is talked about profit. Profit is a severe mechanical test of success. Then when you have done all that, all I want to do is to ask you always to look at your business against the background of the nation's business. In other words don't be narrow-minded. Don't think that this is Ajax defying the lightning. Don't think that this is – I was almost going to speak Latin, but I won't in the presence of the judge – but don't think that this is a matter of fighting the rest of the community, because no business ever yet succeeded which fought the rest of the community. The business that succeeds, succeeds because it does help something that the community wants. In other words, we must all see what we are doing against the background of the wider world and coming back home against the background of a wider nation. The nation's business which is my business, fits into it.

You know, if we were to analyse the events of the first fifty years of this century, we would come across men and some wicked men, among them whose names will live as long as modern history will live, the Hitlers, the Mussolinis. Their names will live just as long as the name of Judas Iscariot. And Why? Because of the good things they did for the world? No. Because they said: "It is my power and my glory which matter". They failed to see their own activities against the background of the activities of their country. But in the long, long run when the accounts are cast up, and they are not cast up in tomorrow's newspapers, somebody or some people, or some hundreds of people and ultimately some millions of people, will say: "This was well done for the nation and for the world. This was something done for humanity"?

Now, I am not attempting to be pontifical about this. I am one of those simpleminded old-fashioned people who believe that an honest business courageously conducted with enterprise is in itself a great service to mankind. If it were not for the men of commerce in our race, we would today be the least of God's creatures in this world. But all the time we must say to ourselves: "How does this fit in with the affairs of the community, of the nation, of the world?"...

You couldn't have succeeded as you have unless you had a sense of responsibility to the entire community. And indeed it does a credit to the Chamber of Commerce which, having a look at a few of my friends around the room, I wouldn't have suspected them to have elected you to be their President. Because you see, Sir, in a rather vague fashion they have seen in you, without knowing it, some of these great things that I have been talking about. A sense of duty, a sense of service, a knowledge that the community is greater than the individual...

Every now and then, when you meet somebody like that, somebody who is able to detach himself from his own natural and proper self-interest and say: "That's what I think would be good for Australia". When I meet a man like that the whole of my faith in mankind is renewed ...

Well, let that be as it is. The truth about this Australia of ours is not that we are a great country, or a great nation. Don't let us be silly about these things. Don't let us make ourselves absurd by putting things out of proportion. All I ever say about my country around the world is that man for man, woman for woman, nine millions of us, we don't take second place to any other country. We have between us all, great virtues. But we will, someday, become a great nation, a great nation in physical terms, a great nation in population, a great nation in material resources. And at this very moment, we can be if we will be, a great nation in the world of the mind and of the spirit, because when you enter the world of the mind and the world of the spirit numbers don't count. It's quality that talks.

But if we are to be as the Almighty designed us to be – a great nation of great people – then we are not to stand with our back to the world, contemplating our internal affairs as if they were the only affairs that mattered. Just as you, John Smith, must look at your business against a background of all the business affairs of the nation, so must we, as good Australians and proud Australians, look at Australia against the background of the world, remembering always we have the singular honour to be British people and brothers of British people all around the world, remembering with pride we have the great honour to be partners in the great English-speaking alliance around the world, remembering with hope, with feeling, that we have the honour to be one of the nations in the world which understands self-government, democracy, freedom all of them being the hope of the world. These are the things, Sir, that I am asking all your members to have in mind.

It wasn't my purpose tonight to make some catchpenny political speech about import licensing. It would be offensive to you and to your intelligence. I was greatly honoured to have your invitation. I had the deepest affection and respect for your President. There are many men in this room tonight whose friendship I enjoy. Therefore, I have taken the opportunity of saying to you something of the thoughts that come into the mind of even a throat-cutting politician, when he is given the opportunity, once in a way, of thinking about his job, the people over whom he happens to be the Prime Minister for the time being, of the country that he lives in – his native country – the great family of nations it belongs to and of the whole problem and ultimate dignity of the world in which he lives.

Liberalism, Speech to Young Liberal Movement Convention, YWCA Hall, Sydney (27 July 1962)

Addressing the youth wing of the Liberal Party he founded in 1944, Menzies reminded his young audience that they were tomorrow's torchbearers of the Liberal philosophy that had given the Party its inspiration. This philosophy was critically important because it was seen by Menzies to embody all of the values and ideals which had made Australia a great nation. According to the Prime Minister, the quest for a more civilised society, the repudiation of class conflict, the pioneering spirit of adventure, the ethic of civic unselfishness and the private enterprise solution represented articles of faith for the Liberal movement, not least its youth wing. In this speech, Menzies called for a concerted effort by the Party's younger generation to champion these principles so that his vision for an even greater and stronger Australia could be realised. Perhaps conscious that his lengthy tenure as Prime Minister was nearing the end, he was resolved that the Liberal philosophy he did so much to nurture would long outlive his own political life.

....

... It isn't so long ago, from my point of view, back before the 1949 election, before the 1946 election, when I, myself, being Leader of the Opposition, had occasion to look over the field in Australia and to say, "Are we putting ourselves into shape to win the election and to govern the country?" This was a serious question but not a very easy one to answer at that time because, under the pressure of adversity, we split up into various groups and factions. There were about three different political parties, non-Labor, in New South Wales. I think there were about four in Victoria, and so it went around Australia until I think, when I convened the original meeting to establish the Liberal Party, I had to send notices to at least thirteen different organisations. I know it well because it was all done in my offices as Leader of the Opposition and by 1944, we were establishing the united party; by 1945, we had it well underway. In 1946, we won a few seats, not too many, we couldn't hope to win an election, but we won a few seats, and in 1949, we were swept into power at what was then almost a record level of majority.

Now all that happened because we had something to believe in, not just something to oppose but something to believe in. If we had fallen into any dangers in the last few years, it perhaps is because we have lost sight of the idea – what is it we believe in – and have perhaps concentrated unduly on dealing with our opponents and demonstrating how wrong they are.

Now, Sir, nobody could be a greater believer then I am in the Young Liberal Movement, and for those reasons, because long after I am merely a dusty memory, there will be plenty of you in this hall tonight who will be occupying leading posts in the political life of Australia and carrying great responsibility in that political life. But you will do it and do it in positions of power and responsibility only if you and all the rest of us from time to time sit down and say, "What is it we believe in?"

Modern history is, as you all know, full of examples of great movements that disappeared because they had ceased to have any genuine reason for existence. I remember – speaking about the British Commonwealth – a penetrating man saying to me only six months ago, "You know, there is a lot of argument about the Commonwealth but the thing I am always trying to discover is what does it stand for, what does it believe in". And this is a great problem. It is not enough just to accommodate the structure to new things or new events, the important thing is to have a faith to live by. And that goes for us, in this Party.

Now, Sir, I don't want to make a sort of theological speech to you, but I do want to say a few things about what I believe in and what, as I hope, you believe in. This is not a matter for some casual, contemporary observations. I want to talk to you about some of the great things, as it seems to me, that matter in our country and in which your mind and your heart and your spirit will be determining factors in the years to come.

What is the first objective, Sir, of national policy in Australia? Not just to be in office or to stay there, but to build something, to build a balanced nation, a strong nation, a progressive nation, a civilised nation in which advances and advantages belong to all the people. Now you may say that is almost platitudinous, so platitudinous that half the people have forgotten it. All the people represent our constituency of thought and of action. We must work for all the people and build for all of the people and have our vision of a civilised Australia for the benefit of all the people.

A good deal has been said in my time, politically, about class distinction. We still have a few hopelessly reactionary people, like socialists and communists (the most reactionary people in the country), who want to whip up something about class distinction. A Liberal regards this country as having only one valid class distinction, the distinction between the active and the idle. If the world belongs to the workers in the words of the Communist Manifesto – and I believe it is true – let it belong to the workers.

Let us believe that it is the industrious people in a country who matter, that they are the contributors to a national life, and don't let us, as Liberals above all things, fall into these easy ideas that the modern conception of life allows you to be idle, to be dependent, to leave it to the government, and between a yawn and a yawn, cast a vote about something. This is a wonderful country; it's going to be more wonderful still, but it will achieve greater wonders on the hard work and efforts of its people, and not by a spirit of dependency, not on that kind of attitude towards governments and what government ought to do that our opponents find so easy,

Sir, it is quite true, we must always remember it, that we have a strong and splendid heritage in Australia. We can all look back, most of us at any rate, except those who have only just newly arrived, on our forefathers in this country. We talk easily about the pioneers. We sometimes forget what remarkable things have been done. It would be a marvellous thing for all of us if, by some retrospective photography, we could be taken back fifty years. That's all. Fifty years, and look at how things were fifty years ago, and then look around us today, and there are those here, tonight, who in fifty years' time will look around them and, remembering how things looked today, will marvel at the achievements of this country.

We come of a great race of people. We have every reason to be proud of them, but our pride in them will be worthless unless we are determined to be an even greater race of people ourselves, unless we are determined that the future that will be looked at, perhaps by another generation in Australia, is going to be as astonishing as the one we look at today.

These things, Sir, don't call for a spirit of quiet acceptance of what a government will do. These things call for a spirit of adventure, they call for a desire to contribute, a rising level of civic unselfishness. Again I say to you, don't take these things for granted. Civic unselfishness. We don't know too many people, do we, who would answer to that description. We know a great number of people who want something, who want to have it, who want to be given it. There are not so many people in the country, outside this room, whose great ambition is to contribute to the nation. And yet, if liberalism stands for anything, and young liberalism above all, it is for a passion to contribute to the nation, to be free but to be contributors, to submit to the discipline of the mind instead of the ordinary, dull discipline of a regimental mass of people. These are wonderful things for us to have in our minds...

We need today, in industry, manufacturing and primary, pioneers, don't we? And we need the pioneering spirit – people who want to do it better and better and better and thereby reduce the burden that their own industry might otherwise cast on the community.

Now, the last thing I want to say to you is this. There will be a lot of people who will want to say to you, "Oh, you know, the government's all right, we have to support it". (Because some people still do). (Laughter) "We have to support it, but you know, they do an awful lot in the public sector" – that's the phrase the economists invented –"not enough in the private sector". Now, Sir, if we stand for anything, it's private enterprise, in this Party – top to bottom, young and old. But do we violate the principles of private enterprise when we assist a State government to carry out public works without which private enterprise could not carry on? Let's be sensible about this. How can you develop a vast manufacturing community in Australia unless you have schools, and schools are in the public sector of expenditure, unless you have roads, unless you have water supplies, unless you have transport of all kinds. If you were to look over the average list of public works that the State governments bring to us each time at the Loan Council, you would be hard put to find one that wasn't directly coming to the aid of the development of this country by private enterprise. You would be hard put to it to find anybody in a great private enterprise who didn't acknowledge that without these provisions, he couldn't possibly develop his factory or his business …

I can sum up my own unsophisticated view very simply. I don't believe that governments provide enterprise. I think governments may provide the condition in which enterprise is encouraged, but if you want enterprise, if you want vision, you have to go to the individual human being. It is human beings right through the community who do things, who think out things, who get on with them. A few of the human beings are elected to Parliament. But to compare the mechanism of government, as if it were some sentient creature with the genius of the human being is absurd. We stand for the human being, we believe that it is on his basis, on her basis, that this country is going to have in the next ten years, a degree of expansion unknown, even in the last decade.

So we look forward, and I particularly tonight, looking at you, look forward, because I don't expect to be around in politics in ten years' time and there are a lot of people who would greet that statement with immense enthusiasm (Laughter), but you will be around, and I warn you that unless you carry this torch on as I believe you will, I shall turn in my grave and reprove you if you can hear me. (Prolonged applause)

Thank you so much. You have convinced me. I think I'll stay for another couple of years.

2

FREEDOM AND DEMOCRACY

Is Democracy Doomed? Broadcast, Melbourne (Mid 1930s)

The following speech represented the first of many public treatises that Menzies wrote in defence of modern democracy. With the ideological polarisation of party politics and the march of European fascist movements in the mid-1930s, a certain pall of pessimism had descended on the Western world about the future fate of democracy. While democracy appeared safe for the time-being in Australia and the English-speaking world, Menzies appreciated that it was a hard-fought tradition requiring eternal vigilance for it to be maintained. In this apologia, Menzies praised the achievements of democracy for ushering in a new conception of human rights and for elevating the dignity of labour and general standards of living. For the future Prime Minister, this was a positive trajectory to be continued, so he refused to accept the proposition that democracy had failed despite the challenges to it in the present day. The great genius of democracy, according to Menzies, was both its realist understanding of the human condition and its flexibility that allowed public opinion to be continually tested, moulded and refined in society's quest to advance the wellbeing of its people.

....

Is democracy doomed? During the next five weeks this subject will be debated before you by five men of standing and authority. It is my function to introduce the debate, or, as I understand it, to prepare your minds by outlining the nature of the question at issue.

Let me, in the best Parliamentary manner, begin with two definitions. "Democracy" I take to be that form of government in which the functions of government are performed by persons freely chosen by the adult community on a universal suffrage, the principle being that sovereignty resides in the people as a whole and not in some privileged individual or class. More particularly, I imagine that this debate will be conducted on the view that democracy connotes a periodically elected parliament and a responsible Ministry or Cabinet. The word "doomed" I take to mean destined for destruction within a measurable distance of time. I say this because we are, most of us, more interested in the possible happenings of the next 50 years than in the polities of a century. Now the Australian Broadcasting Commission is, in my opinion, to be congratulated for having converted a common assertion into an important interrogatory. Whenever I meet a political or semi-political friend and see on his features that wistful look which denotes political speculation, I get ready to hear the result. And it comes in these words: "Democracy is doomed". You are now invited to make the appropriate retort, "Is it"? and to listen in to the arguments which your question provokes.

Right at the outset I might as well tell you that I am young enough in years (though no doubt, as my opponents tell me, old enough in political sin) to be sceptical of this modern cant of failure. It seems to me to be some evidence of poverty of mind, lack of resource and destructive judgement, that we should so readily conclude that symptoms of ill-health are sure precursors of death and dissolution. Because many of us have less money in our pockets then we had once, because our bank credit has been restricted, because the whirligig of extravagant times has brought in its revenges, we at once fly to the conclusion that the monetary system and the banks have jointly or severally failed. Because man's inhumanity to man "still makes countless thousands mourn" we vociferate that the Church has failed. Because the capitalist system, which ushered in and has sponsored and upheld centuries of growth and wealth and human happiness, does not prevent the Great Depression and persists in revealing ugly human features of selfishness and ruthlessness, we take time off from our acquisition and retention of capital to say that the capitalist system has failed.

This is all very depressing. Are all our institutions so inevitably and so rapidly crumbling to disaster? Are the gloomy apostles of failure carrying with them a gospel which we may all preach with conviction in the highways and byways of life? And if this gloom is but the herald of the bright dawn of a new and better age, will the light of that dawn be supplied from the doctrines of the Fascist or the Nazi, the Communist or the constitutionally elected dictator? My friends who are to follow will make some answers to these questions. In the meantime, I will offer a few observations of my own and throw my hat – which I am assured is a somewhat conservative one – into the arena.

I would be reluctant to agree that democracy has failed, because, while democracy has done much, I do not believe that in the full sense it has been completely tried. Though it is founded upon a theory of actual rights and inborn freedom which one dares to hope is almost as old as the English race, it is, as a system of government, extremely young. In the full political sense it has been current for not more than a few generations. For its ultimately effective exercise it calls not only for a machine of government but for a motive force which can be supplied only by widespread interest in the problem of government, a high average level of education, a willingness to appreciate that the interests of the whole are greater than the interests of the part, a sense of social justice. In a word, a good democracy wants good democrats; and the good democrat is not the man who shouts loudly of his own rights and thinks of government in terms of individual or class interests, but the man who realises that the social contract which binds any society together is one expressed primarily in terms of duties and obligations. If I may paraphrase:

"The fault, dear Brutus, is not in democracy, but in ourselves."

To all of which some specially sapient fellow retorts: "You can't change human nature". To which, in turn, I retort: "If you are to discuss systems of government on the assumption that men are inevitably stupid, selfish and ill-informed, you may as well say straight away that the only conceivable and workable system is one founded upon a discipline produced by a central sovereignty, and call for a dictator at once". Which reminds me, as the advocates of dictatorship should remind themselves, that Oliver Cromwell had a son named Richard.

There is another important aspect of this controversy. A single defeat may be magnified into a complete disaster. But if our judgement is to be

47

sound we must see our problem in its proper perspective and against its true background. To vary the metaphor, if democracy today stands its trial at the bar of public opinion, what is its record? Before we condemn it, let us hear it.

Surely it is not a near accident that the era of democracy has given to us a new conception of human rights, of the dignity of labour, of standards of living and of health! It is easy to say that these things have come in spite of democracy; but have they?

It seems to me that the truth is that every human system of government must at some time or other and under some circumstances or other present some features of the absurdity. For example, it is theoretically ludicrous to say that the majority of any given collection of people will on any given subject be right. Indeed, since ignorance is more prevalent and frequently more vocal than knowledge, and since misrepresentation is all too commonly the chief weapon in the armoury of the controversialist, all the chances are that at the first time of asking the majority will be wrong. But the great quality of democracy is that it is flexible and responsive to changed opinion, and lends itself readily to the process of trial and error by which progress comes and the truth prevails. Thus it is that though the majority may be wrong today, that courage and patience on the part of those actively engaged in affairs, with wisdom which is born of bitter experience, will make the majority right tomorrow. If we observe, not the particular decision of the moment, so often vitiated by passion and hatred, but the larger currents of public policy during the last hundred years, we must reach the conclusion that the people have, though slowly and uncertainly enough, been learning to govern themselves with prudence and humanity.

It will, I hope, take more than the not unnatural bitterness engendered by the economic depression of the past five years to make us forget that we owe to those who during the last century established popular self-government. Since the Reform Act of 1832 in England it can be said with substantial truth that the whole face of life has changed. Factory legislation and universal education have opened a new world to the children of the poor; industrial laws, while they have not yet solved the

48

problem of unemployment, have given to the manual labourer a comfort and security of life unknown before; vast and revolutionary advances have been made in the twin sciences of sanitation and health; social barriers have been broken down, and even the foundation of them are buried beneath the maisonettes of Toorak. With it all, the habits and mechanics of life have been revolutionised by a burst of inventive genius not previously approached in the world's history; a development which I, for one, am prepared in no small degree to attribute to the enlarging and stimulating of the human mind brought about by the new standing accorded to man when he began to find himself the master of his own political and social destiny.

With these achievements to its credit, how does it come about that democracy is today subjected to a fierce fire of criticism? As I see it, one possible answer to that question is that we are too disposed to think of the machinery of government as something detached from and independent of our own efforts. Some people think democracy a failure because they think Parliament not representative; a better distribution of seats, more frequent elections (dreadful thought!), and the full use of the referendum – and their criticism would be met.

Some people think democracy a failure because Parliament, they say, comes to be made up of voluble and not too scrupulous mountebanks. But the fact is that Parliament presents a fair cross-section of ordinary humanity – and what more can a representative institution do? And in the result has any nominated legislative body proved itself superior? That some of us in Parliament are poor enough rulers I cheerfully admit; but at least we have the merit of being prepared to try our hand at government while the really first-rate men sit at home and grumble. Some people – and I am one of them – think that the greatest danger to democracy lies in the readiness of the popular elector to be satisfied with low standards of government, to be bribed by promises of political and pecuniary advantages, with the adverse effect which such a readiness has upon the formulation and carrying out of well-considered long-range policies. Indeed, nothing is more disappointing to the political idealist than to see how frequently the only standard of judgement applied by the voter is – "What is there in this for me?" – a standard of judgement, which, when imputed as it commonly is, to the member of Parliament has done much to lower the prestige of Parliament and to discourage the entry into public life of men of character and refinement.

But when all this is conceded, I am reluctant to believe that these diseases of democracy are incurable. Two factors must surely cooperate to restore health.

One is that as economic problems and political problems become more and more interwoven men of all sorts and conditions will more and more realise that an interest in politics is vital to their own wellbeing. The other is that by a process of natural reactions, if not by the more admirable means of developing a community with moral sense and responsibility, men will in time realise that honesty pays; that a democratic country which permits the bribery if its electors must in the long run pay the bribes itself; and that what is taken out of a state by its members can never exceed the sum total of what is put into it by the same people.

One further point I would like to make is this – on the Parliamentary side we hear much of the necessity for reform in the procedure and business of Parliament; on the economic side we hear much of the necessity for planning and control of which my brilliant friend, Mr Macmahon Ball, will speak; on the social side we hear much of the necessity for reconstruction and equality and justice. All these things you can get under democracy if you want them. The need for any of them is no more a valid criticism of the democratic system of government than it would be of the seasons of the year.

So you see I come back to our question, and paraphrase it in this way – "is democracy doomed? Are we unfit to govern ourselves, and is that unfitness permanent? If it is, into what system of bondage shall we deliver ourselves; to what new master or new masters shall we pledge our allegiance?"

The Individual in the New Order, City Hall, Brisbane (21 January 1943)

In this keynote speech on Liberal principles, Menzies told his Brisbane audience that the great principle of individualism had been at stake during the War and that its ensuing survival was essential for the future of a free society. According to Menzies, it was this historic emphasis on the worth of the human individual that distinguished liberal societies such as Australia from the dictatorships of Nazi Germany and Soviet Russia. In such free countries, it was actually human beings themselves and not governments who were responsible for forging the character and prosperity of a nation. It was this innate responsibility and sense of enterprise that accorded individuals with a certain measure of dignity that could not otherwise be bestowed by the state. Foreseeing the ideological contest that would emerge between his creed of liberalism and the socialism of his political opponents in their competing visions for the "new order" after the War, Menzies warned that a future lurch to socialism would diminish the dignity of the individual and the freedom for him or her to contribute to the life of the nation.

....

It is a very great pleasure indeed to come into this great hall in which I have addressed big audiences before tonight, and find that in Brisbane, whether friend or foe, you are still interested in the politics of this country. I am going to talk to you tonight on a specific topic…

My subject tonight will not be at all popular with my friends on the flanks. Tonight I want to say something to you about the place of the individual in this country after the war, the place of the individual in Australia in the new order of which we hear so much.

Now, Mr Chairman, every day when we open our papers or listen to the wireless we find that we are being addressed by elderly gentlemen for that most part on the new order. Everybody who is interested from the Archbishop of Canterbury[10] down has been telling us what the new

---

10 Menzies was referring here to William Temple (1881-1944), the wartime Archbishop of Canterbury from 1942 to 1944. In 1942, Temple penned his influential book, *Christianity and Social Order*, which envisioned a significant role for the State in the coming post-war order.

order is to be when the war is over. Unfortunately, all these people who are vocal from the Archbishop of Canterbury down – and I leave out Roosevelt, Stalin and Churchill who are too busy winning the war – talk about it by saying that when the war is over we in Australia, those in Great Britain and those in the United States are going to enter a world in which the State runs everything. We shall all be neatly regimented, we shall all be on the government payroll. We shall all be attended to and fixed up from birth to death and beyond death. In other words, all the talk that is going on makes you think that all we need is to be completely socialistic and the millennium will come in ...

Now, Sir, let me put another point. We in Australia will be very well advised to confine ourselves to general objectives and to general principles when we talk about this post-war world. We have not won it yet. There are some bitter years in front of us before we do so. Therefore we must talk not as those who are working out plans and specifications for something we are going to build in peace and quietness tomorrow, but as men who know that the voyage in front of them is full of danger, and if they have steering points they will be indeed fortunate.

I want to talk to you about one of these steering points tonight. I want to talk to you and talk to you as fully as possible about where the individual comes in, because I for one believe that the individual is vital to the future of the world. I am not one of these people, and I admit it quite frankly, who believe that you can work out all the problems of life in a laboratory or in an economist's study. I believe that there is one thing that the men who are now fighting for this country would say they believed in. It would be a full life for the individual citizen when the war is over. Indeed, Sir, how do you imagine that we are going to win this war unless it is by the superior quality of the individual which democracy produces? How do you imagine we are going to win if the only question is one of regimentation? Why, if there is any country in the world which understands State control it is Germany, it is Italy. Well, and how shall we defeat them? We shall defeat them by proving once more that a free individual living in a free community with a free tomorrow in front of him is worth a nation of slaves. (Applause) ...

Sir, it is my belief that we are going to win this war because we are a nation of free individuals and I will be very much surprised to discover that Australians, having found that the initiative of the individual has been their sheet anchor during the war, will be prepared to give away the sheet anchor when the war is over and say – "Now that the war is over let us try a spot of fancy planning by half-cooked economists and very, very amateur administrators in politics". I do not believe it.

Let me put this question to you: What is it that the individual in Australia is looking to in life? We are told, of course, by people, some of them very high, at least one of them an Archbishop – that there is something incredibly degrading about the profit motive. I suppose some of my friends here tonight who are acquainted with catchwords will be familiar with the cry – "Produce for use and not for profit". Of course, in our more pious moments we are pleased to say that it is a terrible thing that there should be profit. Is it? Is it a terrible thing that there should be profit? When your union puts in for an increased wage is that a terrible thing? Do the unions consider that it is a terrible thing that munition workers should be able to earn £15 a week? Are they in favour of the profit motive, or are they not? All this talk about the profit motive, ladies and gentlemen, is utter nonsense. There is no representative of a household in this hall tonight who does not exist more or less because of the profit that the breadwinner brings home.

But, of course, you know, Sir, it is characteristic of us that we should become overwhelmed by words. Some of my friends in Australia – and they are my friends, I am devoted to them – learnt many, many years ago a particularly ugly word called "profiteering". Profiteering is a word which connotes taking financial advantages of the emergency of your country. That is all. All the profiteers in this country are not employers. Do not let us fool ourselves with words. Anybody who speaks in parliament and who has taken any interest in the financing of this war knows perfectly well that if any man running any business in Australia has any real volume of profit left in his own pocket when the Tax Commissioner has finished with him, then he is either very, very lucky or very, very crooked.

Sir, I hope to be as good an Australian as the next, and I have lived in this country all my life, but I do not believe that the average young Australian looks forward to a life in cotton wool. I do not believe, Sir, that the average Australian believes that heaven is represented by the universal control of the state. I believe that the average Australian says – "I hope sometime in my life to make a rise; I hope to get somewhere; I hope to be a little better off when I am fifty than I am now; I hope to get about me a wife and family; I want to have a home; I want to buy my own house at a decent price; I want to have reasonably steady employment; and I want to have some adequate provision for my old age".

Yes, all these things, but do not tell me that this country is occupied by a lot of people whose only ambition is to be nice, because it is not. This country is occupied by people whose ambition is to be real men and real women with their lives to live and their own future to carve out.

There is one other thing I want to put to you. It is a very important thing to have in mind. How are we going to be better off in years to come?

I want to know what the new order is, whether it is a new socialistic order or a new order for live, independent citizens. I tell you why I am for the latter, ladies and gentlemen. Anybody outside an asylum knows that if you took the whole wealth of the country today and cut it up among the people who now live in Australia nobody would be much better off. The whole condition of more comfort, and increasing and improving living conditions in Australia is that there should be more production in Australia and more wealth in Australia. If you want more production, cheaper production and better production in this country, will you entrust the job to the dead hand of the State or will you leave it to the ordinary men and women who are battling through the world on their own account.

So, Mr Chairman, with a few dissidents tonight, I, like you, am in favour of using as a vital, a dynamic element, in this new world, the individual element, the enterprise of the citizen, who desires to get an extra reward for doing some extra good job. That, I believe, is still one of the most vital driving forces in human nature, and any government that seeks to put the dead hand of socialism on Australia will produce in this country a flabby community lacking in backbone, lacking in spirit and initiative, that will go down the river in the first flood.

There is another side to that picture, and I want to mention it. The other side is this: If we are to use private enterprise, individual initiative, the capitalistic system if you like, if we are to use that as a social instrument, and we will if we are wise in the new world after this war, than we must say, as we do say to capitalism, to private enterprise, "Look, if you are to have the right to ask for a reward, then you must submit to the obligations that are brought about when you enter a civilised community in which the government accepts responsibility for the weak and the unfortunate. So we must say to capitalism, to private interests, to the employers of Australia – you are a vital element in this new world but you must be prepared as a condition to meet your obligations, to pay the highest wages that your industry can bear, to provide civilised working conditions for your people, and to provide constant employment for as many people as possible". I do not say that every business can have the same number of employees all the time but I do say that businesses must be prepared after this war to carry a certain labour force month in and month out as a condition of their existence. All these burdens must be placed on industry. They are fair burdens in a social world. Profits should not be destroyed as these amateurs would like to destroy them, but they should be made to bear, as they do now, taxes on behalf of the community on the most steeply graded scale. All these obligations I see as obligations of private industry.

The last thing I want to say to you is this: The most important element in any new order – I hope that everybody in this hall will agree with me on this – is not some plan that you work out on a sheet of paper or on a blackboard; the vital element in the new order will be the character of the people who live in this country. The individual in a democratic land, and I say this to you deliberately, is not only the creator of the national character, he is its repository. It is on him that all responsibility rests. For fourteen years in politics I have rarely let a month go by without trying to say something, to some audience somewhere, about the sole responsibility which rests on the individual citizen. I attribute all our troubles in Australia to the fact that people have been prepared to shrug their shoulders and say – "That is somebody else's responsibility; somebody else has to take the responsibility for this and that."

It is our individual responsibility, and let us make no mistake, ladies and gentlemen, all the theories or planning in the world will not of themselves make a better community for us. You cannot make a good community out of bad men. You cannot make an active community out of lazy men. You cannot make a courageous and independent community out of dependent men. The idea that you can have a lot of soft and fluffy individuals who take no responsibility and make no contributions and that you can build a real nation out of them is all utter nonsense. A nation is like a river. It will rise no higher than its source. The success of the new order is going to depend upon the courage and the spirit, the intelligence and the initiative of the individual men and women of Australia who will face their task and proudly carry their individual responsibility for its performance.

"Bond or Free", Pleasant Sunday Afternoon Address, Wesley Church, Melbourne (7 September 1947)

Speaking close to the eighth anniversary of the outbreak of the Second World War, Menzies reminded his audience that "freedom" was a hard fought gain that needed to be guarded in the present by all peace-loving men and women at all costs. This Pleasant Sunday Afternoon address was one of many that Menzies periodically gave at Melbourne's Wesley Methodist Church. As a close personal friend of the Church's Superintendent, Dr Clarence Irving Benson, Menzies was regularly invited by Dr Benson to speak on the moral and spiritual challenges to Western civilisation posed by Cold War communism and secular materialism. In this address, Menzies explained that freedom implied much more than the right for people to enjoy the material necessities of life but the freedom for people to be their best selves and to seek due reward for their efforts.

....

… We are almost today at the anniversary of the outbreak of the last war. I know that without looking at the calendar, because for some time now that has been the practice of this great mission to invite me to come here on this particular occasion and speak to you. My mind has gone back over a good deal, as yours has. It was a war for freedom. The word "freedom" rings like a bell through every utterance made by every leader in the course of that war. Freedom! It was the whole motive of the marvellous orations of Winston Churchill. The word "freedom" was the word which found itself in the most remarkable utterance made by Franklin Roosevelt, while America was still neutral, when he spoke to the whole world about the Four Freedoms.

Time after time, in all the darkness and the miseries that the war had for people, there was comfort out of knowing that in the long run no battle of free democracies against darkness should ever be lost. So that the word "Freedom" was our call. In the last, literal sense we fought for it.

And I want you to ask yourselves: If we fought for it, and as we fought for it, did we secure it? Have we our freedom now? Are we pursuing paths along which we will eventually end up by finding ourselves bond, or free? Why was it that in 1939 we said that the Germans were not free?

I beg of everybody to ask that question. Why was it? What were the characteristics of German slavery? Germany was seeking to impose her own slavery upon great parts of the world. I put it to you: In what did her slavery exist? Germany had full employment. Germany had great hospital services. Germany had magnificent roads, magnificent air services, vast fleets of motor cars. Germany had houses for her people to live in, housing schemes beyond our dreams at this moment in Australia. She had all those things. In what things did her slavery consist? It consisted in that her citizens, in return for that mess of pottage, had handed over to a few men their birthright and said to a few men: "You rule us, you govern us, you order us. We present to you the servile, standardised mass mind".

What I ask the people of Australia to ask clearly today is whether our progress is in the same direction? The only freedom, and I quote now the words of another great man, John Stuart Mill:

"The only freedom which deserves the name is that of pursuing our own good in our own way so long as we do not attempt to deprive others of theirs or impair their efforts to obtain it".

Our own good in our own way! If you want to have the servile mass mind, then seek first the all-powerful state. Because, when you have the all-powerful state, people will then be the servants of that state and the minds of those people will be servile minds, because there will only be one earthly master – the state inhuman but all-powerful!

What do we regard as part of our freedom? What do you believe to be the ingredients in your freedom, the freedom for which your sons and brothers fought? Freedom to worship? – Yes. Freedom to think? – Yes. Freedom to speak? – Yes. These are all obvious enough, and for the most part as yet – as yet – unchallenged.

But there are other elements in freedom. What about the freedom to select and to change your occupation? That is a real freedom. Even as a small boy I should have considered myself in some measure a slave had I been told: "You are not to study the profession of the law," I would have thought, and rightly, that my ambitions were being clipped, that I was being forced into a pattern which was not the pattern I thought I was made for. That is the issue.

One of the great freedoms in this life is the freedom to have some choice of occupation and, not liking it, to change it for another. Can you imagine a state of life in which we would call ourselves the inheritors of British freedom if the all-powerful state came to every boy and girl, and said: "You are to do this, or to do that, and never to change." Would that be freedom? I believe that that must be the position someday if and when we have the all-powerful state, because if there be only one master, and that master the state, how can there be a choice of occupation? How can you leave one employment for another, when there is no other employer? How can you decide that you do not want to be a lawyer, but that you will become a grocer if, in fact, all the activities of the law and the activities of the grocery-shop are in the hands of the one all-powerful state? It is about time we thought of this matter not merely in terms of party politics but with the long view. I have devoted nineteen years of my life in politics to the preservation of individuality and freedom, and opposing the creation of the all-powerful state, and I hope to devote the rest of my time to it.

There is another freedom which is under challenge today, and this is a very important freedom, because without it our mortal souls will be in deadly peril. It is the freedom to do our best and to make that best better. This is a great freedom. Here we have a freedom that goes deep into the very dignity of man. Freedom to do your best; to give of that best so that in the long run that best becomes even better.

That is vital to the world, and yet in this great struggle, and with all that this great freedom means, we find ourselves living in a community where more and more it is said that the man who does his best "is scabbing on his mates", where the man who does not do his best is not only protected but applauded.

That is a dreadful and immoral doctrine, because no man can go on for years doing less than his best without ultimately becoming incapable of doing what was once his best. And so his own standard falls, and his best services to the community are lost. Yet you know, as well as I do, that we hardly ever open our newspapers without reading of some new rule or convention which is designed to prevent men from doing their best! The community in which people are not allowed to do their best is already a slave community.

There is another element of freedom, and that is freedom in this world to seek and obtain a greater reward for doing more. Is that a bad thing? Because, if it is a bad thing, then the whole history of our race is falsified. Is it a bad thing for adventurous spirits to go out into the world, if necessary taking the risks, and looking for the reward of doing a bit more? If it is a bad thing, then there should be no Australia, no British Empire. Let us make no mistake. It is this magnificent instinct to go out after the extra risk for the extra reward that has produced the extra results in history, to the great advantage and prosperity of hundreds of millions of people now living.

And yet, not very long ago, only a few weeks ago in fact, there was a conference in Canberra. It was a conference which was welcomed by thoughtful men and thoughtful women all over Australia. They looked at our industrial set-up now that we are not in a state of war. They saw the mutual antagonisms and dislikes existing between employers and employees and they said: "If only these people could get together and discuss their ideas and their problems, some good might come out of it". And so it was arranged, and with their interests in common, employers and employees met. Various resolutions were carried and one of them was that the ACTU, the most important and representative body in the Trades Union world, was going to make a special study of the problem of "incentive payments", was going to sit down to study the problems of how far you could go towards giving that extra reward to the particularly good man without inflicting injustice on the average worker. It was a fair thing to study, because it will be a crazy sort of world in which you cannot pay the most competent man more than the most incompetent.

Anyway, the ACTU said: "We will study this problem". But, in the last few days, there has been another great conference here in Melbourne, and wisdom has been overthrown, and the new ACTU has repudiated that pledge! It has said: "As for incentive payments, we won't even consider them. We won't even study them. So far as we are concerned, they are gone. In other words, we stand for dull, flat uniformity".

Now, in the name of all that is sensible, do you believe that with two men in a factory, one extremely good, the other not in the same class, but both paid the same amount of money, the best work he can produce will be produced by the better man? Do you consider that the poorer worker will ultimately become like the better worker, or that the better worker will ultimately become a worse worker since, in return for his best he is offered no more than for his worst? Someday those two men will become equal; you are going to get exactly the same amount of work from each of them, the levelling will have been down.

If somebody is prepared to tell me that that state of affairs represents the freedom for which wars have been fought, then I say it is a monstrous perversion of the truth. If freedom means only full stomachs and comfortable beds, then there are millions of slaves who enjoy freedom. If freedom connotes the full use of the powers that God has given men, then there can be no freedom in the all-powerful state or in the servile mass mind which Smuts[11] described as the greatest menace of our time.

---

11 Jan Christiaan Smuts (1870-1950) was a distinguished South African statesman, Field Marshal and philosopher who served as Prime Minister of the Union of South Africa from 1919-1924 and 1939-1948. Menzies deeply admired Smuts for his eloquent defence of liberal values.

"Being a Good Democrat", Pleasant Sunday Afternoon Address, Wesley Church, Melbourne (4 September 1949)

In his last Pleasant Sunday Afternoon address before returning to the prime ministership in December 1949, Menzies reiterated his Liberal creed of unselfish individualism that he regarded as essential to the flourishing of healthy, post-war democracy in Australia and the world. With Menzies viewing democracy as underpinned by the Lockean "social contract", a convention which bound citizens together by a set of mutual rights and obligations, it required the unselfish spirit of its citizens to survive and prosper. In this address, he reminded all citizens that they were their "brother's keeper" and that it was the character of the people themselves who contributed to the strength and vitality of democracy. While the State was vested with important responsibilities to provide security and welfare to its citizens, it was ultimately the people who represented the supreme guarantors of a society's rights and liberties.

....

This afternoon I have been given a topic. I always am by the Master of this mission. And, as usual he has asked me to say something about democracy. I propose to do that, but before my time has entirely gone I propose to say something about a great democrat, about a great democrat who has gone from among us since I stood last in this place, Sir Alan Newton.[12] I shall say something about him after saying something of a general kind, and perhaps of a particular kind, about democracy.

One of the troubles in this world is that although devoted to argument, we involve ourselves in a great deal of unnecessary argument by not defining the meaning of the words that we are using. Even on so well known a word as democracy, we ought to save ourselves unnecessary argument by finding out what the word means.

---

12 Sir Alan Newton (1887-1949) was an eminent Australian surgeon who served as President of the Royal Australasian College of Surgeons. In 1936, Newton was knighted for his distinguished contribution to the medical profession. Menzies lauded Newton as the archetypal democratic citizen for both his strong moral character and service to the nation.

You frequently hear somebody say about somebody else that he is a good democrat. Sometimes what he means is – "This man gets on well with other people" – and yet you can get on, I am told, extremely well with other people and have no democracy in you at all. Sometimes he means – "This man is a good democrat because he believes that the majority are always right" – and yet, though I have known majorities to be right, in fact I am the last man to deny it – in fact, I have some expectations – I am far from conceding that majorities are always right because in truth they are not, so, to be a good democrat you do not need to say that what the majority says is right. I have even heard people say that people are good democrats meaning by this description no more than that his father had no money – and if that is a qualification of the good democracy than I suppose that most of us have a good chance of passing the test. For the truth is that the man may have all those things and be all of those things and not be a democrat at all. Let us get back to the simple truth that democracy means rule or government of the people by the people.

The odd thing about democracy, the thing that distinguishes it from every other form of government that has been tried, is that in a democracy the rulers and the ruled are the same people. The same people have the powers and the responsibilities, the same people have the rights and the duties. You see, Sir, our trouble about democracy is that we think it is simple whereas the truth is that the whole idea of democracy, magnificent and noble as it is, is extremely difficult and extremely complex.

I wonder if I might explain to you a little more clearly what I have in mind. You see, it isn't easy for a human being to be two people at once. It isn't easy to have inside yourself two sets of ideas at the same time, two sets of personalities at the same time. It isn't easy to be a ruler and to be a subject at the same time. You see, the old notion was many centuries ago, long before the dawn of democracy, that one man was ruler and the others were subjects, that one man made the law and the others obeyed. It is the difficult but profound truth about democracy that each one of us must learn to be both ruler and subject, both the lawmaker and the obeyer of the law. Each of us must learn to be the man, or woman, with the rights but with rights that are worthless unless they are also treated as duties. This is not a matter of words, I beg of you to understand. To be a good democrat you must not do what so many of us do here in Australia and go around talking about our rights in a democracy, because there are no rights in a democracy unless they are exactly equalled by the duties in a democracy. You see, I have no rights against Dr Benson unless he has a duty in relation to me, because my right against him is his duty to me and his right against me is my duty to him. Nobody has any rights in this world at all unless they are based upon the duties of other people owing to him, and if they are to have their rights then he must himself say, "What is my duty to my neighbour?"

You see, the oldest expression of democracy – a word which you cannot find in the New Testament – is inherent in the question, "Am I my brother's keeper?"[13] It is because we really believe, at our best, that we are our brother's keeper, that we have evolved this system of democracy under which we, the people, are the rulers of the State and the subjects of the State at one and the same time. Now, it is very easy to give up being a democrat. It is very easy to allow power to pass into a few hands. Most of us, if the truth be known, do not care very much for responsibility. If we can get somebody else to carry the responsibility then life appears to be very comfortable. It is easier to grumble than to perform. It is easier to criticise than to achieve. And so responsibility is something that we like to get rid of, and therefore we are always under an enormous temptation to allow power to pass into a few hands; to allow power to pass, as in Australia, into the hands of a state or a government which we do not identify with ourselves, which we do not sufficiently realise is only the human being which make it up but which seem to us to be some remote, austral body, with power of life and death, with power of benevolence, with power to do things for us. And because we have fallen into that error we are all the time under temptation to let power pass into the hands of a few people. What I want to remind you of is this; if we people of Australia become the mere dependents of the

13 Genesis 4:9. "Am I my brother's keeper?" was asked by Cain when the Lord asked him, "Where is Abel thy brother?"

State, then we are not the masters. We are not the rulers because when you make yourself dependent upon a few people you elevate those few people to mastery and you give away your power of self-government. There is no democracy except where the people are the masters, where government is dependent on the people and where the people are not dependent on the government.

That might be put in another way. We become masters in this life by service. If we are to become masters we must first be servants. We can be the masters of the State only by being the servants and builders of the State.

Now Sir, I do not profess to believe that that is a very simple truth. I do not profess to believe that it is a very easy doctrine, but then I for one have never thought that Christianity was an easy doctrine. If anybody supposes that it is he ought to go back occasionally and read the Sermon on the Mount, and realise once more how almost exquisitely difficult it is to live up to the faith and doctrine expressed in that great sermon.

Now, having said all that in a general way, I just add this, that in a democracy we have constantly internal enemies who say: "Do not worry about that; leave it to the government", meaning leave it to somebody else. The true democrat, when he says, "Leave it to the government", he means, "Leave it to me, because I am the government". But the internal enemy says "Don't you worry; the government will do something about it; somebody else will attend to it". We have an internal enemy who says to us – "the function of the State is to give to you, the citizen, security". Is it the function of the State to give the citizen security? Is it the function of somebody else or something else to provide this object of so much ambition in this world – security? There can be no security in any country which the people have not provided.

No government can give to any human being in this country any solitary thing that has not been sweated for and worked for by some other human being somewhere.

We want to get away from this idea that the government is a mystic thing which exists outside of human effort, human endeavour, human sacrifice. I for one shall never cease to speak in public wherever I have an opportunity against what I hope is only a temporary eclipse of sound, independent, unselfish individualism, which means the recognition by John Smith, Thomas Brown, every ordinary citizen in the country that there can be nothing from government unless he contributes his share. And all that, to put it in another way again, merely means, and this is one of those platitudes which, like so many platitudes, are so currently forgotten, that we can get out of democracy only what we put into it and that governments can distribute to the people only what the people themselves have produced. Now, Sir, considerations of that kind lead me to think more and more every year that we occasionally go wrong in the tests that we apply to governments. At the end of a Parliamentary session I have occasionally read in the newspapers that it was a most "productive" session, that 75 Acts of Parliament were passed. Well, in my better days, I was a lawyer, and I therefore have some conception of the almost immeasurable complexities of the law. I have long since abandoned any attempts to discover what the law is. It has got completely out of hand so far as I am concerned, and when I read that 75 Acts of Parliament represent the proof of a fine, productive session I say to myself, "how fantastic". It is a proof of industry. I should regard a man who built fifteen postholes across Collins Street as a highly industrious man, but I should tend to believe that he had done no more than obstruct the traffic.

Let us test governments much less by volume of legislation and much more by saying – "is there a fair and honest and capable administration of the laws we now have?" Is there strong and imaginative leadership, not from the rear, but from the front? Is there a capacity for inspiring the community with a sense of service?" Do not imagine for one moment that parliaments exist only for making Acts of Parliament. Parliaments exist for leadership, for the expression of opinion at the highest level, for the concentration of ideas, for the exchange of thought, for the total raising of the level of public knowledge and public judgement. Parliaments exist for those things, not just to pass Acts, and yet, we think so much of one and we think so little of the other.

Governments do not exist merely to punish us for our errors, to threaten us with punishment in the future, to exercise rule over us whether it be harsh or gentle. Governments exist in a democracy first and foremost to give fire and character and direction to a country's thinking. We must have more and more leadership and example …

Democracy cannot be and must not be a sterile or selfish thing if it is to succeed. Democracy must demand from all of us, all our skill, all our unselfishness, all our honest independence of mind. If democracy is to be a mere levelling down it will bring with it lower standards and a less noble conception of life. It must be a levelling up, a constant struggle for the highest, an unceasing encouragement to all of us to do our best, to develop our character and skill and energy. The character of a democracy does not depend upon its laws, it depends upon the character of its individual men and women. In a true democracy the State does not and cannot make the people. It is the people who must make the State.

Sir, there is a curious notion that the exceptional man, the man whose uncommon gifts and attainments mark him out from others, is a proof of the failure of democracy. He is on the contrary a shining proof of its success. For as wisdom is justified by her children, so is democracy justified by her greatest men, and not least.

"Participatory Democracy", Pleasant Sunday Afternoon Address, Wesley Church, Melbourne (4 September 1955)

In this Pleasant Sunday Afternoon address at Melbourne's Wesley Church, Menzies was once again prompted to remind his audience of the essence of democracy. Given that democracy was all too often taken for granted as a "given" by most Australians, he felt it was timely to remind them of the social obligations that came with living in a free society. One of these was the principle of "contribution", the idea that citizens were not only entitled to such benefits as social security and healthcare but had an obligation to contribute their talents, skills, industry and resources to the good of the nation. Menzies believed that if Australia was to be a nation of contributors, democracy would flourish and thrive on the spirit of civic selflessness. By contrast, if Australia was to become a nation of self-interested citizens, democracy would stagnate and be in danger of eventually collapsing under the weight of self-entitlement.

....

... I am going to say a little to you this afternoon of a non-political kind about politics. And for that reason, I think I ought to start by telling you all of a politician, of whom I was reminded when my friend, Irving Benson, made his appeal just now. I had always thought that he was as good an extractor of money in a good cause as Mr McGovern, the Federal Commissioner of Taxation. But in New York, a few years back I really encountered, if I may say so, Sir, your superior ...

I do want in a broad sense to say something to you about our democracy because the longer I live and I admit that I am a good deal older than I used to be, the more concerned I become about whether we really understand what democracy is, and how it ought to work, and what we ought to be doing about it. And in order to demonstrate how important that simple question is, one has only to look back over history. Look back over the entire struggle for freedom which has marked the history of our race both here and in the Old Country. After all, when mankind first knew some form of government, of definite government in the modern sense, all power was in the hands of one man. He wasn't called dictator in those days, he was called a Prince or a King, but he had all power. And people did what they were told and were given what they were permitted to have, and held all the small personal freedoms on what the lawyers would call a "precarious tenure". They could be given by the king and taken away.

And then as time went on, as the intelligence of men grew, and his desire for more freedom grew, power went from one man to a small group of men. The king was broadened out into a sort of aristocratic rule – the great nobles became the rulers. And even those who today say something from time to time about Magna Carta, occasionally forget that Magna Carta didn't give freedom to the common people. Magna Carta established the rights of the Barons. It marked the end of absolute monarchy. But it didn't create democracy; it created rights in the Barons, which were, as it happened, so perfectly expressed in terms of language, that they ultimately became known more and more to people and became more and more what we, in modern times, would call the slogan of democracy: "To no man shall we deny or delay justice".

These great observations in Magna Carta were originally made on behalf of, and for the benefit of, the Barons. And so power passed into the hands of a few, then from a few to many. After all, it is only a little more than a hundred years ago, it was only in 1832, that the first of the Reform Acts in Great Britain was passed. Up to that time Parliament didn't represent a democratic voice. It was a pretty competent Parliament in many ways. It happened in the second half of the 18th century and in the beginning of the 19th century. It happened undemocratically, even so it contained some of the greatest names in our history and in our political history – the older Pitt, Fox, Edmund Burke, the Younger Pitt. But parliament wasn't democratic. Those were still the days when a rich man might own a seat in Parliament, and, in effect, present it to some young twig of his family who had political ideas. And it was only after 1832 that we began a process which, after all, didn't end in Great Britain until well on in this century, a process which gradually step-by-step gave every adult person a vote and gave the vote to women as well as to men.

Curiously enough, that last reform did not come in Great Britain until only a few years ago – a handful of years ago. It came in Australia earlier. But it is only in this century, it is only in my own time, that we have seen the full transfer of power from one to a few, to many, to all, completed. And, therefore, democracy is a young thing. Not something we ought to be reading about in history books, but something that we ought to be learning to understand and to employ. You will see the point I am making – it is the hardest thing in the world, for any of us to understand that when the word history arises we are not just referring to the dead past, we don't have to pick up some time in order to discover some history. True we can learn a great deal about the past, and we ought to. But more history has been made in your lifetime and mine then in the history of any other previous generation in the history of the world. Political history, social history, international history, histories of violence and histories of the greatest skill and human understanding, turbulent histories, quiet histories, all made in your lifetime and mine.

And that is why I want to put it to you that if we are to have the benefit of this historic period through which we have lived we must begin to understand what democracy means. Because unless we do not get to understand democracy, we may very well find – haven't you seen some symptoms of it already – that the power passes from the hands of all the people into the hands of some of the people; and from there into the hands of the few of the people. Because – and everybody has an equal chance – power will in the long run belong to the intelligent and the active and will not belong to the sloth or the unaware. And, therefore, the price of democracy, with all the wonderful human benefits that it brings to mankind is that we should all learn to be democrats and that we should know what that means. Being a democrat just doesn't consist of going along to vote once in however many years it may be, doesn't consist of having violent opinions about one politician or another, doesn't consist of going along to some political meeting and demanding something for me as so many people will. The task of democracy is to understand what is good for the whole of the people. The task of the good democrat is frequently to abandon his own claims in favour of the claims of others. Indeed, at its best it is the task of the good democrat to be prepared to vote to injure his own interests if he thinks that what he is voting for is good for the community. And there are a few rare souls about who will do that, and do it like a shot, but there are far too many people to whom democracy is a rare instrument for getting something more for themselves, without any realisation of what the basis of this thing is.

Now, I will just mention two aspects of it because I don't want to be tedious. Every democrat has the task of contributing his or her support to the government of the country. Don't let us leave the thinking to a few people. I have an idea, Sir, I have mentioned this before today. I have frequently met friends of mine who regard themselves as rather powerful minds who have said to me: "Do you know, old man, I have been thinking hard about this problem and in my opinion this is the position". You see. And I have had to smile in that unfortunate manner that I have, they tell me, and say: "Yes old man, I know, I know, I read that in the leading article in the *Sydney Morning Herald* this morning. And all the thinking you have done about it you did coming in on the tram reading the leading article".

It is perfectly true, thinking is hard work. There are a lot of people still living in Australia who think that if you don't work with your hands you are not a worker. But thinking is mighty hard work and it can't be engaged in without preparation. It can't be engaged in without hard study of the facts. There is an awful lot to be done before you can start thinking about a problem. And yet, if Australia were to leave its thinking about political matters to a mere handful of people, would that be democracy? Is the beginning and ending of democracy merely to cast a vote and vote me in or vote me out? These things happen in the normal course with rhythmical regularity. Is that the beginning and end of democracy? Because it is the end of democracy unless most of us try to do our own thinking and to discover what is the right thing for the country. Don't let us delegate our thinking to a few because when we delegate our thinking to a few we correspondingly delegate power to a few.

You see how difficult it is. This democracy is not something you pluck already ripe from a tree and eat and enjoy. Democracy is an enduring task and an enduring challenge to all democrats. And the second aspect of the matter, which is a material aspect, is this: We must get out of the habit of thinking that the government can solve all our problems for us, that the government is some mystical, and indeed almost divine power which if it only had enough goodwill could relieve all of us from misery, from financial troubles, from whatever it is that besets us. Do you know there are lots of people who think that is so; who think that people like myself fall into error by sheer hardness of heart, by failure to understand that all I have to do is to say abracadabra and everything is alright. I wish I could, I have a few financial problems of my own. I would like to be able to solve them as readily as that.

But you see the truth is that we have nine million people in Australia and there is nothing that the government can hand out to anybody except something that the nine million people had themselves created and handed over to the government. Governments don't produce anything. What is a government? The government is an institution which happens to be made of human beings, very much the same kind of human beings as you, I imagine, but all the same – goodwill or bad will or desire to do things properly or not – human beings. But when a Treasurer decides that he is going to spend the equivalent of £1 million on things in Australia – an enormous sum of money – you don't suppose that he whistles for it. He first of all gets it from the people.

The most fascinating thing about a budget which 99 people out of a hundred appear never to have realised is that a budget contains two columns – one that is coming in and the other what is going out. And it comes in from the people and it goes out to the people. And nothing can go out that the people haven't first provided. When you confer what we are pleased to call "social benefits" on people, it is not a matter of saying: "Here are so many coins or so many banknotes". It is a matter of saying: "Here is so much of the means of existence; so much accommodation; so much food; so much of clothing". But accommodation has to be built by human effort; and food has to be grown and manufactured by human effort; and clothing grown and woven and manufactured by human effort. Nine million people will always have what nine million people are willing to produce. No more, unless they want to ruin themselves, and no less.

Now that is, I venture to say, as simple and as clear a proposition as maybe imagined. And yet, I believe it is the least understood. And the reason it is least understood is this: There will always be some people in the community who for reasons of one kind or another will actually get from the government more than they put in, because they are not capable of putting in more. For reasons of illness or of their economic position, or whatever it may be, it turns out that they draw more from the government than they pay into the government; that they collect more services than the services they actually render. That may be true. But if that is to happen, and it ought to happen, then there must be a lot of people who will contribute more than they take out. Because, we can't all take more than we give – that just doesn't make sense. And if we all give more than we take, then the government, that mystic being, will be gorged with financial resources and the budget will not be a balanced budget, and, therefore, by and large, allowing for individual variations, let us understand that the government is ourselves; and that we help ourselves best by contributing to government so that we may obtain from government what we need in a social way.

Now, that is the simple and immutable law of contribution in a democracy. And no democracy that doesn't understand that is a democracy at all. I have heard more nonsense talked in my lifetime about some marvellous financial theory under which money is whittled out of the blue sky. No more dangerous nonsense can be imagined. What is money worth to anybody unless there is something to buy with it? And if there is far more money than there are things to buy, then surely it is clear that the value of the money is going to fall, because money is only worth what it will buy. And therefore, if we want to raise our standards as a democracy, we want to get out of this habit of thinking that the main business of the democrat is to ask for things; and to come back to the plain truth that the main duty of a socially responsible democrat is to contribute to things, to give things, to hope that at the end of his life he will be able to say to himself without self-righteousness and without hypocrisy: "I think I have put more into this community than I have taken from it". That is the only way in which communities rise, that is the only way in which living standards grow, that is the only way in which great histories are made; We are proud of our history, aren't we? We will look back over the history of the British people, and allowing for all the errors and imperfections we know, don't worry that it is a proud history, that no race in the modern history of the world ever stood more consistently for good things or contributed more to the good things of life and the good things of living in the world?

How did it happen? It didn't happen because hungry generations – hungry in the sense of being selfish generations – trod down the history; it didn't happen because in Great Britain, among the English and Welsh and Scots and Irish, people were all the time concentrating upon what we want and not bothering about the other fellow. We are not going to contribute to him. They couldn't have had a great history under those circumstances. When Churchill spoke about their "finest hour", as indeed the Younger Pitt might have spoken about over a hundred years before, he wasn't talking about people who had, in the great trial of history, being taken up by their own desires, their own selfish interests, their own comfort. He was speaking of people who regarded sacrifice of comfort, the going hungry, the accepting of daily dangers, the helping of their neighbours under bombs and ruin of every kind, as their contribution to their country and to their race. They were great democrats. We must all learn from them.

3

POLITICS, PARLIAMENT AND GOVERNMENT

The Communists, Broadcast, Melbourne (2 July 1943)

Remembered for his unsuccessful attempt as Prime Minister to ban the Communist Party of Australia in a 1951 referendum, Menzies stood as an avowed foe of communism but what were the actual reasons behind his revulsion of this Marxist ideology? As Communist activity continued to fester in the Australian Trade Union movement during the War, Menzies used this speech to alert his audience as to why he regarded communism as inimical to liberal values and a menace to the Australian way of life. In particular, Menzies took issue with the deceptive nature of the movement which he saw as adept at concealing its true ideological colours from the public. As a liberal who aspired to class harmony and cooperation between employer and employee, Menzies denounced the divisive Marxist doctrine of "class warfare" as anathema to fostering a spirit of mutual understanding in society. Communism was deemed illiberal because its dictatorial quality denied ordinary people the freedom to be themselves and contribute to society. Accordingly, it represented the enemy of free enterprise, free association, free expression and religion. For Menzies, communism was particularly anti-Christian because its fanning of class envy ran counter to the Christian ethics of "brotherly love" and mutual responsibility that Menzies regarded as critical to the flourishing of liberal democracy.

....

In the last Labor conference at Melbourne, the Communists had a victory. The events of the last six months have to a large extent prepared us to do this because they have shown us a steady rise to power of Communist leaders and Communist-controlled trade unions. One would need to be singularly blind not to say that before another year has gone, the Trade Union movement will have fallen entirely into the hands of the Reds.

It is essential that people should understand this and remember it when they go to the polls.

Tonight I want to give you some reasons for my own detestation of the Communist policy and viewpoint. It is not based upon any mere catchwords about such elusive matters as "Russian gold" or "orders from Moscow". On the contrary, it is based upon a real conviction that Australian communism is the enemy of Australian democracy and that if our liberties are to be preserved and our development planned and carried out in an orderly way we must set up and take notice of the activities of those who stand for disorder, dictatorship and the class war.

At the outset, it is time that it was plainly stated that the Australian Communist Party has been in the most dishonest fashion trying to make political capital out of the suffering and struggle of the Russian people. "Why", they say, "look at Russia, look at the great fight she is putting up. Communism must be responsible for it. Therefore communism must be a good thing". It would be just as logical to say that capitalism or conservatism was responsible for the even more marvellous fight of Great Britain in 1940 or that Confucianism is completely vindicated by the struggle which the Chinese people have carried on for years. The truth is, my friends, that the war by the Russians in Russia is founded upon an old-fashioned quality which the Australian Communist despises – the quality of pure national patriotism; love of country; a resolute determination to defend Russia's independent existence. The claim that the Russians are fighting for some complicated set of Karl Marxian ideas is to ignore all the realities of human nature. It is, of course, unreasonable to ask the Australian Communist Party to understand this because it regards patriotism as a bourgeois sentiment, and boasts of the fact that until Russia came into the war it had no use for the war at all.

I wish I had time tonight to read to you some lengthy excerpts from the published views of some of the Union leaders who are in the forefront of the Communist campaign. They would make it clear to you that when this war broke out in September 1939 the Australian Communists were opposed to it and did their best to organise strikes in industry; did their best to impede war production; argued strongly for a negotiated peace; used all their poisonous old claptrap about this being "an imperialist" war like, (so they said), the war of 1914-1918.

The people of Australia need to be reminded that in the middle of 1940, at the most critical period in our history, when the British people stood in the military sense substantially alone, when the face of humanity was in the balance, and when the only second front that could be opened was one that we would open ourselves, the Australian Communists were either indifferent or hostile to the tremendous struggle. The Australian people need to be reminded that according to the Australian Communist philosophy the immortal young men of the Royal Air Force in the Battle of Britain gave their physical lives for a sordid and unworthy cause; that when young Australians died in Libya or Greece or Crete they died in a cause which became noble only when Germany subsequently attacked Russia, and Russia resisted.

It is no answer to all this to tell me that there are communists in the AIF. Of course there are. There are men of every possible political view in the AIF. I am not talking about individuals; I am talking about communism as an organised political body in Australia. It cannot escape condemnation and contempt simply because it has attracted some decent individuals to its banner.

Immense efforts are been put forward to dress Australian communism up in orthodox garments. In particular we have been witnessing the most ludicrous efforts to prove that communism, so far from being anti-religious or irreligious, has a really jolly and Christian quality in it. The Communists in this country have always been artists at camouflage. They organise themselves under different names and have a penchant for appearing in respectable company. At a Communist rally, it is always possible to induce two or three warm-hearted and simple-minded clergyman to appear on the platform. But a few minutes reflection will tell any thoughtful person that communism is and must be anti-Christian. Its founders in a philosophical sense, Karl Marx and Engels, would turn in their graves if they were told that the Australian Communist Party was seeking to obtain the votes of church people by claiming that communism is merely a pure manifestation of Christianity. Certainly the founders of Russian communism had no illusions as to where they stood, for they denounced religion as "the opium of the people", drove many churches out of existence and developed a marvellous propaganda technique, not in prohibiting religion, for that would have been impossible, but in seeking to persuade people, that it was a lot of irrational nonsense.

What is the essence of communism? If those who established it knew anything about it, we must assume that communism is a political and social doctrine of violence and conflict, of the class war leading to the dictatorship of the proletariat. It is founded upon the belief that there is an inevitable conflict between the so-called economic classes that the conflict must be carried on if necessary and indeed probably with arms and bloodshed and that as a result of a great clash of hatreds and of wills, we will ultimately emerge into a classless society in which all men will be equal in the eyes of an all-powerful state. Its thesis is entirely material. Christianity, on the other hand, sets out an entirely different philosophy. It denies the inevitable mutual hostility of social groups; it preaches the obligations of mutual understanding and love; it does not see the progress of men as something produced by the class war, by the violent clash of economic interests, by the surging to and fro of purely material movements. It calls on human beings to love their enemies and to do good to those who misuse them. It subordinates the purely material factors of life to the spiritual factors. It seeks to make men understand that there will never be a brotherhood of men over all the world except by the acknowledgement of a common fatherhood.

Now I ask you how can any intelligent human being pretend for a moment that there is any point of contact whatever between these two philosophies?

In an epoch-making statement published in Sydney this week the

two archbishops of Sydney, Dr Gilroy[14] and Dr Mowll[15], have condemned communism, in common with fascism and Nazism, for just
such reasons as I have been trying to put to you. Their statement has
of course been criticised and usually for this entirely sentimental and
irrelevant reason that the Russians have been fighting magnificently.
But really, if we are to be so stupid as to confuse Russian patriotism
with Australian communism then we don't really deserve to have a
vote at all. The sound men in the Australian labour movement and in
the trade union movement have understood this question all through.
That is why they have fought the Communists. That is why they had
resisted all specious applications for a "common front". Your true
Trades Unionist, while he may quarrel with me violently on many political matters at least agrees with me in thinking that of all the world
systems of government that of a liberal democracy is the best because
it alone recognises the infinite variations of human nature and the unlimited potentialities of the individual human being. Communism in
this country is the enemy of these things. It is illiberal, pagan, violent,
and essentially dictatorial. It does not believe in parliament. It does not
believe in cooperation or understanding. It does not even believe in the
country that shelters it and that has given it the privilege of shouting
its garbled nonsense from the street corner and through the wireless
microphone.

And yet, who knows – the Communists may very well be in control
of labour before we are twelve months older.

How do you like that prospect? And if you don't like it how are you
going to vote? It is going to be very important, isn't it? Your vote on
polling day may represent the one chance you will have in the next three
years of influencing the political and economic and social destiny of
Australia.

---

14 Dr Norman Gilroy (1896-1977) was the first Australian-born cardinal of the
Roman Catholic Church and served as Catholic Archbishop of Sydney from 1940
to 1971.

15 Dr Howard Mowll (1890-1958) was an English-born Anglican Evangelical who
served as Anglican Archbishop of Sydney from 1933 to 1958.

Opening Speech at Camberwell Town Hall, Melbourne (23 July 1943)

In a bid to commend his vision for a post-war Australia to the public, as the 1943 election approached, Menzies delivered a wide-ranging speech at Camberwell Town Hall in his East Melbourne electorate of Kooyong. While still on the backbench, Menzies used his speech to outline a broad policy agenda to his constituents that touched on such matters as regional and national security, trade and industry, post-war reconstruction, education, social security, housing and infrastructure. With quiet ambitions to eventually return to the Prime Ministership, Menzies maintained his intense interest in the future direction and development of Australia after the War. He desired the country to have a robustly competitive, private enterprise economy free from the clutches of socialism but one that was civilised and mindful of its social obligations towards the vulnerable, particularly the employees of businesses and firms. In his speech, he revealed his confidence in the character and resource of the Australian people to take their country forward.

....

Three years ago, on September 2, 1940, in this Hall, it was my duty as Prime Minister of Australia to lay before you the policy of the then government and ask for your endorsement of it. It was a policy which called for effort and sacrifice. It made no promises and offered no cash rewards. It declared that whatever our hopes for the future, our present task was to win a war which would determine "whether our problems should be solved by free people or by despotic power". From the point of view of traditional political strategy some pessimists thought that it was too bare and harsh a policy to succeed in a democracy. Yet, on polling day of 1940, five states out of six supported the government, though New South Wales crushingly defeated it ...

I pass over such important matters as industrial arbitration, the treatment of strikes, the necessary review of our over-abundant, complex and confusing wartime regulations, and such matters, with a mere mention – because Mr Fadden[16] has already outlined the Opposition's

16 Sir Arthur Fadden (1894-1973), Leader of the Country Party, 1941-1958, briefly succeeded Menzies as Prime Minister in 1941.

policy in relation to them. I would like, however, to offer some words of my own on the question of socialisation. I am no great believer in words or labels. We all have, I suppose, a socialist outlook up to a point. Few of us would have any quarrel with government control of railways or tramways or water supply or such other great public utilities. To me, the real question is whether we assign any and what place to individual or, as we perhaps wrongly call it, "private" enterprise in any reconditioned industrial order: Certain high ecclesiastics have made it fashionable to sneer at the profit motive as something faintly or even strongly discreditable. Yet I suppose everybody in this hall seeks to make such fair and modest profit as he can out of his business or his salary or his wage. So far from it being wrong to endeavour to secure a material margin in life, it is in my opinion the great solvent and stable element in proper society. Profit enables savings, thrifty people are the repositories of that spirit of individual enterprise and ambition which is the motive force in a progressive society.

Show me a nation in which everybody lives on the government and I will unhesitatingly declare it a nation whose decline and fall are at hand. It is impossible for any person who speaks with knowledge of the events in this country in the last few years not to realise that but for private industry and the many thousands of persons who have ventured their money in it we would have made few munitions in Australia and would have been almost naked to our enemies. Whatever else we do, we must not destroy this priceless element. This does not mean that we are to be reactionary and endeavour to go back to a state of affairs in which the government merely keeps the ring for the competitors. The post-war period will hold more government control then pre-war years. The element of reward, of initiative, is vital. Scope must be given to it.

Businesses, if they are to provide secure employment, must be permitted and indeed encouraged to be profitable, that is, to be successful. But in a just world, no business can be allowed to be successful except on terms that it pays proper wages, that it affords civilised living conditions, that it contributes adequately to the social security of its employees, that it stabilises employment as far as possible and that it admits its employees to the greatest possible extent to some share in the benefits which it may yield as a result of a cooperative effort.

For myself, I should like very much to see steps taken to break down the traditional, and in many cases unreasonable suspicion which exists between great enterprises and those who work in them. I believe that if employees had the means of accurate knowledge of the problems and financial results of their employers' operations there would be far more cooperation which is the thing to be produced only by knowledge and never by mere exhortation.

Finally, I would like to say a little to you about the future: It is difficult to discuss with any detailed accuracy plans for the post-war world when we are still at war and when we cannot see more than a shadowy outline of the shape of things to come. I have a lawyer's distrust of arguments divorced from facts. But at least we can have in our minds some vital principles to which we have decided that we shall do our very best to adhere. What is more important, we have 7 million people of great stock, full of the traditional British qualities of courage, cheerfulness and generosity. There is no task which we cannot assay with high hopes and quiet confidence.

It is unfortunate that so much of the discussion on post-war reconstruction should have centred so exclusively about purely material and monetary matters. They are of course extremely important and we should all be prepared to devote years and energy to solving the problems associated with them. But they are not everything.

The first problem that will confront the world, which includes Australia, when the war is over will be not how much we are to carve up the chicken – because the chicken by that time will be an emaciated bird at best – but how we are to prevent a repetition of the war. This will at once plunge us into a consideration of international politics which many of us in Australia have recently been studying with new eyes. With full knowledge of the inherent weakness and failures of the League of Nations, I affirm my own view that in some form of collective security resides the world's only real hope of permanent peace. The League of Nations failed not because it was too modest but because it was too ambitious. It tried starting from scratch, to have universal membership and universal discipline, founded upon nothing better than a contract.

This time, we shall have to begin more rationally. We shall, I believe, have to look for regional security pacts over the grouping of great nations which instinctively share common ideas and common desires. If it is my privilege to have any association with these matters, I shall work untiringly for a functional and if possible an organic association between the English-speaking democracies of the world. If they were automatically and under all circumstances together on the issues of peace or war there could be no greater guarantee of future stability.

Our next great task will be to clear out the channels of international trade, for without prosperous international trade there cannot very well be that domestic prosperity which this war generation is earning so splendidly. Such historic documents as the Atlantic Charter and the Lend Lease agreements are of great value but they do not solve problems; they state them. We in Australia for example are not to be expected to abandon the development of our vital secondary industries and therefore there must be some practical limits upon our acceptance of the doctrine of the universal sealing down of tariffs; a doctrine which in any case over-simplifies a tangled question. At the same time our primary industries are equally vital, and whatever internal policies we may pursue in relation to them (and I hope they will be liberal) it will still be true that their adequate recovery will largely depend upon the restoration and development of world markets.

It is thus clear that we must at the conference table be prepared to contribute more than a mere assertion of economic self-sufficiency. If world trade is to be restored we must play our part as contributors. There is nothing in our past tariff history to suggest that we cannot adequately protect sound secondary industries while at the same time remaining buyers from other countries of those commodities which they will seek to sell us in exchange for our wool and wheat and butter.

Before the war ends I should like to see the manufacturing, importing and primary producing interests of Australia breaking new ground by getting together to see just what sort of common contribution to world recovery can be presented when the time comes. Unfortunately in the past our primary industries have been dealt with almost exclusively in the political arena. The tariff ceased to a large extent to involve prolonged political arguments when the Tariff Board was set up and by its skill and character gains prestige and authority with the people. Why should there not be either an extended Tariff Board or some similar body to take the economic handling of the primary industries away from the political arena and onto a ground where it could be dealt with justly and on its merits.

These problems – and I might well add to them the problem of migration, on which I hope our short sightedness of the last 25 years will not be repeated after this war – are in reality international. You will permit me to refer to two internal problems of reconstruction:

The first is that of education, which is today a state matter but which I hope will increasingly become a Commonwealth matter, as indeed it must be if adequate expenditure is to be incurred in relation to it. To me education is the fundamental of post-war reconstruction.

Democracy cannot succeed merely by grace of the few leaders or a few thinkers. It must develop its citizens to that limit of their individual intelligence. It can never rest on its laurels while any boy or girl lacks the opportunity to become a trained and qualified citizen. This means two things: as a famous author has recently reminded us – "instruction teaches us to work; but education how to live". We must look to both things. Despite the efforts of zealous departments and enthusiastic men, our technical and trade training lags behind that obtained in other countries. We have done good things in elementary education, but by washing our hands of the average child at the age of 14 or 15 or 16 we have all too frequently converted one who might have been a good plumber into a bad clerk.

I could say a good deal about this problem but at this stage I content myself by saying that nothing less will do than a most resolute determination that after the preoccupations of this war we shall make a real and progressive attack without hesitation or false economy upon the problems of giving to each child a full chance to develop his or her nature and aptitudes; extending and improving the facilities for adult education, about which we have so far done practically nothing; multiplying the means of technical training; and improving the status and remuneration of teachers.

The other internal problem is the great one of social security. I am no believer in encouraging the notion that the citizen is simply dependent upon the state. It is a notion which is out of harmony with the tradition of the resourceful and independent Australian people. It is infinitely better that the State should be dependent upon the citizen. That we must do far more than in the past to give decent people some security in the face of sickness and unemployment is of course true. But in my opinion we must to the greatest possible extent do it upon the principle of contribution.

Unemployment allowances or sickness allowances or medical provisions should where possible not be made on any basis which to the slightest degree smacks of charity. A worker who falls out of employment should be able to collect his unemployment insurance not as if he were going "on the dole", but with self-respect as a man who collects something which is his right and to which in his days of employment he has made a contribution. Quite plainly, when the war is on us, and I may say that its expenditures are already more than double what they were when I spoke to you three years ago, it is not practical to make vast changes in every direction.

As you know I was a warm supporter of national insurance just before the war, and resigned my seat in cabinet because the scheme was not proceeded with. But it would be difficult to establish at this moment a complete health insurance plan at a time when a large proportion of the medical practitioners of this country are engaged in war duty. But there is no reason why a complete national insurance scheme should not be ready for immediate post-war execution. In some cases such as unemployment insurance, we ought to act right away because, there being no unemployment at present, a properly designed scheme would require such reserves that it could face possibly lean periods in future with strength and success.

Similarly there are, for reasons of material and manpower, great difficulties at present about homebuilding; but I should like to know that when the war ended we would have ready properly considered rehousing schemes which could be a valuable feature in the immediate post-war period.

The same is true of water supply. The proper conservation and distribution of water is one of the crying needs of millions of acres of land in Australia and there is nothing to prevent us from being ready for an attack upon the problem when the fighting ends.

These are particular instances of what I believe to be the general truth that some things permit of present planning and should therefore be planned now; that other things, and great things too, will depend upon the condition of the world and our place in it when the war is over. In relation to these things we must guard against any temptation to relapse into slackness when the emergency has passed.

We shall need good minds and flexible minds. We shall need to be ready to try new things and, what is more startling still, to think new thoughts. Many of the wartime controls will inevitably carry on for some time into the days of peace, for to terminate them suddenly might well produce chaos and would certainly produce injustice.

> But if we are conscious of our greatest destiny,
>
> if we aim steadily at international cooperation,
>
> at a revival of trade,
>
> at a marked increase in the population,
>
> at the encouragement of enterprise,
>
> at the maintenance of proper living standards,
>
> at the development of good brains in good bodies,
>
> at a proper sense of social justice and the dignity and importance of every individual

we shall not have any doubt about coming out from the trials of this war into a world where justice, that greatest of human elements, saved from its attacks by the blood and sacrifice of millions of simple people, will set up its throne in peace and honour.

"The Choice" Broadcast, Melbourne (1946)

The Federal election of 1946 represented the first electoral contest for Menzies' freshly-minted Liberal Party. With the post-war Chifley Labor government taking a decidedly socialist turn with its proposals to extend the reach of government, Menzies was determined to present his Liberal Party as an attractive alternative for the millions of Australians hungering for greater personal freedom from wartime controls and government regulation. In this broadcast, Menzies told his audience that it was impossible to reconcile "big government" socialism with the ethic of individual freedom and that voters were faced with a choice between the two at the ballot box. Menzies argued that his Liberal vision offered electors the assurance of benevolent and just government, but one which gave individuals the necessary scope and freedom to live their lives without undue interference from the State. While Menzies did not win the 1946 election, his message resonated with the electorate as his Party made up considerable ground to be in a winnable position to eventually claim government in the 1949 poll.

....

All politics involves a choice of men and of systems. But above all of systems. All parties realise that behind and beyond all systems are men and that the nature and spirit of man are all important. But however the nature of man may develop and improve, there will still be conflict about systems. That is why we have Parties and Governments and Oppositions.

This year Australia, with the war over, will face up to the decision as to the system under which it wants its post-war policies worked out and executed. As sensible people, we are bound to make a choice. It is ridiculous to vote for some member or candidate simply because we like him or respect him. For if he is elected his real significance will be derived from the kind of government he supports, the policies he advocates, the kind of laws he helps to make. It is worse than ridiculous, it is suicidal, to say, as some people are now tempted to say, that it doesn't matter what government is in so long as there is plenty of money in circulation, and that when the money begins to run out it will be time to make a change.

Now, what is the choice before us? Broadly, and I certainly don't intend to name them in order of merit, we can choose between communism, state socialism, and democratic liberalism.

Communism, as I will endeavour to prove in subsequent broadcasts, is to some people a vague expression, denoting a sort of kind-hearted materialism, a strong impulse towards drastic reform, which can find its expression by sending communists into Parliament and ultimately installing a sort of democratic Communist government.

The idea will not hold water. True communism is revolutionary. It aims at the overthrow of the existing system, political, social and industrial, by direct action, that is to say, by force. It rejects democracy in parliament, just as the Soviet Union has done. It is an alien doctrine, quite hostile to individual freedom, and quite foreign to the Australian tradition and character. If you doubt this, I just ask you to consider whether, if communism stood for parliamentary government and Constitutional action there would be much real difference between communism and socialism.

State socialism, our second choice, is espoused by the Australian Labor Party. Its classic objective, supported in writing by all Labour candidates, including that good-natured MP of yours who would like you to believe that he is so moderate that he is just as good as a Liberal or Country Party man from your point of view, is the "Socialisation of industry, production, distribution, and exchange."

This does not mean that you have to be a Socialist to believe that the State should run the railways or the tramways or some big source of electrical power, or any one of a dozen public utilities. Any Liberal, judging each case on its merits, may do that. What it means is that the Labour Party sees the way to human happiness is through more and more government action and control all round. Wherever some problem crops us, the Labour Socialist's immediate reaction is to pass another law, create another department, enlist another army of government servants, proclaim another set of regulations containing more rules and restrictions, and give us another set of forms to fill in.

That some substantial measure of government direction and control is necessary, nobody will deny. Industry must be compelled to discharge modern and civilised obligations to its employees and its customers. Business success must not be allowed to grow into monopoly because monopoly breeds tyranny and injustice. Competition must be kept within fair limits. Measures of Social Security must be enacted, and contributions to them secured.

But, while all this is admitted and warmly supported, we should remember that every increase of government activity means a reduction of individual freedom. Under the final, complete socialist system, when the State conducts all industry and we are all its servants, the real freedoms will have disappeared. For there can be no real freedom in a community in which the government controls our employment, and directs our lives, and runs newspapers and the broadcasting stations, and tells us when we shall work, and how. This is no exaggeration. It is futile to set out along a political road without asking about our destination! And the destination of the Socialist Road is a state in which there is only one employer – the State, and therefore no choice of alternative employment for the servants of the state. Socialism is government by authority and not by free individual will, and it is none the less authority because its source is to be found in the votes of a majority instead of in the decision of one man.

We need constantly to remind ourselves that democracy can produce tyranny just as readily as any other system of government unless the individual democrat has learned to attach supreme importance to individual freedom.

As for liberalism, its essence is its concentration upon individual freedom which it regards as being not only the most important element in our civilisation, but also the most endangered by the socialist advance.

Some of you may tell me that Labour socialism also believes in freedom and is only concerned with removing the physical and social barriers to its enjoyment. This is quite wrong. A Negro on an American plantation who happened to have a kind-hearted master in the slavery days before the American Civil War enjoyed certain freedoms. He had freedom from want, and freedom from fear, and indeed freedom of worship, but he was not a free man. He could not choose his own employment. He had one master, and one only, whom he was bound to obey. He could not move about and choose his residence at his own will, but only by permission of the prescribed authority, his owner. And without the choice of one's own means of life, there is no real freedom as we know it.

To liberals, the practical issue for the years to come is plain. Are we to have a government which, exercising central and complete authority, plans and directs our lives for us according to the notions worked out by largely theoretical planners and administered by officials who are necessarily more concerned with general rules than with individuals? Or are we to confine the activities of government to those matters which lend themselves to general rules, to industrial policy, fiscal policies, the gathering and collating of information, the reinforcement of obligations to pay good wages and observe proper conditions and provide adequate security against economic misfortunes, the adoption of measures designed to encourage enterprise and reward thrift, leaving the actual conduct of industrial affairs and the actual planning of business activities to those who are, competitively, best qualified to the task.

We do not ask for unrestricted competition or uncontrolled private enterprise. We are not apostles of the old *laissez faire* idea. But we do say that unless the enterprise and freedom of the individual are recognised and aided as the dynamic of progress, the end will be disaster.

In my next few broadcasts I propose to deal further with the question of communism, and having, I hope, cleared our minds of that pestiferous growth I will then proceed to discuss those great practical issues which exist between the Labour government and His Majesty's opposition.

New Year Message, Broadcast, Canberra (1 January 1952)

In this New Year broadcast, Prime Minister Menzies exhorted his fellow Australians to be positive contributors to the security and prosperity of a nation that he regarded as being singularly fortunate. With the spectre of the Cold War ever present, the Prime Minister warned Australians to grow neither weary nor complacent about the present, but to use the present as an opportunity to build an even better future by channelling the selfless, enterprising spirit of the nation's early pioneers. He reminded Australians that economic hardships, such as inflation, were basically human problems that required a reserve of national determination and discipline to be successfully overcome. Essentially, the strength and prosperity of a democracy such as Australia was contingent upon the character and resolve of its own people. This was not something that governments could produce, but only something that individual citizens could cultivate.

....

Let us look at the New Year together. Let us forget our differences and concentrate on our points of agreement. For if men and women remembered nothing but their disputes, and strove only to disagree, it would be a mad world and a bad world and human society as we know it would disappear.

We live peacefully in civilised communities simply because in most things we agree. What a moving thing it is that, wrangle as we may about what the law should be, practically every one of us obeys it instantly when it is passed. Intolerant as we sometimes are of those of other creeds, we all find comfort at Christmas time in the common thought of an all-wise creator whose tolerance and justice we all aspire to receive.

Unity is strength. But the most important unity is in the spirit, in the consciousness of community. Never was this more true than today, when so much is happening to vex the peace of the world and to threaten the ancient freedoms. "A house divided against itself cannot stand".

I speak for my colleagues. But in particular I crave your leave to speak for myself as your Prime Minister speaking to his own people. It is the glory of our democracy that the head of the government is the servant of the people, not their master. It must be his constant duty to seek the good of all. If he is called upon to speak of the need for hard work, he must work hardest of all. If he urges a spirit of self-sacrifice, he must set an example.

I am myself very conscious of these matters, and of a high responsibility to which you have called me. Your problems are mine in a very particular way. For not only does the burden of taxation and of the falling value of money fall upon me as upon you; it does so with the added force that comes from the fact that you have placed upon my shoulders the responsibility of leadership and guidance and wise judgement. You have a right to expect of me toil and honest thought, and courageous decision, and a willingness to accept unpopularity in what seems to me to be a good cause. All these things are part of my duty to you. I can only say that I pledge myself to that duty to the limits of my capacity.

We Australians are attacking some great and formidable task under circumstances of grave shortage of both men and materials. And these tasks are made doubly difficult because the national income, expressed in terms of money, out-runs the volume of our production and procurement of goods, with the result that what we call inflation is proceeding to reduce most grievously the value of the pounds that we earn.

Now, I am not going to inflict upon you, on New Year's Day, a political treatise on the treatment of inflation. But I do want to make one point: Inflation is a common enemy. It attacks everybody's pound alike. It is monstrously unjust, for it does most damage where there is the least power to resist it.

When we have a common enemy in war, we get together to fight him. The nation strives as one for victory. The free world could not have won the last war if the soldiers had said, "leave it to the generals", and the people had said, "leave it to the politicians". That war was won by scores of millions of ordinary men and women who were prepared for sacrifices, who had endurance, who are not dismayed by dangers or defeats. And if, today, inflation is our common enemy, are we not to meet it by national unity and common effort? How can we defeat it otherwise? We have put into action our programme. You may think it harsh and uncomfortable. But it is not so harsh or uncomfortable as the widespread misery and bitter injustice which would come from national financial disaster. There will be economic casualties, just as there are more vital casualties in war. But I have yet to hear from anybody of any other plan of campaign; and without a plan of campaign this fight cannot be won.

It must be won, and it will be won. Whatever temporary hostilities it may provoke, we are determined to go on with it. For our duty is to the ordinary men and women of our country and not to any vested interest, whether capital or labour. It is fatally easy to become so taken up with our difficulties that we fail to count our blessings. After all, it's the optimists who get things done.

Let us each carry his own burden. Let us each do more and produce more. Let us not yearn too much for life's fripperies or sink into the spiritual bankruptcy of always wanting "something from nothing" or even "as much as we can get for as little as we can give".

We are a great people, and have a great and honest inheritance. We are still only on the threshold of our national life. We are the pioneers of the future, not the mere remittance-men of the past. If our problems are great, let us remember that our race became great by the overcoming of problems, and that the civilisations of the past weakened and perished only when they sought to ignore or to avoid them.

Judged by material standards, 1951 was a prosperous year for most of our people. For those whose money incomes did not keep pace with the rising prices it was a hard year. That is the real bitterness of inflation; it bears most harshly on those who live on more or less fixed incomes, often the result of thrift and a spirit of independence. That is the big reason for our concern over inflation. It creates an illusion of wealth, for money becomes more and more plentiful. But, unless checked, it leads first to hardship for a valuable minority, and then to hardship for all. Inflation cannot be defeated by some artificial law. Laws are useful things. But no law can improve the spirit of man; no order can be a substitute for a strong will; no government can do for us what, as eight million individuals, we cannot or will not do for ourselves.

As a nation, we have been trying to do too much too quickly. But as individuals too many of us have been trying to do too little too slowly. Let us make a national effort in 1952. Let it be founded upon the individual effort of every one of us. I assure you that I have a serene confidence that with such an effort, we shall, in this new year, this Royal year, in which the king's daughter comes to us, have such a victory as will bring to us a rich growth, a new stability, a broader social justice than we have ever known before. I wish you all a Happy New Year.

New Year Message, Broadcast (1 January 1953)

Prime Minister Menzies began 1953 with another address to encourage the Australian people to be the builders of a better tomorrow. Mindful that the relative peace and stability that Australia enjoyed in the present-day owed much to the received institutions of the past, the Prime Minister began his address by welcoming the ascension of Queen Elizabeth II to the throne. For Menzies, the coronation of the young Queen in 1953 would represent the rejuvenation of an ancient institution that served as the fulcrum to Australia's tried and tested system of responsible government. In addition, she would emerge as a worthy successor to the sovereign who had done so much to lift the spirits of his people through the darkest days of the Second World War. Turning to the present and the future, Menzies anticipated that the challenges of 1953 would call for all the strength and character of the Australian people to maintain peace, prosperity and good order at home and abroad.

....

New Year's Day is much more than a trick of the calendar. We are all interested in it. It is the beginning of something new, the first dawning of an unknown day of hopes and fears and joys and sorrows.

What are we all thinking about?

The Queen, whom I saw only the other day in all her radiant youth and beauty, is thinking of her Coronation; a Coronation which for fortunate millions will be a dazzling spectacle, but for her, our Liege Lady, a solemn act of consecration to duty.

Could I say two things to you about the Queen? The security of the throne rests more and more upon the personal quality of the throne's occupant. In this respect, we have been and are most happy and most blessed. But the throne is, of necessity, as lonely as it is exalted. It has to sustain burdens, not of legal power, but of high example and inspiring leadership. It is the beacon of unity for hundreds of millions of people for whom the flame must burn with a clear and steadfast light. To these high tasks there has come a young woman, trained, poised, an arresting blend of gaiety and responsibility; in the great tradition, but yet modern, and eager, and warm-hearted. Rich though she is in her husband who matches her own youth with his own and gives her an incomparable companionship, and in her children, she still needs our prayers and our love and our encouragement. She must know, as indeed she does know, that we are proud of her, and have faith in her, and will ever be her loving and faithful people. God bless her! May she reign over us for fifty years!

For the great statesmen of 1953, the Churchills and the Eisenhowers, the New Year will be one of saving a peace which they did so much to earn and to secure. Let us think of them, and put up our wishes for them. They will need all their strength and all their human understanding. They will need our support, even when we do not quite understand all the facts, or see quite clearly the current of their policies. I can assure you that there is magnificent character at a higher level in the free world; let us support it with all that we have and are.

For us, in our own homeland, the outlook is good. How good, will depend on us. We can consolidate our prosperity by honest endeavour, by accepting each of us his own responsibility, by avoiding the easy cynicisms of politics, by restoring our faith in the sturdy and simple virtues which have made us the nation that we are. If we have one weakness, it is that we are occasionally tempted to think that governments can do everything and that if there are difficulties they arise from malice or incompetence on the part of governments. I beg of you to cast such thoughts aside.

Properly considered, governments do not create; they direct. They provide nothing for the people which the people themselves have not provided by work and integrity and skill and pride. We are all engaged in a joint enterprise in which the failure of any one of us places some extra burden upon the others. It is a marvellous thing to live in a free and democratic land. How free and how democratic we shall be in this bright New Year will be decided by our own actions, the high and unselfish level of our thinking, our cheerfulness and good humour, and our sense of brotherhood.

It is with confidence in Australia, and the abundant hopes of peace and order and growing prosperity for the world that I offer to you, on behalf of the Commonwealth government, warm good wishes for the New Year.

Role of Government in Society, "Australia Today – Man to Man", Broadcast, Canberra (4 November 1953)

In this radio broadcast, Prime Minister Menzies articulated his liberal philosophy on the proper role of government in society. He reminded his audience that while government had legitimate functions to perform in a modern society, particularly with respect to the provision of health care, law and order, defence, education and social services, Australians must not fall into the trap of depending on government at the expense of individual initiative and self-reliance. In an age where post-war socialism in Britain, Australia and New Zealand had popularised the concept of the welfare state, Menzies warned citizens of the danger in regarding government as some kind of all-powerful deity. At best, government could function as a "machine" to provide the necessary conditions for responsible, self-reliant individuals to freely pursue enterprise and contribute to the good of the nation.

....

Good evening ladies and gentlemen:

If you were to say to me: "What is the greatest change in basic political thought that has occurred in Australia in your lifetime?" I think my answer would be: "Our people are now willing to be more dependent on the government. I sometimes wonder whether the old fine independence of spirit which built Australia is beginning to disappear!"

This, I agree, seems such a sad thing to say that I am reluctant to believe it. Reluctant, because of the great pioneering efforts which made Australia were the efforts of individual men and women; because the whole military reputation of Australia, a high and splendid reputation all around the world, was founded upon individual courage, resource and initiative.

Are these great qualities really disappearing, or are they just temporarily under a cloud? Have we really got to the stage where we say instinctively and automatically, about any trouble of any kind, "What is the government going to do about it?" Has self-help ceased to be the first of duties, and one of the greatest of social virtues?

Now, having put these questions, let me attempt an answer. And, to make an answer, let us first face the facts, frankly and simply. Beyond doubt, we look to government now more than our grandfathers did.

This is, I admit at once, partly because our taxes are higher, and we think we are entitled to our money's worth. But, as we make this excuse, let us admit that our taxes are higher very largely because we expect the government to do more and more things for us, and that means more government expenditure and more taxes.

But this is not the whole answer. My own belief is that there are two tremendous errors in our public thinking, and that unless we clear our minds of them we will encounter no end to our trouble in the future.

The first error is that of thinking that "The Government" is an artificial but benevolent sort of body, quite detached from ourselves, which can produce money without effort and jobs without difficulty and can ease our paths through lives of complete security. "The Government" has become a sort of pagan God, possessing all power, a power quite independent of our own contribution, but sometimes, through sheer perversity, inflicting upon us depressions and shortages and unemployment. This conception of government is a most grievous error. In a democracy, the government is ourselves, and nobody else. Your prime minister was a boy born in the bush, and trained to earn his living by the development and use of his own mind. Your ministers are normal Australians, whose language you understand and whose experience of life is very much the same as yours. Your government cannot serve its personal interests at the expense of yours, partly because it is made up of honest men, and partly because if it tried to do so it would cease to be your government. It has no money to spend on its own account. It pays no pension that the taxpayers do not provide. It borrows no money except from the people, and the people themselves accept the obligation to repay the loan. It spends nothing that the people have not earned and entrusted to it. Once these facts are stated, and you will at once say that they are facts, you will all begin to realise that instead of saying, "What will the government do for us?" We should be saying, "What will we do for ourselves?"

There is a great moral truth in these simple remarks. If we think that an abstract body known as "The Government" is going to carry our burdens, we will be tempted to slacken our own efforts. If we think that "The Government" is the other fellow, always so much better off than we are, we will be tempted to leave the job to him. But when we realise that we are the government, and that no government can do more for us than we, the sum total of the people, can do for it, then we will find ourselves acting as those who know the dignity of labour, the just pride of work well done, the spiritual elevation of a duty performed, not simply for ourselves, but for our neighbours.

Let us get back to the ancient virtues, one of the chief of which is sturdy independence and an unwillingness to lean upon the efforts of others.

The second error is, at bottom, the classical socialist error; the error of thinking that the State – meaning by that "The Government" – can always do things for us more effectively than we can do them for ourselves. Sometimes, of course, the State can. It can organise defence better than you and I can. It can plan and carry out public works. It can devise and carry out the education of the young. It can keep the peace and administer justice. But the dynamo, the driving force of human progress is in the heart and mind and energy of the individual. Government is at best a machine. It must be driven by men and women; not by men and women as mathematical figures in the year book, but by John Smith and Mary Jones, who may know a little about yearbooks, but who do their work and have their ambitions and see some vision of the future. It is by the encouragement of John Smith and Mary Jones that the world moves on. The moment the thing we are pleased to call government responsibility destroys the much more vital sense of individual responsibility, we will be lost indeed. This is of the essence of all religious faith, of all true social service, of all enduring democracy.

When I was a child, living in what was then called the Victorian Mallee, near the banks of the Wimmera River, there came the great drought of 1902. There was, for all practical purposes, no rain. The grass dried and was eaten or blew away. The earth was brown and dry. There was no harvest. The red pall of dust covered the sky, day after day. In this state of utter disaster, the then government of Victoria made advances to farmers for seed wheat for the planting of the next crop. The advances were taken up. The next harvest was a great one. Within a few months of that harvest and the collection of the proceeds, all the advances were repaid. To be in debt or under obligation to a government was felt to be a sort of subtraction from individual independence. We have moved since those days – backward or forward? I sometimes wonder.

Of course, times change, and we change with them. Vast government responsibilities are here to stay, and inevitably to grow. But the whole point of my talk this evening is that before we ask the government for more we should pause and remember that we, as 8 000 000 individuals, must produce the goods before the government can distribute them, must earn and pay our taxes before the government can spend them. In brief, the government has no divine creative power; but men and women have.

"Medicine, Politics and the Law", Arthur E Mills Memorial Oration, Royal Australasian College of Physicians, Sydney (11 May 1955)

Invited by the Royal Australasian College of Physicians to deliver the annual Arthur E Mills Memorial Oration, the Prime Minister spoke about the intersection of three professions, two of which he had had first-hand experience and one of which he deeply respected. In this lengthy address, Menzies drew out many of the similarities between these professions and how they each had a mission to serve the best interests of humanity. His insights into politics and the law had been gleaned from years of practice as a parliamentarian and a barrister where he had witnessed the contest of policy ideas in the parliamentary chamber as well as the pursuit of justice in the courtroom. While Menzies himself was no medical man, he took pride in the achievements of his government in healthcare policy, particularly during the early years of his second prime ministership. Working with his Minister for Health and old Country Party nemesis, Sir Earle Page, Menzies had introduced the *National Health Act* (1953) which instituted a new medical health scheme for Australians. While this scheme brought medical treatment within the reach of every citizen, it differed from Labor's policy of socialised medicine by preserving the freedom of choice for patients and the personalised doctor-patient relationship. Proud of this legacy, Menzies maintained an abiding interest in the medical profession and the evolution of healthcare which was evident from his observations in this lecture.

....

I thank you for the great honour you have just conferred upon me...I read that the purpose of the Arthur E Mills Memorial Oration is "the promotion and encouragement of medical education" (on which I must confess my incompetence at once) "and general culture and dissemination of knowledge" (a phrase which gives me a small chance but smaller comfort). In a genial and expansive moment I chose for my subject, "Medicine, Politics and the Law". Here is indeed a wide canvas on which to paint; much too wide, as I now realise, for my pigments or my brush. For the truth is that my title embraces three topics, each of vital importance and each, therefore, deserving of more than sketchy treatment.

For the truth is that in this strange, mad, clever, but in many ways uncivilised century, some of the greatest and best things in civil life have been the development and triumphs of curative and preventative medicine, the spread of the rule of law to new nations, and the adoption in many new areas of the political institutions of democratic self-government ...

Take politics. If we give all our time in headlines to the antics of cheap and noisy demagogues, and to occasional outbursts of vulgar abuse in Parliamentary debate, we may conclude that politics is rotten; that "politician" should be a term of reproach; and that Parliament ought to be abolished or drastically reformed. Yet abolition is unthinkable; and Parliament is reformed every three years, anyhow, by you and millions of others at a general election. The truth is that Parliament should be judged by its best; by the quality of its law-making; by its statesmanship.

To speak of Australia is to speak of men and events too close for detached judgement. But, to take an example, can there be much wrong with politics in Great Britain when we see, in a brief half century, a Balfour[17] , an Asquith[18], a Haldane[19], a Birkenhead[20], a Milner[21], a Lloyd George[22], a Salisbury[23], a Churchill? Democratic politics may have

---

17 Arthur James Balfour (1848-1930) was a British Conservative MP who served as the Prime Minister of Britain from 1902 to 1905.

18 Herbert Henry (H H) Asquith (1852-1928) was a British Liberal MP who served as the Prime Minister of Britain from 1908 to 1916.

19 Richard Haldane (1856-1928) was a Scottish Liberal, who served as British Secretary of State for War (1905-1912) and Lord Chancellor (1912-1915; 1924).

20 The Earl of Birkenhead (1872-1930) was a British Conservative MP and barrister who served as Lord Chancellor from 1919 to 1922.

21 Alfred Milner (1854-1925) was a British statesman and colonial administrator who served as Secretary of State for War, 1918-19, and Secretary of State for Colonies, 1919-22.

22 David Lloyd George (1863-1945) was a British Liberal MP who served as the Prime Minister of Britain from 1916 to 1922.

23 The 3rd Marquess of Salisbury (1830-1903) was a British Conservative MP who served as Prime Minister of Britain, 1885; 1886-92; and 1895-1902.

shown, here and there, folly, corruption, avarice, moral cowardice or gross ignorance. So does mankind; and a representative system may well reflect that fact.

But the glory of democratic self-government is that it has not only lifted the status and expanded the horizons of ordinary men and women, but has also produced some of the greatest and wisest and bravest men of modern times. It is only by remembering this and rejoicing in it that we can hope to escape the deadly cynicism about politics which, with its clammy hand, reduces enthusiasms and discourages generous effort.

And so of medicine. That there are charlatans and rogues and bunglers, nobody can deny. But only as aberrations from the standard are news, and vice more readable than virtue, we hear about them, and we exaggerate them. It is now many years since I discovered that in the great professions (except politics, which, in its nature, must be carried on in the fierce light of publicity), the finest exemplars are frequently the least known and the least advertised. Of no profession are these remarks more true than that of medicine.

There have, on the very summit of skill in Australia, been hundreds of medical men of the rarest ability, of the most generous and devoted impulses, great servants of sick humanity, miracles of energy and endurance, without leisure and the regulated life of others, whose very names are, and will continue to be, unknown to the overwhelming bulk of their fellow countrymen. Yet, they are the proof of excellence. There can be nothing basically wrong with the profession which produces them.

And so, judging by the best, I turn to my own profession of the law, and to the list, for example, of the Chief Justices of the High Court – Griffith, Knox, Isaacs, Gavan Duffy, Latham, Owen Dixon. It was no mean profession which produced such men, taking their places among the greatest lawyers in the English-speaking world.

Having said this, I propose to say something about the interaction of these great professions, of Medicine and Politics, of Medicine and the Law.

Medicine and Politics

No profession has in modern times made such strides as medicine in skill and in public respect. More than three centuries ago, it was possible for Francis Bacon in his "Advancement of Learning" to say: "Medicine is a science which hath been…more professed than laboured, and yet more laboured than advanced; the Labour having been in my judgement rather in circle than in progression". He may have been right. Certainly less than a century later, we find Samuel Pepys describing an operation for the "stone" in terms of sheer barbarism.

For more than two centuries after Bacon, the physicians were as busy reducing bodily afflictions by drawing off the patient's blood as they are now busy pouring blood into the patient. Until the bio-chemists enlightened the 20th century with their painstaking genius, the sedative drug was the prescription and nature the healer. Until this modern revolution occurred, surgery, backed by the discovery of anaesthetics and introduction of anti-septic and aseptic methods, seemed to have taken the lead.

In the present century the physician, the chemist, the engineer have wrought wonders in preventative medicine; antibiotic and related drugs have eliminated some diseases and drastically reduced the mortality of others; literally millions of lives have been saved which 60 years ago would have been lost.

The effect of all this is, even now, difficult to estimate. That it has been of benefit to mankind is beyond question. That it has added to the problem of politics I have no doubt; for though politicians, having this in common with ordinary mortals, live longer (physically at any rate) than their predecessors of the 18th century, they find increasingly that the growth of numbers in the old age groups is proportionately so much greater than that of numbers in the earning and productive age groups, that the relation between government social services and the national product is achieving a new significance, bringing with it the most remarkable changes in our social, economic and financial structure …

As I have already established some association between the work of the physician and the problems of the politician, let me develop the nature of the political problems a little more clearly.

There was a time not so long ago when many men thought that it was easy to draw a clear line between matters which it was appropriate for governments to undertake and those which should be left to the ordinary citizen. The consequences of that assumption, put into practice, was that the functions of government were restricted, the burdens of government were light, taxes were almost negligible, great fortunes were made and poverty and misery came to be regarded as the natural lot of the great number of good people.

There were in the 19th century notable reformers who set about to change that state of affairs by political and industrial and social action.

The 20th century has seen the most radical changes. Today many of us, indeed I would hope most of us, still think it important to draw the line, but we no longer think it easy. For complexities of modern life are astonishing, and the methods of democratic self-government inevitably lack subtlety.

Governments and parliaments cannot deal with individuals or exceptional cases except to a minor degree. Parliamentary law has of necessity a fairly rigid form. It deals with people and transactions in the mass. It achieves the paradox of being at one and the same time sharp in its incidence and yet, humanly speaking, a blunt instrument. For example, a law providing for a pension or some other social benefit must have precision when it defines eligibility for grant. This very precision, because it excludes the exceptional case, will exclude some deserving people and include some others whose merits are dubious. Such anomalies cannot be avoided in terms except at the risk of an over-elaboration and over-refinement of definition which in the long run may hurt more than it cures.

The alternative to over-elaboration is to create in the Statute a wide area of administrative discretion. This is a process which gives too much uncontrolled power to officials, leads to grave uncertainties, and renders it impossible for most people to know or enforce their rights. Government by regulation has been much attacked in recent times as constituting the "new despotism". Sometimes it has been attacked with good reason. But government by administrative discretion is much worse, for it runs counter to all the lessons of history and is deeply opposed to sound democratic theory and practice.

The end result of 20th century laws and policies is what has been styled the Welfare State, some of the implications of which deserve some clearer public understanding that now appears to exist. The most important practical implication is one to which I have already alluded, but which needs repetition. A community of individuals who expect and receive, at all stages of life, assistance and protection from the State must of necessity, by proper fiscal measures, accept the economic and financial burden of providing that assistance and protection. Many individuals may properly get from government more than they pay to or provide for government; some may even get "something for nothing", though I doubt it. But the sum of what all the individuals get cannot exceed the sum of what all the individuals pay or provide, for the government has no money of its own! ...

I do not believe that any sensible observer could doubt that for years to come at least we must accept as part of the burden of our life relatively high levels of taxation. As production grows, as our creation of wealth increases, so we all hope to see the proportionate burden of our taxes reduced. But, reduced or not, they will continue to be relatively high. The effect of high taxation is, of course, to limit personal savings; and, as the personal savings which enabled many people to assure their own independent future, and which provided capital for expansion, became more difficult, so will there be further demands upon governments and upon government action. All these things mark, as I have said, a social revolution. It is idle to protest against it. It has many aspects which are admirable and some which are magnificent. Our task is to make it work, and not to allow it to develop into a vicious spiral terminating in the elimination of private capital and initiative and the creation of an all-powerful State.

I have dwelt on this point in order to emphasise that we are not just to cry for the "good old days" when governments, so it was said, attended to "their own business". We have to try to weave into this new fabric some of the old virtues and good things which all of us want to preserve. In brief, if governments are to do more and more, let us at least see that they act in such a way as to preserve the greatest measure of independence of spirit and do not sink into the area of creating a universal feeling of dependence upon government, or a willingness to accept as inevitable the complete regimentation of life by political authority.

You of the medical profession have every reason to be concerned about this problem, and deeply interested in its solution. For whatever the scientists may have discovered about the causes and treatment of disease, whatever the new techniques that have evolved, whatever the immense subdivision of skills which appear to mark modern times, I affirm my belief that there can be no proper medical services to our people unless it preserves freedom of choice, the personal relationship, and some obligation of self-help. I adhere to my conviction that there is a definite therapeutic value in the confidence of the patient in the doctor of his choice. There is on the doctor's side a potent humanity and a real enhancement of his understanding and skill in the personal knowledge that he has of the patient whose doctor and friend he has frequently been for a long time.

I am very proud of the fact that, after years of conflicting views and sometimes of sharp dispute, my own government has been able to institute a medical health scheme which, while it brings medical treatment within the reach of everybody, has set out to preserve these precious elements to which I have referred. The whole thing indeed is a splendid example of how by hard work and co-operation between government and profession, the existence of a high degree of government action can be reconciled with the preservation of the private enthusiasm and independent activities of the citizen.

Twenty years ago it was a common experience for me to be told by bankers or by doctors or by many other people of various groups and occupations that they took no interest in politics. More than once I remember replying that the day would come when politics would take an interest in them. That day has come. The fact that it has come does not mean that you must all become politicians in the sense that I am one, engaged in daily controversy, drawn off from private life or private interests, but it does mean that you must all become politicians in the sense that you give serious thought to what I have endeavoured to describe as the great internal problem of our times; the problem of reconciling the growth in the power and responsibility of government with the power and responsibility of private citizens ...

Law and Medicine

So there we have politics and medicine, and something of their inter-relation. I will now say something about medicine and the practice of the law; about doctors and lawyers ...

For the true object of the true lawyer is justice; justice according to the law; the application of the rules of law to facts affirmed, cross-examined, established, fearlessly and objectively. That is the justice to which the medical man, a defendant to some action, is entitled. Do our present methods reasonably guarantee such justice to him? Speaking, not as Prime Minister but as a lawyer, I take leave to doubt it. It is one of the oddities of human nature that those we fly to most readily for help in time of trouble, or for protection against the threat of future trouble, are frequently those whom we abuse most roundly when all seems well. It is not uncommon to hear lawyers described as sly and cunning cynics, whose prospects of a satisfactory hereafter are dim. Yet they are the first resort of those in trouble or difficulties, and are the trusted custodians of the confidences and secrets of many thousands. And this is even more true of doctors. But let a doctor be accused of negligence, and sued in damages, and some juries will (or did in my experience) give a verdict against him, and damage his reputation, on the earthy principle that "the plaintiff is a poor and suffering soul, and could do with the money". The whole point about British justice is that it is justice according to the law. LEX EST REX. It is not to be swayed by passion or prejudice or admirable but irrelevant social motives.

I believe in juries in criminal cases, for they acquit unless satisfied beyond reasonable doubt, and a layman is as qualified to have reasonable doubts as any lawyer. But where the issues involve the examination of highly technical problems, as in an action of negligence against a doctor, I will take leave, impertinently, to believe that a judge, accustomed to understanding new bodies of knowledge and to judicial consideration of them, would produce a sounder justice according to the law. Juries are an admirable and worldly-wise instrument in libel, in slander, in all matters in which the sensible judgement of ordinary men is, in reality, the standard of judgement at which the law aims. But in complicated technical matters, I doubt whether the jury is truly "the palladium of English liberty". Well, I have come to an end. I am sorry to have taken so long, and, as I fear, to have said so little. But if anything I have said has increased in any way "the dissemination of knowledge" – I say nothing of "general culture" – then the purpose of the establishment of this memorial to a great and good and wise man will not have been entirely defeated.

Australian Federalism ("Passing the Buck"), "Australia Today – Man to Man" Broadcast (30 April 1958)

On the theme of Australian nationhood, Prime Minister Menzies drew attention to the fact that Australia functioned as a federal democracy. As such, this implied a special relationship between the national government and the constituent State governments in the shared responsibility for managing the economy and other national affairs. As Prime Minister, Menzies practised a doctrine of "balanced federalism". As an Australian patriot, Menzies envisaged a strong role for the Commonwealth government in directing the progress and development of the country as a whole. With his liberal philosophy of smaller government, nonetheless, he was also an instinctive federalist who favoured the devolution of power across several state jurisdictions. In this address, the Prime Minister acknowledges the practical complexities of Commonwealth-State relations, but ultimately defends federalism as the ideal system for governing a geographically expansive country such as Australia.

....

Good evening ladies and gentlemen:

Some of you may have heard me say before that, if we want to have a free society and a non-socialist economy, we must not fall into the habit of going to the government for everything.

Tonight I want to speak about what that expression, "the government", means.

In Australia, we have lived under a system of government which it took many years, and many great men, to fashion. We have been a Federal Commonwealth for 57 years.

Our Federation is a system under which, by a written constitution, certain powers of government are given to the Commonwealth Parliament and others are left with the State parliaments. So that the Commonwealth Parliament will not exceed its powers or State parliaments go beyond their powers, we have a High Court which decides such matters on proper principles of legal interpretation.

This division of powers is vital to a federation. There have been many instances in which the High Court has declared a Commonwealth law invalid, e.g. the bank nationalisation laws, the Act to outlaw the Communist Party, the Acts which attempted to give the government Air Line a monopoly.

The Commonwealth Constitution is the fundamental law of the nation, binding on all governments and parliaments as well as on all citizens. We cannot laugh it off nor can we sensibly describe any reference to it as a mere "legal quibble".

It is for these reasons that you have sometimes heard me or one of my Colleagues say, in answer to a request that the Commonwealth do something or other, "This is a state matter". And then somebody says – "Passing the buck!"

The suggestion is, of course, that the Commonwealth can do anything it likes as if the Constitution did not exist! If that were the true position, we would not be a federation, but a unified country in which States and State parliaments had no place or function. You cannot brush off respect for the Constitution by using funny expressions about "buck passing".

Under each State Parliament, and created by it under statute, we have local or municipal governments. The Commonwealth Parliament cannot either create or destroy them; nor can it direct them how to do their work. But a State parliament can.

This may seem, to outsiders, a complicated and inefficient system of government. But it suits Australia, which has an enormous area, a relatively small and scattered population, and an immense variety of climates, living conditions, and local problems. Most of us feel that it would be a grave mistake to concentrate power in Canberra. State governments and local governments are physically near to the people with whom they deal, and the local problems with which they deal are in their nature not appropriate for remote control.

If we had a referendum asking us to approve of all power being handed over to the Commonwealth, the vote would clearly be overwhelmingly NO. Yet there is a growing tendency to take all difficult problems to Canberra by deputation or letter or propaganda, and then to become either contemptuous or annoyed if Canberra says, "This is not our problem, under the Constitution; it is a state problem!"

As one of the objects of these talks of mine is to promote clear thinking, I will illustrate my point by very brief reference to education.

Except in the Commonwealth territories, power over education is not one of the powers granted to the Commonwealth Parliament. It is purely a State matter, and the States have in fact done a great deal about it. Long experience has convinced me that it is a good thing that the States should have this power. What is a good and sensible state educational system in Tasmania maybe quite inappropriate to North Queensland. A continent-wide uniformity of education would be a bad thing; we badly need the development of individuality if we are to meet the challenges of the mass mentality which is doing so much harm in the world. Again, I think that most people would, on reflection, agree with this.

Yet hardly a week goes by without some representations for huge Commonwealth Grants for primary and secondary education in the States. We are not at present getting requests for grants for universities, because our efforts in this field, are I believe, recognised as so generous that they have opened up a new era for the universities. What we are repeatedly asked to do is to make grants, out of revenue, to the States for their own schools, ear-marked as such. We already, of course, find scores of millions for the States both for works and for ordinary expenditure, and much of this no doubt finds its way into education, which constitutes a large fraction of state spending. But this is ignored by some of the campaigners, who want us to make additional grants for the specific purpose of meeting the States' educational charges. This would mean that the Commonwealth Parliament would be carrying all the responsibility, but would have no power at all. Surely this is a bad principle. It is the chief vice of uniform taxation, and we should try hard not to extend it. For if the States had complete command of the building, staffing and teaching of their own schools, as they have now, but had not to find the money with which to pay, the temptation to irresponsibility or extravagance would be almost irresistible. And if the Commonwealth, in its turn, found that it was completely paying the piper, would it not soon want to call the tune and demand that power over education be transferred to it? And that, as I said at the beginning of this example, would be a bad thing for education and the future of our people.

The division of powers and responsibilities between the central and local parliament has great merits. It would be a pity if, by not thinking about what we are doing, we drifted into a complete centralisation of power and gave Federation away. Good night to all of you.

Looking Around at Eighty, Recorded Speech, Melbourne (12 December 1974)

As Sir Robert entered his ninth decade, he felt that it was a timely occasion to both reiterate his Liberal philosophy and share his reflections on some of the developments in political life that had transpired since his exit from the public stage. After twenty-three years in the political wilderness, the return of Labor to power under Gough Whitlam had precipitated a major transformation of Australia's political climate with ripple effects for both major parties. At the same time that the Whitlam government embarked on its ambitious reform agenda to end conscription, recognise Communist China, abolish tertiary education fees and replace *God Save the Queen* with *Advance Australia Fair*, the winds of change were also felt within Menzies' own Liberal Party. In this recorded speech, Menzies expressed his concern that in the interests of modernisation and political expediency, the Party he had founded was drifting away from its core principles and softening its longstanding positions of opposing communism and defending the Crown. With vivid memories of the Great Depression from his early political life, he also feared that Australia's economic turmoil in the 1970s would visit a similar fate on the present generation. To overcome this pending crisis, Menzies argued that Australia needed not only wise economic policies but a moral resolve of "unselfishness". Although the general tenor of Menzies' speech was somewhat downbeat, his faith in the good character of the Australian people remained undented.

....

1. Introduction

I should make it clear at the outset that I am not and have not been for some years since my illness, associated with the Liberal Party or with its policies, nor have I in fact been consulted by that party nor would I expect to be.

It follows that I am not professing to express the views of today's Liberal Party. These are matters which are naturally outside my control and influence. But I do think that it might be useful to me, in my old age, to say a few things about a few aspects of political policy which will express my own views, but which will not be attributable to any other person.

My 80th birthday is just about to arrive. For the last three years, I have been an onlooker, vastly interested and frequently greatly disappointed.

I was the founder of the Liberal Party in Australia and have, of course, a personal interest in its future. But many things that I believe in, many of the principles which made the Liberal Party, have so far been forgotten or put on one side that I am deeply concerned about the future. When we commenced the Liberal Party we had principles. Principles are apparently nowadays things that are not to be insisted upon because to insist upon them is to demonstrate that you are a reactionary or a "Conservative". This, of course, is the most pernicious nonsense. Principles do not change. In the whole of my political life, I have never arrived at something that I thought to be a matter of principle lightly or casually. They have represented deep beliefs on my part; and I am old-fashioned enough to believe that principles adopted after much thought and much consideration do not change. The circumstances to which they are to be applied, of course, will change with the change of circumstances, but the principles remain. I would just like to take a few examples of what I mean.

The first is that we have a system of government – responsible government under the Crown – which is, in my opinion, the best form of government that has ever been devised. And yet there are some people who talk glibly about a republic though not, I think, quite as many as there were a year ago. A republic – do we want to have a system of government like that in the United States – heaven forbid! It may suit them but it doesn't suit us. Do we want to have one of the other kinds of Republic that we see around the world, very largely old colonial areas which are, for the most part, dictatorships, or, in the case where they maintain a little gesture towards the parliamentary system, countries in which only one party runs the candidate for parliament. I hope that in Australia we will never succumb to any temptation to be like them. Yet, the fact is, as I sit in my study at home – rather handicapped physically

116

but still able to read, still able to think, I sometimes wonder whether the party which I helped to create has retained its belief in responsible government under the Crown. I say this because, though I admit that I rely entirely on the newspapers and the television – and that's a bad form of reliance, with great respect, Sir, sometimes wonder whether the Liberal Party of today really believes in its heart in "responsible government under the Crown".

I am, of course, well aware that there are many people in the present government of Australia who in their hearts believe in republicanism, and who are disposed to speak disparagingly about the Crown. Well, all I can say is that in this century, and particularly since the beginning of the reign of George V, we have been fortunate in our monarchy. We have had, and today above all times, we have a Queen and a Royal Family who, in the colloquial phrase, "do us proud!" I would love to think that someday in the Federal Parliament, the Opposition would make an issue of this matter of the Crown and bring it to a point.

Well, that is one principle in which I believe and about which I have my unhappiness at the present time.

2. Foreign Policy

The second principle in my time, though I suppose it is now to be called a conservative view, is that our foreign policy was built around certain basic elements, and these were that we must be friendly and understanding with our neighbours in our corner of the world, but, if we should become involved in warlike operations we should always be able to feel that we had great and powerful friends. The phrase, "great and powerful friends", is now a matter of ridicule to half-baked political commentators but it is so true. God forbid that, it came to the point that this wonderful country of ours is attacked, we should not have great and powerful friends – the United States and Great Britain – and all those people in the Commonwealth who really believe in the kind of things that we believe in. We must have them. But yet I am now told by the government that the real purpose of foreign policy is to nestle down with the communists, to make great friends of China, to make great friends of North Vietnam, to speak disparagingly of South Vietnam; that all these things are good because they mean we have been taken out of the old world of alliances and friendships and put in what I am now told is called "the Third World". "The Third World" is apparently so significant that we have alliances with our erstwhile enemies and can afford to speak disparagingly about our old and proved friends.

I was horrified quite recently – a few months back – looking at the television, to see that the Shadow Minister for Foreign Affairs in the Opposition was prepared to say that, apart from a few matters of detail, he had no great quarrel with the foreign policy of the present government. No great quarrels? Heaven help us! The foreign policy of the present government is the very antithesis of the foreign policy of the Liberal Party in my time. Of course, if our foreign policy is based upon a new friendship with the Communist powers in Asia, then it follows, so they say, that we don't need any real defence in Australia, because defence is the other aspect of foreign policy. We are told that we don't need it. We can look forward to fifteen years, so they say, of peace. This is, of course, the most abysmal and dangerous nonsense. We do not have fifteen years to look forward to. When we look around the world today and see all the boiling up that is going on, we may be lucky to have twelve months, two years, not fifteen years. If we succumb to the comfortable belief that all is for the best in the best of all possible worlds, we will be prepared to run down our defence forces. But this is the very ecstasy of suicide. I would hope the Liberal Party in the Federal Parliament would devote the attention to it that it urgently deserves.

3. Internal Security

Then, of course, there is the internal instrument of our security, the Australian Security Intelligence Organisation – ASIO – well, we know what has happened to it. It has been attacked by this government. It has been raided. It has been reduced to a state of futility. Does this make you happy? Does this make you feel that everything is going on very nicely, thank you? Of course not. The abolition of internal security, the writing down of external security, are both aspects of something which I would like to say something about, and which I regret to say I seldom hear mentioned when I am listening in either directly, or indirectly, to the Federal Parliament.

4. Communism

Communism is today, the greatest menace that it ever has been in our country. I know it is not fashionable now to attack the communists. To attack the communists is to demonstrate that you are an "old square", that you are an old conservative or some other rubbish of that kind. All I want to tell you is that the communists were quite a menace in Australia in the early 1950s when I failed in an attempt to outlaw them, but today, they are ten times as significant because they are ten times as powerful. The best advertised unions, the most effective unions I suppose, if you care to put it that way, are those run by the communists. They have long since gone past the idea of arguing for industrial benefits on the part of their members; they are now undertaking to tell governments what they must do about conservation, about town planning, about power stations, and so on. They are, in their arrogance and influence in the government, tremendously powerful; and, so long as there is no such thing as a secret ballot in union matters, they will continue to be more and more powerful. And what does this mean? Let it never be forgotten that communism is a destructive agency. It foments strikes and foments all sorts of industrial problems because it wants the present economic system, based upon private enterprise, to come to an end. It is out to destroy. When it has destroyed, well, I suppose it hopes that it will promote some sort of communist government in Australia, whether it is on the Chinese model, or the Russian model, who knows. But, in the first place, the communist says "we must destroy the present system".

Now this is, I think, the greatest issue now confronting the Australian people. Either allow these wicked people to go on with their villainous

119

work of destruction or stand up and fight them and be counted in the fight. Now, of course, when I say these things, I am just an "old square". I am a Liberal who still entertains principles, but, apparently, I ought to have more sense than to be raising the issue of communism which, while it is the most vital issue in this country today, is regarded by little "l" liberals, and people of that kind, as being rather reactionary and something that ought to be forgotten about.

5. The Economic Issues

The next matter I want to speak about, though it is by no means the least, is the great economic issue that is not presented to our people by the government.

Liberalism has always stood for private enterprise, not an uncontrolled private enterprise, but a regulated private enterprise, because we have always believed (or we did in my time) that increased production is the best guarantee of economic stability, and that production is largely, if not wholly, to be achieved by private enterprise. I suppose that of all the wealth that is created in the country, over 90% is produced by private enterprise. Governments have a part to play. They may regulate, they may distribute, but they do not create; and, therefore, what happens to private enterprise is of vital importance to the people of Australia. I would like to see it made one of the great political issues at the present time. Quite plainly, the present government does not believe in private enterprise, except in a somewhat condescending way. All its budgetary provisions have been clearly designed to transfer investment from the private to the public sector, so that the government may have more and more and more to spend, and private enterprise will have less and less reward for the effort that it puts into production. This is, of course, a disastrous state of affairs. If anybody imagines for a moment that by transferring expenditure to the public sector, and by starving private enterprise of what it needs to produce and to develop, something is being done for the Australian economy, he will find that the result will be a very painful one from the point of view of the Australian people.

We do not hear quite so much now, though I would hear nothing else if I were listening to the ABC, that well-known instrument of the Left Wing of the Labour Party, of talk about "multinational corporations"; the multinational corporations who were apparently responsible for inflation and unemployment, and who were, of all wicked people, the most wicked. Well, I never read or listened to such nonsense in my life. The fact is that the whole of our development in recent years, of our mineral resources, of our allied resources in that field, has been due to the fact that we have had a great importation of overseas capital. Without that fresh capital, we could never have developed the capital that was needed for the development of our national resources. Never. And yet it became the mode to say that these people were wicked people, that they ought to be kept off the ground. Well, for two years, I have listened to this drivel, this well-advertised drivel about the multinational corporations. But it is only in the last few weeks that I have discovered that the new economic ruler of Australia (Dr Cairns) who, in my opinion, believes what he says, has just been in America – in New York – at the head office of a big multi-national corporation, and has sat there and explained to them that he eagerly desires that they should invest money in Australia. Well, this is wonderful, isn't it? This is going around not full circle, but half circle – to go half circle means you go astern. But there it is. And yet, Australia will learn, I hope not too late, but I hope at not too great a cost, that the entrance of new capital into Australia, where after all, it has to pay its taxes and be subject to government rules, the entrance of overseas capital into Australia has in the last 15 years, meant all the difference between national progress and national stagnation.

Well, I apologise, of course, for being such an "old-fashioned reactionary", but these are things I believe in, and I have not yet discovered any good reason why I should abandon my beliefs because somebody else tells me I ought to.

6. Inflation and Unemployment

We are, of course, confronting problems that have not come before us for a very long time. I can remember when I was first a Member of Parliament in the State Parliament of Victoria, the Great Depression and its aftermath when there was almost a financial collapse, and where we had in Australia at one stage, not 1½ per cent or 2 per cent of unemployed but 25 per cent of unemployed. The younger people here today will, mercifully, have no recollection of this at all, but you may imagine what a disaster it was for Australia to have one quarter of its workforce without earnings, without a job to do, without any dignified interest in life. I, for one, would never want to see that come back again. It took a few years to recover from it, to beat back those unfortunate events which produced those results.

But, here today, we are in a great country. I think the most lovely country in the world. I think a country more rich than perhaps any other in natural resources and in human resources. A wonderful country; and, yet, each day, inflation and unemployment go-ahead from a new base at the rate of 15 per cent or 20 per cent, and so on, that our people are beginning, very properly, to become deeply concerned about what ought to be done about these great problems. We dealt with a similar problem. We, meaning by that, my government in 1951 and 1952, and we dealt with it successfully. But today's circumstances are more severe. But I do not want to say this as I look forward and I see this great tremendous tide of inflation and unemployment going on and on and, if unchecked, leading to an economic disaster in Australia, I do remind myself of a few things.

Now here, I just want to say that I have no more desire than the next man to be accused of being sanctimonious – I don't think I am sanctimonious – but I am a great believer in the moral values of life. And one of them is this, that every now and then all of us citizens ought to have a square look at ourselves and say, "I am a citizen, a citizen of a self-governing country, a citizen who, because he is a citizen, has duties as well as rights". And, if we are to talk all the time about our rights, how much more we want, how much a bigger price we want for our goods, or for our services, if we are going to narrow our horizons to that extent that we think only of rights and not of duties, not of the country, not of the interests of the country as a whole, then we are very bad citizens. What is needed most today is not some economic theories of which there are as many, of course, as there are economists, but a great mood of unselfishness in our country, a great realisation that unless we are prepared to be on the list of contributors, we can complain not a bit about other people who pursue selfish interests. This is a great moral issue and it means, of course, and I think this is a fair thing to say, that an economic crisis of the kind we are contemplating, has tremendous moral significance. The citizen must give himself furiously to think. We must more and more realise that unless he is prepared to make a little sacrifice, to withhold a little of the claim he otherwise would make, restrict the advantages he seeks, unless he is prepared to do that, then he cannot expect that anybody else will. And if there is one thing that can bring us down, it will be unbridled greed on the part of all sections of the community. I don't believe for a moment that Australians need very much to be reminded of this.

I, myself, was sustained in my political life for over 20 years, by one firm belief, and that was that the vast majority of the Australian people are good and decent people. This was a thing that sustained me. Otherwise, I would not have bothered about politics. You don't go into politics in order to play a game on behalf of this group, or that group, and with no idealism in you. But, when you know your people are decent people, then you owe them in your turn decency, an appeal to decency, an appeal to moderation.

I think it was the Apostle Paul who said, among many other good things, that "We are all members of one another". It is a lovely phrase, a beautiful expression. It means that no man lives to himself; that every man who lives in a community is a member of that community. He shares his membership with other people in it, and, political friend or political foe, he owes them every good thing that he can contribute to the life of the country.

Politics and the Media, Recorded Speech, Melbourne (26 March 1975)

In one of his last recorded speeches, the former Prime Minister appreciated the power of the modern media but did not believe that its influence on present day politics had been wholly desirable. According to Menzies, the demands of the modern media for quick "sound-bites" and "headline-grabbing" pronouncements would compromise the art of authentic statesmanship. This was because true statesmanship demanded leaders to take a considered, long-range assessment of the public policies that they determined to be in the country's best interest. With Menzies regarding the preservation of sound statesmanship as intrinsic to the flourishing of healthy democracy, he feared that the brash, "bullying tactics" of the modern media would bode ill for the future of democratic self-government. As prime minister, Menzies had valued the important role of the media but insisted it must honour the people by affording due deference to the democratically elected government.

....

This is a synopsis of something I would like to write before I finish. It concerns the deplorable development of the activities of what they now call the "media" in public affairs.

In my time, we had not entered the era in which brash young men shoved their microphones into the teeth of their victims and tried to persuade them to make Kerbstone announcements on policy.

Let me go back to an older day when political leaders expected to have an opportunity to do some homework and to read hard and think hard before announcing anything that might be a matter of policy. In those good old days, political leaders did not speak on matters of policy until they were ripe for the ultimate pronouncement. This meant that those who spoke on politics would, first of all, do their homework, would (if necessary) as I did in my time, lock their doors and read the documents and, in the quiet of their own study, arrive at some conclusion, or, at any rate, some conclusion worthy of pronouncement.

This, of course, was essential, because the first thing that any political spokesman must do is to read documents, to study the problems, and after a day or two locked in their offices, make some announcement about their conclusions.

It was, of course, clear to us that Kerbstone opinions are worth nothing except headlines. Therefore, we did our homework and when we finally announced something, it was considered something and would stand up to examination and criticism.

Nowadays, all this appears to have changed. Eager young men, of doubtful literacy, besiege people on their way to a meeting, or on the way from a meeting, or at any other time that suits them, and demand that something be said which will give them a headline. And so, during recent years, I have been accustomed to the new order. The interviewers are, of course, interested not in getting at the facts, but in getting a headline and, unfortunately, too many political people have fallen for this and give to the interviewers the opportunity of distorting what is said, of treating today's casual remark as if it were a considered matter of policy.

Now the truth is that statesmanship, as distinct from day by day *ad captandum* remarks, are of enormous importance. I would like to think that more people today were prepared to brush these impertinent interviewers on one side, to explain to them that matters of statesmanship require thought and study, and that no statement would be made until that study and that thought had been engaged in.

Statesmanship requires the long view; and no yielding should be made to the pressure of people who want only a headline for tomorrow's newspaper. Statesmanship in modern political practice requires that the long view should be taken. It is not a matter of what tomorrow's newspaper may say, but a matter of how the country will feel in a year's time if some particular policy is adopted. Of course, I know because I have come to realise that the scribblers and spokesmen of what are called "the media" are not interested in the long-range impact of policy, or, for that matter, are prepared to encourage a thoughtful approach to these matters.

Unfortunately, most politicians appear to me to feel that they must be obliging to the interviewer, instead of putting him right back in his box. The impertinence of interviewers is beyond all words. So long as political leaders are prepared to help them play their own game in their own way, nothing but disaster can ensue.

In America, as in Australia, the arrogance of the interviewer is completely inconsistent with true statesmanship. I remember some years ago at a meeting of the body to which I belonged in the United States, a very eminent newspaper writer from the *New York Times* offered the view that nowadays the rule would be to have a one-term President and of the prospects against having a two-term President. I told him that I feared that he was right but that one of the disasters of his thesis was that from now on only short-term policies would prevail. This, I said, was disastrous for democratic government because only long-term policies represented statesmanship and short-term policies represented only a catch penny idea of how to influence votes tomorrow morning.

Yet, I fear, that under today's bullying tactics by the media, only short-term policies would be resorted to. This, I thought, and I think, was a disaster for democratic self-government.

I understand, of course, why the young men of the various media engage in these tactics. They like to think that they are, in effect, running the country, whereas the truth, of course is that unless the democratically elected Parliament, or Congress, or whatever it may be, assumes responsibility for the future of the country, nothing but disaster can occur.

It is a melancholy fact that the assumption of power by the media is completely inconsistent with democratic self-government. The interviewer is usually a brash young, or middle-aged, man whose qualifications are unknown but whose impudence is unlimited. A public man, who is worth his salt, must do a lot of serious thought and study. It is ridiculous for him to be bashed around by semi-literate people whose qualifications are unknown, but whose vanity knows no bounds.

I retain my old-fashioned belief that the people who, in a political sense, have a duty to offer leadership to the people, must spend many hours in the study and in reading and in reflection, and that they should arrive at their conclusions only after these processes have been gone through. The present system is consistent with this proposition, and, if it continues, will bring nothing but disaster to the democratic self-government which is the greatest inheritance of our people, and represents the greatest assurance of sensible long-range policies for the future.

4

AUSTRALIA AND THE WORLD

Broadcast to the People of the United States of America, Broadcast (4 July 1941)

Even before the United States joined the allied war effort on 8 December 1941, Menzies reached out to the American people on Independence Day 1941 with this broadcast. While the United States lay outside the British Commonwealth of Nations, he recognised the great Republic of the United States as an integral part of the English-speaking world to which he was devoted. With its English language, free institutions and traditions of liberty, it stood beside Britain as one of the two great pillars of human civilisation. In addition, his affinity for America and its people was based on the peculiar similarities he saw it as sharing with Australia. To a considerable degree, the history of the two countries had been analogous with waves of immigrants from Britain and Europe arriving as explorers, settlers and pioneers to new worlds across vast oceans. In each country, these new arrivals had exhibited the pioneering qualities of adventure, enterprise and determination to build new civilisations that would emerge as beacons of freedom and opportunity. In Menzies' succinct phrase, the nations of Australia and America were "united by the Pacific and not separated by it".

....

Independence Day has long since ceased to be the mere celebration of a successful revolt by some American colonies against a stupid and short-sighted British government. It has become rather a day upon which the minds of English-speaking people the world over turn to the United States of America as the home of a people dedicated to freedom and richly furnished with the institutions of unfettered self-government.

I was in your country a little more than a month ago. During every hour that I was there I felt entirely at home. I think that every Australian who visits America has the same feeling. Not only do we speak the same language, but to a large extent we have the same thoughts and we act in the same way. We are both equally devoted to the rights of man. We are both unhesitatingly and resolutely opposed to the overthrowing of those rights by any tyrant. Both of us – you in your large way; we in our small way – have had a similar history, a history in which industrial skill and power and rising standards of living have followed upon a pioneer age in which foundations were built by brave and adventurous people who knew how to dare the unknown and greet the unseen with a cheer.

Two peoples in whose veins there still courses the blood of rugged ancestors who conquered the wilderness, not by grace of government but by the grace and vigour that was in themselves, are not likely to submit readily to a world order in which the rights of the individual ceased to be those things that were born with him and became a mere charitable allowance from an all-powerful state.

You and we may live in vast countries, separated by thousands of miles of sea, but on the matters that count in this world we stand on common ground. On these matters we are united by the Pacific and not separated by it. We Australians have entered, like you, into the rich inheritance bequeathed by Washington and Hamilton, and Jefferson, and John Marshall, and Abraham Lincoln. We, like you, responded to the noble words of your President, Franklin Roosevelt, when he recently spoke to us of the four freedoms which are now at stake.

True, we are a nation at war, and in the most immediate sense we have all to lose, just as we have all to preserve. You are not at war, but day by day the activity of your war factories grows; day by day American aeroplanes and guns and munitions of war pass in an increasing stream into British hands. Day by day we are becoming increasingly sure that you mean us to win and that you will never tolerate a Nazi domination of the world.

All this is tremendously important to us. As I said to some of you in America, it has never occurred to us to think that we cannot win, but we know that the speed of victory will be immeasurably increased, and the evil and dislocating consequences of war immeasurably reduced, by American aid on the greatest scale.

And so I say to you plainly but without impertinence on this Independence Day, that Americans – like Australians – have a trust to discharge. It is a trust not only for those who are alive but for those who are to come. As trustees we have learned that there are powerful enemies in the world who would destroy the inheritance. Freedom, as you know and as we know, is not lightly come by, and free men do not lightly abandon it. It is the privilege of this country to fight for freedom, not only for Australia's freedom – but for your freedom and the world's freedom. Our armies are in the field; our air forces in the sky; our warships on the deep. Our factories are expanding and producing day and night. Our taxpayers, our citizens, are digging deeply into their earnings and their savings so that the last penny maybe spent for victory.

It is my honour as the political leader of the nation which is doing these things of its free will but also of a sense of universal obligation to send greetings to a great nation which looks at us and at all the British people, I am sure, not with distant benevolence but with a clear understanding that in this great world combat between light and darkness those who live under the Stars and Stripes are to be numbered "among the children of light".

Australia's Trade Relationship with Japan, "Australia Today – Man to Man" Broadcast (16 September 1953)

The first significant trade agreement Australia struck in its own right was the historic commerce agreement with Japan on July 6, 1957. In John Howard's assessment, the agreement gave formal expression to Australia's most enduring trade relationship with any country since World War II. In this 1953 broadcast, Menzies not only defended Australia's existing trade relationship with Japan but desired to consolidate it by increasing the quota of Japan's exports to Australia. As the British Empire dissolved in the post-war years, Menzies understood that Australia's trade base would need to be sustained by fresh markets. Accordingly, he set about pivoting Australia's trade focus towards Asia, not least to the burgeoning post-war economy of Japan which had an appetite for raw materials such as wheat, wool, iron ore and coal. Menzies' farsighted approach to trade with Japan was welcomed by domestic primary producers but opposed by local manufacturers who feared that their products would face overseas competition. Whilst Menzies was attentive to their concerns, he believed, on balance, that it was in the best interests of the nation for Australia's export markets to benefit from more open trade with Japan.

....

... There is much organisation of special interests for political pressure. This is inevitable. But some men, because of such organisation, tend to think exclusively of the problem of their own industry. If the government does what they want, they are happy; if not, they will be hostile and bitter. Yet, no government can please everybody, because many pressure groups are in conflict one with another. And a government should not try to please everybody, for it ought to have principles and a mind of its own. The ultimate responsibility of a government is to do what it thinks is best for the nation as a whole. Political leadership therefore requires considerable strength of character and patience and hard work, and much study and tenacity. If these were not so, we would not need or expect men of talent and industry and character to go into Parliament.

All political judgements must be made on balance. Somebody will think he is hurt by the decision, but a balanced judgement founded upon the interest of the nation must prevail. This is undoubtedly the hardest thing for most of us to understand. I will just give you one illustration. How should we deal with trade with Japan? Japan is a country with which we were recently at war, and whose conduct of the war was such as to produce immeasurable bitterness among our own people. But we are now at peace. Are we to say that we will not trade with Japan? Trade involves selling and buying.

Last year our trade with Japan was so lopsided that whereas Japan bought from us no less than £84,000,000 worth of goods – the largest item being wool – we bought from Japan under £5,000,000 worth of goods. Now that kind of thing simply cannot go on. Japan cannot buy our wool without paying for it. She cannot have money abroad with which to pay for wool unless she earns that money by exporting and selling goods herself. Her presence in the wool market has been of value, for it increases competition, builds up our national export income, and therefore increases our capacity to sustain our local industries.

You would at once agree that if we want to continue to be a great trading nation and maintain those exports which are our life-blood, we must be prepared to buy more things from Japan. Yet the moment it is proposed to increase the quota of Japan's exports to Australia, somebody will very naturally say that the goods coming in will compete with his products, and he will be very vocal about it. Now I don't want you to think that I fail to understand his case or to sympathize with him, but what is the duty of the government in such a case? Is it to please the affected local manufacturer and sacrifice a substantial share of our wool market, or is it to preserve our export markets in the interest of the entire nation, including the great mass of manufacturers whose success is affected by every increase in the national income.

I give you this illustration to show that the problem of determining where the true Commonwealth advantage lies is one of great difficulty and that no government could hope to solve it merely by giving way to special pressures within its own boundaries. The longer I live in public affairs the more satisfied I am that political leadership does not require the kind of mind which is blown about by every wind, but requires in full measure those very qualities of work and thought and determination and enterprise which we like to believe are the characteristic of the best elements in our nation and our people.

Speech at Dinner Tendered by His Excellency, First Minister Djuanda, of Indonesia (2 December 1959)

At the same time as buttressing Australia's traditional relations with its North Atlantic allies, Menzies was keen to develop Australia's ties with its South-East Asian neighbours through the Colombo Plan, the regional SEATO pact and new bilateral links with nations such as Singapore and Malaya. In 1959, Menzies became the first Australian Prime Minister to visit Indonesia where he met the President, Dr Sukarno. In this speech to an audience in Djakarta, the Prime Minister spoke of Australia's desire to cultivate a warm friendship with its northern neighbour. He welcomed the great number of Indonesian students coming to Australian universities under the Colombo Plan and assured his Indonesian audience that Australia took a warm interest in the development of their country. While conscious that the two nations had obvious differences in background and culture, Menzies saw this as posing no barrier to building a healthy relationship of goodwill and understanding, wherein Australia and Indonesia could work together to advance the ideals of freedom and self-government in the region.

....

Your excellency and ladies and gentlemen, before I conclude, I am going to give you the toast of the President, but before I do that, I hope you will allow me to say a few words in answer to what has fallen upon the Chief Minister.

It is quite true that all our contacts between our two countries develop friendship. We have had proof of that in our own country. I hope you may feel that you have had some proof of it in your own. But, after all, in a sensible world, why should not we be friends? On the whole, it is rather more comfortable and pleasant and sensible to be friends than to be opponents and, so far as we are concerned in Australia, the one thing that we dislike most is to be opponents of somebody and, therefore, we reach that state of mind with great reluctance. In my own lifetime, twice, Australia has been involved in War, in enmity, but neither time because Australia wanted to be anybody's opponent, but because somebody wanted to be the opponent of Australia and what Australia believed in, and there it is.

In other words, we are a peaceful people. We are capable of being warlike for a time, but always with the ambition for peace. And I would rather think, Sir, that that typifies your people. I haven't yet heard of you conducting a War of aggression against somebody and I don't suppose I ever shall, but when it comes to things that you believe in, that you have to defend and hold to, then you face up to what is involved in that, and that is exactly the same with ourselves.

I have had the most interesting day. I had a long talk with his Excellency the Chief Minister, whose mind I was delighted to find was running on what is to be done in Indonesia to develop the production of food, the production of power, the production of industry, all the things that a modern people with pride and self-reliance expect to have. And what you were saying to me, Sir, is not only exciting to me but gave me immense satisfaction because, after all, in Australia, particularly in the last 30 years, 40 years, we have been setting out to make ourselves self-reliant so that we produce iron and steel and base metal and all the things, or most of the things, that we need for our own life and sell our surpluses to the world and buy from the rest of the world the things that they have to sell to us so that we may be a great trading nation. And this, to us in my country, and in my period as a politician, this has been a great and exciting adventure. It has given us some feeling of pride. I am happy to say that it has never given to us any feeling of hostility. We have always felt that our own success would be part of the success of the world. And so, when we look across these little narrow seas that divide us from Indonesia, from the Old East Indies, I was saying to my wife the other day, "Do you remember that dressing that used to be put on a salad called 'a thousand islands dressing' you see? And we have been looking at the thousand isles, romantic, historic, full of charm, perhaps in my earlier youth we looked at it as a sort of holiday place. I don't know.

Not that I ever got there for a holiday, but I think a few people perhaps thought of it in that way, but today we know perfectly well that this great Republic of Indonesia, lying there on the northwest of Australia, is our greatest and most powerful neighbour, and we are interested in what goes on. Not interested in a protective or defensive way, but interested because we know that so many millions of people are managing their own affairs, working out their future, their own culture, their own scholarship, their own training, on people, their own administration. These are remarkable and exciting events. And, Sir, you may be tempted occasionally to feel a little defensive about that. To feel that the world is critical. I beg of you, don't feel like that. Forget about criticism of me. I am not unaccustomed to being criticised myself, but it doesn't make me feel ill, or go to bed in a bad temper, all that is the law of life. What you must understand, if I may put it in that way, is that here you have a great population of happy people who deserve to be happier and happier. Of people who deserve to feel that life has something to give them. A people who love the idea of freedom and want to keep it. A people who want to have a freedom of government in which the chief end of government is the happiness and prosperity and intellectual enlightenment of the people themselves. Nobody will disagree with you on those matters.

So little would my country, or myself, disagree with you that we wish you every conceivable success in that work.

You were good enough, Sir, to refer to a collection of Australian omnibuses which run on the streets. I noticed them and think that is very good. But, personally, I belong to the school of thought which says that the best thing that you can do for another country, if you are friendly with it, is to help it in the development of the people and the skills which it will need. Every time we have some of your students, and we have a great number coming to Australia, I am delighted because I know that they will not only learn what we may have to teach but that they will learn something even more important. They will learn that friendship is easy between different people if they have the right approach and I am perfectly certain that every one of them comes back here and says, "I enjoyed it". It was great fun. I loved it and I used to go into their home and they called me Tom, or Bill, or Jack or whatever it might be. Now this is very good. And in the same way, when they come to my country and mix with undergraduates in Universities, or other students in technical colleges, these other people come to regard them on their merits and they say "he is very good. He understands this. I must get him to explain it to me". In other words, it produces a kind of brotherhood which is immensely important.

And the moment two nations like yours, so much more numerous than mine, and mine get to understand each other, get to understand that they have so much in common. They both have pride, they both love freedom, they both believe in ordinary men and women, neither of them believes in the right of anybody to dominate anybody else. The moment all these things become understood, we suddenly discover that we have so much in common, that we might as well reduce our differences of opinion to size.

Of course, we have some differences of opinion.

We have one in particular. It is purely a difference of intellectual judgement. There it is. We think we are right, you think you are right. Well, we have a difference. You know, if a husband and wife concentrated on their mutual dislike for a sister-in-law, the marriage would break up, and therefore, when you are in that state of affairs, put the sister-in-law, if you don't mind, in the spare room (Laughter). Just leave her there, we will deal with her in due course. But do let us concentrate on the things that unite us.

Sir, would you mind if I made a somewhat phlegmatical remark on that subject. You, as the Chief Minister, and so many of your colleagues here tonight, have been connected with the winning of freedom and independent self-government for your own country and this is the great chapter in your history. We understand that. We know something of the pride you feel in it. This is a great and exciting and historic event. It is like the old Roman notation from the founding of the city. This is dramatic and important. You would never have achieved it if you had taken time off to argue among yourselves on other matters. If you had not concentrated on the main thing, you would not have achieved this result, but it is because you saw with complete clarity that the greater not only includes the less, but disposes of it, that you concentrated all the powers of the finest minds in your country and said we must be free. We must govern ourselves, we must devise our own future system of government, and we will do it in the face of the world and with courage, and with our inherited national character.

Sir, we admire all that. We like that very much. We would desire in Australia, through myself, that it should be understood that we are your friends. We may occasionally exercise the privilege of friendship and have some argument with you. A friend with whom you cannot argue is not worth having. He is not a friend, he is a piece of blotting paper. But of the great things that count, Australia has a lively friendly warm interest in the development of Indonesia and my wife and I have both been delighted to have the opportunity of coming here and trying to explain as best we can by word, or look, or deed, how warmly we feel about what has gone on and how much we wish well to those who have the great responsibility like yourself, Sir, of leading the destinies of this country. (applause)

I always rely on my wife, she gives me the slight lift of the eyebrow, which reminds me, you know, what I said at the beginning (Laughter). The President.

"The Cold War, Freedom and World Peace", Pleasant Sunday Afternoon Address, Wesley Church, Melbourne (3 September 1961)

In this address, the Prime Minister largely avoided the topic of domestic politics to instead reflect on the significance of events abroad, particularly those relating to the Cold War and the division of West and East Germany. Menzies reminded his audience that the geopolitical contest between the Western alliance and the Eastern Soviet bloc was much more than a mere conflict of power but a clash of two radically different worldviews. In essence, it represented a spiritual battle for the soul of the human race in which the very notion of freedom lay in the balance. Menzies appreciated that slavery could manifest itself in both a physical and spiritual sense and, as such, the free world needed to resolutely stand against both by defending democracy and religious freedom. With the ominous spectre of nuclear war casting its dark shadow across the world, Menzies made it clear that he sympathised with the objectives of the contemporary peace movement but believed that it was somewhat naïve if it expected free, Western nations to suspend nuclear testing whilst turning a blind eye to the real threat of nuclear attack posed by the Soviet Union. Accordingly, he appealed for a peaceful yet realist Cold War foreign policy that would never compromise the interests and values of the free world.

....

Sir, thank you very much, indeed, for your kind introduction. I would like to thank, through you, Dr Benson, for the very courteous references that he made to me; and I would like to thank my fellow-Presbyterian who has just spoken about me.

He said that I must have a record score for Pleasant Sunday Afternoons in this place. I am quite sure that is right. The first time I was beguiled into coming here by the late Mr Cain[24] must have been at least 30 years ago. And the only thing that is evidence to me that time marches on is

---

24 The Rev James Henry Cain OBE (1866-1940) was a Methodist minister and Army Chaplain who served as Superintendent of Melbourne's Wesley Mission from 1914 to 1939.

that, although now I must have come the better part of 30 times, the audience has a tendency to get a little smaller each time. And I don't blame them.

In all those years I have never undertaken the improper task of talking about Australian politics because this is not the place for that. I have in various ways over the years tried to say something to you about the problems of the world and our relation to those problems; and our duty as individuals, in relation to them. This afternoon I thought I might, following along that line, say something about the current state of the world, because it is a cliché today that we are living in a very critical period in the world's history.

You may well say that we have been living in critical periods of the world history for most of our lives. It is quite true. We have, perhaps, become so accustomed to headlines, to riots, to outbreak, to little wars, to rebellions, that we have almost become accustomed to them; and perhaps a little bit disposed to say, "Well, that's happening somewhere else and I mustn't concern myself about it too much". But while all that is going on, we ourselves are presented, almost every day, with false statements about false issues, with propaganda of various kinds, and with a good deal of so-called sentiment, which is rather bogus. And I thought that I might help you, and help myself, if I put a few questions this afternoon and endeavoured to answer them. As I once rather mischievously said to a political opponent in the Federal Parliament who had prepared a series of questions and answers, "there is one great advantage about answering questions if you prepare the questions yourself, as well as the answers". Therefore whatever I say on this you must discount to that extent.

But you know what we are hearing time after time: we read and we think about what is called the "Cold War". We don't have to go down into that matter deeply enough to find out: Is there a Cold War? Who is causing it? What can we do about it? Therefore, perhaps, one ought to begin by saying something about what a "Cold War" is?

We now talk about war – it is a very strange development – in the broad, as meaning a great global war, a war in which great powers are hurled at each other. And anything that stops short of that, anything which is local, which is hot propaganda, but not actual fighting, any actual fighting, such as the fighting now going on in Laos, in Southeast Asia, we call these things the "Cold War" because we do that to distinguish them from the great war which we all pray may never come. But that is not to say that we ought to have an affection for the Cold War.

There are great conflicts in this world and they are not just conflicts of power. Don't let us succumb to the idea that the great conflict in the world is a conflict between the power of the United States, for example, and the power of the Soviet Union. This is a false picture. The conflict in the world is a conflict between basic principles, profoundly important ideals, differences of outlook on the spirit of man, and the significance of man; a conflict, as we would wish to believe, between what, from our point of view, is the Christian conception of the freedom of the human mind and of the human spirit, and the dictated, dominated, unfree human spirit that exists under totalitarian government in the Communist regime. And this is a tension which will never be quite removed, and never can be quite removed, until other people have the same outlook on the human spirit as we have ourselves.

We must remember all the time that while physical slavery is a terrible thing, spiritual slavery is much worse. We must be free or die who speak the tongue that Shakespeare spoke. This is it: freedom of the mind, freedom of the spirit. The great Communist leaders, men of immense power, of immense authority, take advantage of the fact that our very freedom tends to divide us. We argue with each other. Believe it or not there are 49½% of the people of Australia who would love to get rid of me (Laughter). I'm not sure that sometimes I don't agree with them! But this is part of our freedom: to approve, to disapprove, to have ideas of our own in the political field, and to defend them with vigour, and sometimes a little roughly. This is part of our inheritance. It will be an ill day for Australia when that sort of thing comes to an end.

On the other side you have leaders who need consult no parliament, who need respect no public opinion; but who, with the sheer voice and power of authority can decide what they are going to do. And this is an unequal contest. I will illustrate this by reference to Berlin, this great problem that is going on today – Berlin. What is it all about? Just let me put it to you in a few sentences.

When the last war was being fought to its successful conclusion the powers, the victorious powers – the United States, France and Great Britain, and the Soviet Union – achieved rights in Berlin; a series of sectors in which they were to establish themselves pending the execution of a Treaty of Peace with Germany as a whole. And in the meantime the Soviet forces had come in and had occupied East Germany in which Berlin itself is a mere island – you can't reach it except through or over East German territory. And of course West Germany was there, and has become a free, independent, self-governing and tremendously prosperous country.

Well, Berlin presents a spectacle that we are in Australia would never hope to see ourselves. Can you imagine Melbourne divided down the middle? No connection between one half and the other except by permission, except by authority? And at this moment, of course, lined with temporary walls actually to prevent people in one part of the city from going to their work in another part of the city. Here is the division of a great historic city: it is almost symbolic of the division in Europe, and the division in the world.

Are the Western powers to say to the 2½ million people who live in freedom in West Berlin that they are no longer interested in them, that they propose to withdraw? Because if they do, then this island in East Germany will be absorbed as certainly as anything could happen, absorbed by the surrounding Communist authority. And here is the terrible thing about it: one portion of Germany not free, controlled with a puppet government, but controlled by the Soviet Union with the aid of Soviet troops; and on the western side of Germany, as I have said, freedom, hope, happiness, prosperity. It is little wonder that over recent years hundreds and hundreds of thousands of people from East Germany have fled across the frontier – not to escape into slavery, but to escape from it. And in Berlin itself, there have been many, many thousands of people crossing from one side to the other, in order to get out into a state of freedom. West Berlin, rebuilt, prosperous; East Berlin still with its ruins and rubble on view, and people living in a state of poverty. This is a tremendous point of conflict, and a tremendous point of crisis for the world.

Well, what does the dictator have to say about it, Mr Khrushchev?[25] He doesn't need to consult a parliament – he hasn't one to consult; he needn't worry about electors because that is a species that you don't find in the Soviet Union. So he can engage in the great tactics of the Cold War. He can threaten. He can say, "unless you go out of Berlin, unless you agree to my proposals in relation to Berlin, I will sign a separate treaty of peace with East Germany; I will perpetuate the division of Germany; I will make it impossible for you to conduct your affairs in Berlin. Because once I have signed a Peace Treaty with East Germany, which surrounds Berlin, then, whether you can go into Berlin or come out of it will depend upon the government of East Germany, which will be a Communist government". Now he can do that.

What are the Western leaders to say? This is a great problem. They can, as they have already made clear, indicate to him that they are always prepared to sit down and have a sensible discussion about the position of Berlin, but that they will not respond to threats or to violence. That is a hard thing for democratic leaders to do. Never forget that. It is very hard for a President of the United States, or a Prime Minister of the United Kingdom, to say, "If certain things happen, then we will do so and so" because he must carry with him public opinion; he must carry with him his Parliament or his Congress; he must be sure that he is speaking with authority and his authority is derived from a wide area. But the authority of Khrushchev is his own authority; he may bluff; he may threaten; he may advance; he may withdraw at his own free will.

Now this is a great crisis in the world. I don't need to tell you that you can't dismiss the Berlin problem by saying, "Well, is it worthwhile to have all this argument over one city?" We have an interest in it here in Australia, strange as it may seem to some. If Berlin goes, if Berlin goes into the Communist maw, if they have this enormous triumph in the Cold

25 Nikita Khrushchev (1894-1971) led the Soviet Union during the Cold War from 1957 to 1964.

War, the same kind of triumph as that which has subdued Hungary, a country older than ours, a country of a great ancient civilisation, if these tactics succeed in Europe, then you will have an encouragement all over the world to people who don't believe in the freedom of the spirit, who don't believe in the divine right of man. Because they don't believe in a God anyhow. And we will find in South East Asia the pressure growing, more triumphs in the Cold War. Time after time we will be told, "Well, is Laos worth worrying about? Is South Vietnam worth worrying about? Is Thailand worth worrying about? When will we start to worry about it? When we have to say 'Is Darwin worth worrying about?'"

You see this as a matter of immense significance. We are not only looking after our own interests; I believe that we are, all over the free world, trustees of matters of imperishable significance. We are not to allow the enemies of freedom, the enemies of a free religious faith, to trample over more and more people, more and more ground, in order to achieve their ambition dominating the whole world.

Now I am not saying this because I want to rattle the sword. This is too grim a matter. I don't believe, myself, that the Soviet leaders want a great world war. The very power of destruction that exists today in these dreadful weapons, the nuclear and thermonuclear bombs, to say nothing of the intercontinental ballistic missiles that are now being practised, the very power to destroy is mutual. It is quite true. If a great war broke out a country like Great Britain could be practically eliminated in a few minutes. But so could all the great centres of Russia. Action, reaction, both sides equally powerful, both sides equally alert.

It is not a matter of waiting for months, you know, to find out what happens, but a matter of minutes, in attack and counter-attack. This means that the nuclear war will, beyond question – it is not a mere matter of metaphor – destroy both sides in the conflict and leave the outskirts of the world to some extent untouched; but the great centres of the world eliminated. And this is something that can't seriously be contemplated by any man, whether he is Russian, British or American. Because there is a good deal of human nature in all of us. Therefore I feel, myself, that Khrushchev has the great advantage of knowing that he doesn't want to have a nuclear war, knowing that we don't want to have a nuclear war, and feeling all the time, if he can divide our councils, that he can press forward a little, pressing forward, not taking the final risk of a great war, knowing that we don't want one, feeling that we will be prepared to abandon a few positions in order to avoid having one. This is an immense game of bluff in that sense. And people can be easily bluffed in this world if they have confusion in their minds, they are not clear about what goes on. Just let me give you one illustration of that because I can't hope to cover all this ground in one short speech. But let me give you one example of it.

Every now and then quite worthy people in Australia associate themselves with ideas of having a petition, or a deputation, for example, to me, about banning the bomb, about peace – as if I didn't want peace, as if I had any atomic bombs around the corner, because I haven't, and I don't want them. What is the use of coming to me? Where does the threat come from? Who started the Cold War? Who is going to initiate a great war of destruction? The old country? how stupid! The United States of America? Ridiculous! France, bled by two or three wars? Of course not! Well, who is going to start it? And yet people will come to democratic leaders like myself in the free world and speak earnestly about the atomic bombs when I would very much prefer that they went to the Soviet Union and talked about them to the Kremlin. Let us go to where the real danger exists.

All this idea of making armaments unpopular in the free world is exactly what the Soviet Union wants. Because armaments will always be popular in the Soviet Union until it has got all it wants in this world. So don't confuse this matter, don't let us think that we are going to solve all these problems in the world by weakening our own position, or by appearing to accuse ourselves of being responsible for world positions for which other people are responsible.

Now my one illustration of that is the question of the further testing of atomic weapons. Back early this year we had a Prime Ministers' Conference in London and we passed a very significant resolution, unanimously – and it is very seldom we pass a resolution – a resolution on disarmament in which we endeavoured to get down to the reality of the matter. We decided that the first step in the direction of disarmament, the first proof of good faith, the first ray of hope for mankind would arise if the powers concerned agreed that they would suspend all further testing of nuclear weapons.

Now that was simple enough. Great Britain has a few; America has a great many; the Soviet Union has a great many; France has two or three perhaps. But there is a limited number. There are four nations that have these terrible things. All right, let them all agree that they will stop testing anymore. That would be a wonderful step, wouldn't it? This would, to that degree, remove a feeling of threat from the decent people of the world. What difficulties are there about it? Only difficulties of good faith.

The Western people went to the conference at Geneva. They said, "Yes, we are prepared to suspend the testing of atomic weapons. Of course, if you are", because it has to operate both ways. "Of course we will need to arrange to have this agreement supervised; we will need to be sure that not one of us is doing it secretly behind the other fellows' back so to speak. Therefore let us have a system of inspection, and a committee to conduct the inspection and scientific people from both the Soviet Union and the free world side, to conduct their examinations to see that this agreement is being honoured". What is wrong with that? All that is perfectly fair? And for months they have been sitting there getting nowhere, with the Soviet representatives refusing to agree to this or that, playing for time.

And now, at the very moment, I repeat, when there are good people in England and in Australia who want to talk to us about suspending atomic tests, they are now reading the last news that Khrushchev has said, "we will resume tests". And to illustrate the utter insincerity of the whole thing, within 48 hours of him indicating that they are going to resume tests, they have one. Now I am no scientist but I don't think you can get ready the testing of a new weapon in 48 hours. Experience indicates that the preparation for this must have been going on all the time these talks were being engaged in at Geneva.

You see the hypocrisy of it. Play for time: If you can get the West to halt while you go on, quietly, and then say, "we don't have an agreement" and then be in a position, at once, to test your new developments, you may ultimately get ahead of the West; and you may ultimately be able to threaten more destruction than you can receive. And on that day you will be master of the world. This is the way; this is the approach. You and I can't understand this; we haven't been nourished in such a creed. This is not part of the conduct that we understand, that we aim at, not at all. But this is it. This is the kind of thing that you are up against.

So, while I am a great believer in persuasion, and am always willing to receive complaints, criticisms, or advice, I hope that on these matters we will clear our minds and know really who are the people who are responsible; and that while we talk, anywhere, at any time – because I am sure the democratic leaders will – in order to resolve these difficulties like sensible people, we are not going to let down our own defences and accept a risk which, if it materialised would make us guilty of abandoning some of the most vital things in the world.

Australia-Britain Society Inaugural Dinner, Wentworth Hotel, Melbourne (26 August 1971)

In the five years since his retirement from public life, Sir Robert's affection for Britain had not wavered as this heartfelt address to the Australia-Britain Society illustrates. Indeed the course of domestic and international trends since 1966 served only to strengthen Menzies' resolve to preserve the British connection. Shortly after his departure from politics, Britain once again signalled its intention in 1967 to join the "Common Market", a shift that would reorient its trade policy away from the Commonwealth of Nations to the European Economic Community (EEC). While Britain's second attempt was vetoed by the President of France, it remained its ambition to eventually join the EEC, which it eventually did in 1972. As well as a diminished trade relationship with Britain, Australia switched the peg of its dollar in 1971 from the pound sterling to the United States dollar. By the early 1970s there were murmurs of Australia possibly cutting ties with the British monarchy. These developments perturbed Menzies and, in this address, he affirmed the need for Australia to cherish the traditions it inherited from Britain, together with the maintenance of existing cultural ties with the UK. Appreciating that Australia was a maturing nation in its own right, he argued that the continuing affinity with Britain was not about a subservient child-parent relationship but rather about two adult nations pursuing their own interests as members of one family.

....

Sir, Your Excellencies, ladies and gentlemen…

I come before you tonight in my own right because I have long since politically expired – but I had a great interest in this and a small hand in it since it all began. I know that you will be told (I'm told frequently by some of the commentators, with a sort of derisive note) that I have said that I am "British to the bootheels", and by Jove I have said it and it has only one inaccuracy in it – I don't wear boots, I wear shoes – but that I'm British to the bootheels, British right and through and through, I not only don't deny but I proudly assert. (applause) And I

149

have two reasons for that assertion. One is that under the Citizenship and Nationality Act which was passed at the end of 1948 and early in 1949 when I was a respectable Leader of the Opposition, by the Chifley government with, I think, completely bipartisan approval in the House. In the result we are all "British subjects" by our own Act of Parliament and "Australian citizens" by our own Act of Parliament. This was not a gesture of subordination – I took that legislation as an expression of pride. Australian citizens – what better could we be? British subjects – all subjects under the Crown – and what more wonderful position could there be than that? So that legally I am right when I say I am "British to the bootheels". But more than that, this statement is fundamentally and sentimentally true. And there is something to be said, isn't there, for sentiment? Not sentimentality but sentiment is one of the rich things that makes the world go on. I don't suppose anybody will deny that I am entitled to claim myself as an Australian through and through – after all, I have devoted the great bulk of my adult life with such talent as I might muster to the service of my fellow Australians – I stand here unashamedly as an Australian through and through (applause) and the whole purpose of this exercise which we begin tonight is to prove that you may be Australian through and through and British through and through, and that we should continue to have the same elements in us for long, long years to come.

We are all British, here, tonight, and this is a fact of which we are all reminded if we care to look about us every day. We have a common allegiance to the Crown. Now, I know that there are a few bemused fellows who think we ought to have a Republic in Australia. Why? Just to show that we're really independent. The poor Queen bullies us. The Queen, the Royal Family, assert authority over us! Did you ever hear anything more childish? The Republicans won't gallop very far in Australia because they have never made up their mind what kind of Republic they want; and that's a very important question. But we stand within the allegiance to the Throne and it's a proud place to be in. It doesn't lower us; it raises us in our own sense of our place in the world and the position of our country in the world. And then we have, of course, in common with Great Britain, our language – I allow for some vernacular differences but we share a common language with them, with Britain, and may I commit myself to say this to you that I say Britain, but it is occasionally conceded that the best English is spoken in Edinburgh and Dublin (applause). But there it is, this marvellous, flexible language of ours. Even when we are abusing each other at a football match, even when violent scenes are occurring on some occasions, the language that is spoken is English and sometimes Anglo-Saxon! (Laughter)

Our literature in Australia, though we've added to it in many notable ways, is overwhelmingly the literature of Britain and it's as much our inheritance as it is of a normally educated Englishman. This is a great treasure to have in common, and all these things are treasures that enter into the mind certainly and into the heart – they mean something to us, they make us feel something. And then, of course, if I may, Your Excellency, as one who once had the pleasure of being a colleague of yours, remind everybody that our system of government was brought by our predecessors from Britain. It wasn't created by us; it's worth thinking about, isn't it? A system of government. Now what is our system of government? Forget about all the things that you read from day to day here and there. What is our system of government? Well, in the first place, we have Parliamentary democracy. I know that half the democrats complain the other half are undemocratic – that's very healthy and sometimes true – but Parliamentary democracy, created at Westminster, was brought here and has made us, perhaps more than anything else, a free country. Freedom is easily lost, as we all know, as we look around the world. There are countries that had some form of self-government that have none today. The great hope of the world in this century has always come back to the people who had a Parliamentary democracy which meant that the Parliament spoke for the people and had a strength derived from their people. It is the sovereignty of Parliament which we have inherited – responsible government.

I wonder if I could say a word about that because we sometimes think that our system of government is modelled on that of the United States. It isn't. The United States has an entirely different system of Presidential Government from the one that we have. We have derived, from Great Britain, "responsible government". That is to say, every minister sits in Parliament and is questioned in Parliament and can be dealt with in Parliament and the government that he belongs to can be wiped out in parliament and at any tick of the clock. In a presidential system a president has four years for sure and sometimes a hostile Congress for three years out of the four.

But here, as in England, responsible government ensures the most flexible approach to the questions of the day and the most responsible attitude, by and large, on the part of the people we choose.

We have here the basis of the common law. The common law sounds to a non-lawyer a rather tedious sort of thing – rather, well if not tedious, at least faintly rhetorical. But the common law is, I think, the greatest contribution that the English genius has made so far in the history of the world. It exhibits all the genius of the English and of ourselves in the inductive method of moving from precedent to precedent, of not being dogmatic about something, not being codified but proceeding on a basis of the common law and its superb inductive methods. We have the common law, we practice it, we read the English law reports, we apply them, more or less successfully, in Court. They have some on the east coast of America; South Africa has none, it operates under the Roman-Dutch law and that makes it difficult for them to understand other people. But we are in the full stream of the English rule of law and the common law.

I see a number of men here tonight who have been eminent public servants in my time. I just like to remind them and you that one of the great things in this inheritance of ours is the tradition of the integrity of public administration. (applause) This is no commonplace – there are countries and countries all around the world, where the corruption of administration is a commonplace. We, as in England, have no such tradition – we have a great tradition, well lived up to, of complete integrity in the administrative Public Service. We have inherited also the marvellous tradition of the independence and character of the judiciary.

I hope I'm not boring you by talking in this way, but really more things are lost in this world by neglect than were ever lost by outright opposition. We must remember these elements if we are to continue to be what we regard ourselves as being – one of the great future nations of the world. Why? I for one, and I am sure you and others, believe in the inheritance we have from Great Britain and in the imperative necessity of upholding it, building it, making it grow. Now, Sir, ten years ago I would have thought that it went without saying that all these things were understood. We had and have a splendid America-Australian Association and I am a member of it, and it has done great work, and we have had other associations of an international kind. Ten years ago I wouldn't have thought that we needed to have a British-Australian or Australian-British society, but I think today it is under challenge – very superficial challenge in many quarters, but sometimes a well-advertised challenge. Too many people are indifferent to this great issue, and indeed say, "Oh well, what does it matter? They're going into Europe. They're going to have the Common Market, they don't care about us. This will hurt us this way, this will hurt us that way." I don't need to be told much about that kind of thing myself because I have been in a few of the arguments about them. It's never occurred to me in an argument with the British government about any of these things, that I was talking to them, however critically, in any other capacity than that of a friend – a friend, an enduring friend.

This is tremendously important – Britain becomes more economically involved with Europe, yes. The old structure of Commonwealth preferences disintegrates and fades away.

We have our own problems in trade and we are developing new trade in new directions. But what does that mean? That we must now become hostile? That we must now become no longer the inheritors, conscious of our inheritance? That would be absurd. All it proves is that we're an adult nation and if you come to look back on it, that's been the whole object of the exercise ever since the beginning of the century. We've become an adult nation – we have our own interests, our own economic interests, our own trade considerations; but that doesn't remove us from the family. You might as well say that when the son grows up and develops a business of his own and occasionally argues with his father (a not unknown phenomenon) that the family is at an end. On the contrary, the family is merely at a beginning. It's adult, it's vigorous, it grows in understanding. But it does not grow, I hope, into a state of hostility or indifference.

I think that's all I have to say to you – very badly I'm afraid, very badly. But that is why I am here and that is why many of you who have done so much on this matter are here and that's why I am going to give myself the pleasure of asking a very great Australian, the Governor-General, whether he will formally inaugurate this society. (Applause)

Speech at Melbourne Scots Dinner for St Andrew's Night, Melbourne (24 November 1973)

As a proud Scots Australian and an esteemed President of the Melbourne Scots Society, Sir Robert in his retirement was frequently invited by the Society as a guest of honour. At this 1973 dinner, Menzies lauded the Scottish contribution to settler societies such as Australia, particularly in the realm of education and learning. To be sure, his attachment to his Scottish roots was romantic but also informed by a studied appreciation of the historic contribution the Scottish people had made to literature, philosophy, theology, economics, education, medicine, science, politics and the general enrichment of Western civilisation. No doubt attributing his own love of learning to his Scottish heritage, Menzies reiterated the point he had made in his famous *Forgotten People* speech that Scotland, and Scottish homes in particular, had made an enormous contribution to the flourishing of education. In this speech, Menzies took singular pride in the fact that the Scottish zest for learning transcended class, with the "poor proud homes of Scotland" proving capable of producing station masters and cow-herders who could happily study Latin or Greek. Rising to great heights in the law and politics from his own humble origins in country Victoria, Menzies had hoped to be a worthy exemplar of this Scottish tradition.

....

... Now my task tonight is to propose the toast of Scotland...

I have been President of the Melbourne Scots, through some inadvertence on the part of the Melbourne Scots, for some 12 or 14 years, quite a long time anyhow, but I have never before had the opportunity of proposing the toast of Scotland and so I do it tonight with great goodwill.

Let us now praise famous men, and our fathers who begat us. This is a wonderful theme on a night like this. Sir, it isn't an uncommon error nowadays to think that the world began in our time and that we have nothing to learn from history. This is, you will all realise, a very common error. You have only to read the newspapers to realise how common it is. And yet, of course, it is completely untrue. The Scots have made a positive contribution all around the world. They don't suffer from the unhappy disease of looking back on their grievances and living on their grievances. On the contrary, they look forward, and the Scots throughout modern history have shown that wherever they go in the world they make a contribution to the country to which they have gone and to the good order and government of that country. The Scots are forward-looking, not backward-looking, and that is tremendously important.

Now there are various reasons for this. The first is that the great traditional Scottish desire for learning and for making a contribution to learning has never quite faded away. The other day I received Alec Fraser who is not only a parson but, in spite of that, a great student of Scottish history and who knows about Scottish history, and Alec rejoiced me, as he always does, by telling me the story of two men who worked at the Caledonian Railway Station in Edinburgh. Most of you, I hope, have been there and, therefore, you will appreciate the pure juiciness of the story. The Station Master in his spare time read Greek. Think of it! I found Greek frightfully difficult myself, but the Railway Master, the Station Master, he read Greek for pleasure. And one of his Porters, read Latin for pleasure. Now, can you imagine it in any other station but Scotland, a Station Master reading Greek in the Classics and a Porter, a Porter pushing barrows along the platform reading the *Iliad*[26] for fun. This, I think, is a tremendous illumination of a true Scottish tradition. "There must be learning in this land" as J M Barrie[27] said when he made that famous speech of his at St Andrew's. And, similarly, one year when I was Prime Minister – a time that some of the older among you may remember (Laughter and Applause) I was up in Scotland and was staying with Billy Rootes, the motorcar man. I know I must speak very carefully about motor car manufacturers, you understand, I say this with all reservation, but I happened to be a friend of Billy Rootes and a guest in his home in the high country running down into the valley at Aberfeldy, and so it was almost my own country, you

---

26 Attributed to Homer, the *Iliad* is an ancient Greek epic poem describing the siege of the city of Troy.

27 Sir James Matthew (J M) Barrie (1860-1937) was a Scottish playwright and novelist.

see. And on the Saturday morning I went out into a field and there was a man, a cowherd, looking after the castle. And we got away to one side and we leaned against a fence and we talked together. He was a cowherd in Scotland and he was a philosopher, he was a man of learning. He discussed problems with me both philosophical and metaphysical which strained my own imperfect powers to the very limit and I thought, where could this happen except in Scotland. His job was to look after cattle, his mind was to look after the magnificent mysteries of thought and the entire philosophy of human life, and I went back to lunch feeling that though I had been speaking to a cowherd, I had met my better. Only in Scotland, I think, could that happen.

Now J M Barrie made a great speech at St Andrew's, the rectoral address at St Andrew's. I hope everybody has read it. I hope everybody has appreciated its immense humour and penetration and wisdom. And at one time in the speech, Barrie said he was speaking about the "poor proud homes of Scotland". That is a lovely expression, isn't it, "the poor proud homes of Scotland". But many of us today want to be sympathised with, want people to be sorry for us because we are poor but he saw, with penetrating wisdom, that to be poor was not to be obscure, was not to be a nonentity, that you could be poor but proud and it is because the Scots have given to the world this feeling that a poor proud people can do great things for the world, and they have lived to our time, and lived here with us tonight as people who understand, who understand that it is wise, it is proper, to feel some sensible self-satisfaction about being both poor and proud. This is tremendously important. The poor proud homes of Scotland.

You know, the only man who ever understood this properly, unhappily was not a Scot. He was Rudyard Kipling who was a man of Sussex and who wrote the most lovely things about Sussex. Do you remember what he said when he was adapting to his own purpose the lines with which I began:

Let us now praise famous men,

Men of little showing

But their fame continueth

But their work continueth

Long beyond our knowing.

This makes me proud to be a Scot, a person of Scots descent, a miserable descendant, an unworthy descendant of the most remarkable race of people that the world has ever known and, therefore, Let us now Praise Famous Men, rise up and let us drink the health of Scotland.

5

NATIONAL IDENTITY AND CITIZENSHIP

Broadcast on Australia's Golden Jubilee of Federation, Broadcast, Melbourne (9 May 1951)

Pitching his message to a largely British audience through the BBC, Prime Minister Menzies discussed the significance of Australia celebrating its first half-century of nationhood. He first of all affirmed that Australia, as an autonomous nation, was adding to its British foundations with its own character, experiences and achievements. It was evident that while Menzies was a staunch Anglophile, he took pride in what Australia had accomplished in its own right since Federation. His description of Australians as "British" appears archaic to modern sensibilities but it reflected the legal reality of the time that all Australians were classed as "British Subjects" under the *Nationality and Citizenship Act* (1948). For Menzies, a key tenet of this Australian British identity was allegiance to the Crown and something of a fraternal bond with the then British Commonwealth. It was beyond doubt that Menzies saw the "Britishness" of Australians as not only the product of a legal technicality, but as an inerasable trait in the inherited DNA of the nation. Returning to a popular theme of his, the Prime Minister reminded his audience that the struggle for democracy could never be taken for granted and that with the onset of the Cold War, the British Commonwealth stood firm as the bulwark of freedom and civilisation for the modern world.

....

On May 9th, 1901, the first Parliament of the new Commonwealth of Australia met in Melbourne.

We are now celebrating that historic event with pride and thankfulness, with hope and resolution. I will not, in a brief speech, attempt to describe with either fullness or accuracy our emotions on this occasion. I shall therefore say no more than three things: First, we are Australians; not remote and scattered colonists but a closely-knit nation, building our traditions for the future upon the noble traditions of the past; adding to them, as we trust, the products of own character, conflicts and achievements. These are matters for pride. Second, we are British. We are the king's men. We spring from an ancient race; but we are members of a modern British Commonwealth which has been called upon twice in this war-scarred century to keep unbroken the gates of the strongholds of human freedom. Our Mother Country has not failed. Our sister nations have not failed. We have not failed. These also are matters for pride. Third, we have played our own part not only in the defence of liberty but also in the carrying of its torch into new lands.

Those who are either unable or unwilling to understand the true nature and quality of the British Commonwealth have not yet realised that the great new nations of the Commonwealth have not grown to their nationhood against the British will. On the contrary, they have by British precept, example, and encouragement, come to know and to practice the arts of self-government, the magnificent self-discipline of the rule of law, the brotherly humanities of social and industrial justice.

Democracy is neither accidental nor inevitable. It is the product of generations of self-sacrifice, of conscious struggle, of belief in the vital significance of individual men and women, of a sense of Divine order in a distracted human world. These also are matters of pride. You may wonder why I have spoken in this way of pride; a quality so much misunderstood, so frequently confused with arrogance. The answer is simple. It is my conviction that we of the British family are not yet discharged from duty. The war for freedom still goes on; and in the old words: "there is no discharge in that war".

The world, if it is to be free, still needs – and needs more than ever – a bold, proud, wise, confident and active British Commonwealth.

We in Australia reject the poor notion that this great association is just something for the historians to write about. There is much history to be made before it is written. What is our contribution to be? What does the world need? Let us answer without fear. The world needs something better than resignation, or cynicism, or the fading of great dreams, or the easy abandonment of great responsibilities.

It needs courage and resolution and endurance and faith. It needs in particular that decent pride which gives to a nation or to a race a sense of destiny and continuity, of feeling deep in the heart that it stands for great things that those things must not be surrendered or abandoned.

I would like to say, for Australia, to the King's subjects the world over, that, fifty years young as we are, we are still the off-spring of an ancient kingdom, the votaries of an ancient faith, the servants of an enduring cause. It will be an ill-day for us and for the world when our emotions grow feeble, when we fear to be great, when honest pride is put away.

It is my honour to speak for a peaceful and friendly nation, not given to bitter enmities, nor to sustained hatreds; a nation living in a land of sunshine and cheerfulness and goodwill.

We send out our greetings to all men. But on this day especially do we send our message of love and understanding to the Mother Country and to her children wherever they may be.

Australian National Identity, "Australia Today – Man to Man" Broadcast (26 August 1953)

In this radio address, Menzies identified some of the personal characteristics that made Australians unique, the chief of these being a robust individualism. This "Australia Man-to-Man" broadcast was one of many radio addresses in a 1953-54 broadcast series that the Prime Minister used to speak directly to ordinary Australians on topics of national interest and importance. In this broadcast, Menzies spoke of individualism as a positive Australian trait that was character-building and eminently conducive to national progress. While the notion of individualism in today's context is often regarded as a selfish, atomised philosophy that overlooks the notion of community, Menzies affirmed it in his time as a welcome corrective to the collectivist ideologies of socialism and communism which tended to diminish the dignity and freedom of the individual. In a world where these conformist, "big government" ideologies were seen to subordinate the interests of ordinary citizens to those of the State, individualism affirmed the freedom for individual men and women to cultivate their own talents, to pursue their own enterprises, and to contribute fully to the life and wellbeing of the country.

....

In my early broadcasts after my return to Australia I spoke to you about events overseas and particularly those associated with the Coronation. Tonight I want to say something to you about our own country.

There is an old saying that travel broadens the mind. I do not know how true this is. Perhaps I'm not a good judge, because I have travelled a great deal around the world, and whether my mind has been broadened in consequence not even my best friends will tell me. But I really think the benefit of seeing other countries and other people is that one comes back to one's own country with perhaps a better informed and more just and critical eye. I am a dyed-in-the-wool Australian, and I believe in Australia. I think that we are a good country and a good people. There are of course, as in other lands, some self-seekers and some evaders of responsibility, and some crooks, but the test of a nation is whether it contains a clear majority of decent, honourable, competent, industrious and self-reliant people. That test Australia will pass as handsomely as any country in the world.

You will remember an old and interesting expression about a man "having the defects of his qualities". What does it mean? I will answer by giving an illustration. A man of action, with the qualities of decision, and drive, may frequently have a defect of those qualities, in that he is not considerate of other people's feelings or rights. Similarly, every country which has qualities is apt to produce the corresponding defects of those qualities. The English, for example, as they have shown magnificently during this century, have patience and endurance and a sense of discipline which are the marvel of intelligent onlookers in other lands. The defects of those great qualities are that they may sometimes be accused of taking things too quietly, or relying perhaps too much on the notion – the historic notion – that though they may lose the battles they always win the war.

The Americans have enormous qualities of generosity and idealism. The defect of those qualities is that some Americans, in discussing international relations, are apt to think that there are certain principles which govern the conduct of nations and that once those principles are enunciated the nations will fall into the appropriate pattern. The trouble is that things do not happen that way. You cannot lay down a set of principles and squeeze human conduct into them. You will be far more profitably employed in dealing with men and nations as they are, seeking good decisions and just actions as opportunity occurs, and leaving the principles to evolve themselves as a result of conduct.

What about our own country? How do you suppose we look to the eye of the intelligent and critical onlooker? Well, I think that he would at once say that for our numbers we are a great and fortunate people; who live a free kind of life, mostly in climatic and domestic conditions which would be the envy of most people in the Northern Hemisphere. The expression of that freedom is that we are uncommonly good at games of skill, we produce great cricketers, great tennis players, great runners. One of the reasons why we do this is that whatever we may say politically, we are at heart great individualists. In time of war, we produce fighting men whose fame spreads all over the world. And they are great fighting men because they have courage and self-reliance and initiative. All these things are the expression of a free individualism. Now, I am a great believer in individual self-reliance. I think it is of the essence of strong nationhood. It may occasionally express itself in what some people regard as undue aggressiveness, but that is merely what I have called the defect of the quality. But much more importantly there is perhaps another defect. We do not take too readily to discipline. We occasionally fall into the error of thinking that discipline has something to do with tyranny and, thank heaven, we won't have tyrants at any price. But it is still true that democracy, which ennobles the individual and which depends for its success upon his efforts and sense of responsibility, cannot succeed without discipline; not discipline by a dictator or by a small group, but self-discipline.

When, as with us, the people are electorally the masters of government, they are masters because they can periodically make a government or break a government at their will. But while the government is an office we all have an instant and meticulous obedience to the law; all the more so because we have made that law through our chosen representatives. That is why in a free democracy, people who wangle their way out of the law, or beat the tax commissioner, or conduct black-market operations, are not clever people to be applauded because "they have got away with it", but are to be regarded as undemocratic people who are weakening the authority of democratic self-government.

Let me take another matter, the more individualistic we are, the more we treasure our right to grumble. No sensible person quarrels with this; Divine discontent is of the essence of progress. But if the grumbling habit becomes too strong, we will find ourselves persuading ourselves that things are worse than they are, and we will inevitably tend to get our benefits by contemplating too closely our burdens.

There is a well-known revivalist hymn which begins, "Count your blessings, count them one by one". It is a good sentiment. More, it is a good principle of action. Every time in the last few years that I have come back to my native land after contemplating the state of affairs in Great Britain and in Europe, I have found myself wondering if we know how fortunate we are. I would sooner live in Australia than in any of those old countries that you could name. I feel that I am living a free and better life, and that my children have a happier inheritance. Visitors to Australia sometimes say that we think too much about our grievances and too little about our prosperity and our future. It is, of course, inevitable that public attention should be constantly attracted by criticisms. For criticism is vocal and therefore news, while contentment is silent and is therefore not news. We have black spots upon our national life which it is our responsibility to remove, but by and large we enjoy a level of employment, of income, of living conditions which are the envy of most people overseas. We gain a great deal politically by dissatisfaction. But we gain nothing from pessimism. Pessimism is a bare, negative thing which never gets anything done and which, in fact, if it becomes widespread, is positively destructive.

There is no reason whatever for despondency or evil prophecies. I for one am confident that the next 50 years in Australia will see a growth and development which would have been thought fantastic at the beginning of the century. So I say to you; let us count our blessings; let us think about them and be thankful for them; let us harness our resourceful individualism to the service of our community, for it is abundantly clear that if we are determined to put more into the nation than we can take out of it, we are destined to be one of the great nations of the world. In my next broadcast, I will continue to look at our position in Australia, and to give what I hope you will find a true and balanced account of how our condition has been improving, of our national achievements, and of our opportunities for the future.

Notions of Nationhood, "Australia Today – Man to Man" Broadcast (23 April 1958)

In this "Australia Man-to-Man" broadcast leading up to Anzac Day, Prime Minister Menzies began by paying tribute to the valour of the Gallipoli Anzacs before explaining what it meant for Australia to be a modern nation. For Menzies, nationhood did not simply imply that Australia was technically a sovereign State with its own national borders, but rather a body of Australians imbued with a sense of history and animated by a spirit of national pride in their cultural identity and achievements. Moreover, nationhood was about community and a sense of mutual responsibility among citizens for the wellbeing of their country. According to Menzies, Australian nationhood did not entail an insular and parochial nationalism, but rather an outward-looking Australia that had a responsibility to contribute to the peace and prosperity of the world by cultivating amicable relationships with its allies and neighbours. In short, he envisioned an Australia that was both proud of its national identity and conscious of its important place in the world.

....

Good evening ladies and gentlemen:

This week we celebrate Anzac Day. It is more than a holiday; it has a great place in Australian history and national feeling.

On the original Anzac Day 43 years ago, Australia by the bravery and devotion of her soldiers achieved a new nationhood, a new place in the world.

What does nationhood mean?

It means first of all a sense of national unity.

Have we, although converted into a federal Commonwealth in 1901, really become a united nation? Do we think of ourselves first as Australians and only second as citizens of a State? Have we got rid of interstate jealousies? Have we realised that there is one internal sovereignty in Australia; that of the national will?

Second, nationhood means a sense of common destiny. What is good for any part of Australia is good for the whole. Do we always recognise this? Do we in our hearts admit that the development of Western Australia or of North Queensland is of real concern to the resident of Melbourne or Sydney? I confess to being occasionally disappointed to find that we still think too much of ourselves as citizens of the State and not sufficiently of ourselves as citizens of the nation.

Third, nationhood means a common pride.

In Great Britain there can be no question of the local pride of the Yorkshireman or of the man from Sussex or of the man from Somerset. This pride expresses itself when the cricket season is on. But the pride of the English is something much prouder and deeper. It is because of that national sense that the old country has over so long a period of history contributed so powerfully to the safety and well-being of the world.

National pride is deeply founded on a sense of history, of self-respect, of achievement. The nations which have contributed most to the history of the improvement of mankind have been those in which a sense of national identity was predominant.

Fourth, nationhood means a sense of common responsibility. It is one of the great things about democracy that the government is ourselves and that what the government has to provide for citizens must first of all be provided for the government by the citizens. This is the inexorable democratic law. There is really no such thing as something for nothing. What is provided for the total of our people must be supplied in greater or lesser individual degree by the total of our people. So regarded, a democratic nationhood is a state of affairs in which a sense of social responsibility has become paramount.

What are the modern tasks of a self-governing nation?

One is to keep the nation free from foreign invasion and the establishment of an alien tyranny. The achievement of this end is not a matter for a few people sitting at Canberra but for the nation as a whole. The defence of the country is a task for all of us. We are not to grumble if the cost of this defence, either in terms of money or of professional inconvenience, seems high. For if we lost our independent freedom, we have lost the whole foundation on which all spiritual, and mental and physical freedom rests.

Another is so to conduct our relations with other countries, both political and economic, as to develop friendships and arrive at mutual accommodation. Just as citizens in their dealings with one another cannot always have it their own way, so in international transactions, the task of statesmanship is to get the best that we can without impairing the rights of other nations to have their own existence, their own future and their own pride.

Sometimes this kind of policy may appear to cost us money; sometimes it will cut across what we believe to be our own rights; but in the end we will be a respectable and respected nation in the world if we realise that our responsibility is not exclusively to our own interests but extends to a joint responsibility for the peace and prosperity of the world.

The other matter that I would like to refer to is that of our internal responsibility to see that our living standards are high and improving; that poverty and social injustice are eliminated; and that the great treasures of our native land, of which we are the trustees, are discovered and developed and used for the benefit of our people.

This calls upon all of us to realise that we as individuals have the responsibility of doing our best in whatever task we are called upon to perform.

It is difficult to understand that there are still some people who fail to realise that rising living standards require more and more production and not merely more and more money. Material living standards express themselves in terms of actual goods and services and if they are to rise there must clearly be more goods and more services. This is a great national task. It is one of the great responsibilities of nationhood.

It is a good thing that we should think about these elementary but frequently forgotten matters at a time like this.

Believing as I do that our country has a wonderful record of achievement and that that record has not been achieved without great skill and hard work and a sense of pride, a sense of destiny, I think it not inappropriate to point out that the greatest cause of the magnificent pioneering that has gone on and still goes on in Australia is a feeling in the hearts of all pioneers that they are discharging a common national responsibility and helping to build a greater Australia for the future. Good night to all of you.

Speech at Naturalisation Ceremony, Perth (24 July 1961)

As Prime Minister, Menzies enthusiastically supported and indeed expanded Australia's post-war immigration scheme initiated by the Chifley Labor government. Like his Labor predecessors, the Menzies government aimed to fully absorb immigrants into Australian society and encouraged them to take up citizenship as "new Australians". In his address to a naturalisation ceremony in Perth, Menzies assured Australia's newest citizens that they were just as much a part of Australia as earlier arrivals – and, indeed, their present-day descendants – in what was essentially a nation of immigrants. In the face of community disquiet that new immigrants often failed to integrate, Menzies remarked on how rapidly these new arrivals had adapted to the customs of their new home, particularly in their language habits. Far from viewing these immigrants as a strain on the community, Menzies welcomed them for their potential to become great contributors to Australia. The Prime Minister lauded Australia's lack of class consciousness and natural friendliness as endearing characteristics that would instinctively draw newcomers into the national fold.

....

Sir, Parliamentary colleagues, and ladies and gentlemen:

I want to say a few words to those who are, tonight, taking a step which in the life of any human being is a very, very important one. Those of us who have had the good fortune to be born in a country, to live in it, to enjoy its life, to take our citizenship for granted, can't know very much about what is involved in pulling up the roots of the family and moving into another country, moving right across the world and entering into a new life, and a new citizenship. This is a very remarkable event.

Whenever I think about it I say to myself, "What does persuade people to move from one country to another?" I might ask you ladies and gentlemen tonight, what was it that persuaded you to leave your ancient home, and to come here? There have been times in the world's history when people have left their own country because they were, in effect, driven out of it – we have seen something of that in the modern world; we have seen something of that in the last 30 years of human history – people being compelled to leave home, so to speak, because home was no longer home, no longer the kind of home they wanted to live in. These are the tragic events of modern history. And when that event happens to anybody there must be one passion in the heart, and that is to go to the country where those things can't happen to you, to come out of a country whose freedom has been snatched away from it, and to come to a country where freedom will be defended by everybody, whatever political party he may belong to, whatever religion he may profess, where everybody is agreed that we are free people, free, as Mr Cash[28] says, to pray as we want to pray, to speak as we want to speak, to assemble as we want to assemble.

Well, of course, there have been other movements in the world's recent history – or modern history – in which people left and came to another country because they saw in that new country an opportunity which they didn't see at home: not driven out, but drawn out by the prospect of a new life.

In case any of you who are being naturalised tonight think that we political fellows here on the platform are treating you as if you were something apart, let me say this to you: there is not a man on this platform, and not a woman on this platform, who didn't have a grandfather or a great-grandfather, who came to Australia – he might not have been called at that time a "migrant" or a "new Australian". (Laughter, applause) – so you know we are all the same, aren't we?

Don't let yourself feel that you are a sort of something apart, something odd in the Australian community, because you are not. Let me tell you – I'll speak only for myself: on my father's side, my grandfather and my grandmother came to Australia from Scotland. Now any Scot here tonight would say "what a mistake". (Laughter) "To leave Scotland to come here". But they came here and looking back on it I have no doubt they said, "A very good country to go to, Australia, because although

---

28 Mr Doug Cash (1919-2002) served as a Federal MP representing the Perth-based division of Stirling from 1958 to 1961.

171

we will be "new Australians" when we get there, our grandson will be Prime Minister". (Laughter, applause) You make a note of that. Put little Willy's name down. (Laughter) Stranger things have happened. On my mother's side my grandparents came out because my grandfather on her side thought that there was gold in Australia. Instead of looking for it in Kalgoorlie, which might have been a rather successful thing to do, he looked for it in vain in another part, in the state of Victoria. He was, I suppose, a new Australian. I don't know.

You see the point I am getting at? Your grandchildren will be as much old native-born Australians as I am today. (Applause) And so I want to say to you: don't feel odd. Some of you may face language difficulties, although I am staggered at the skill and speed with which people learn to speak, not only English, but Australian (Laughter) – you know, a slight complication upon standard English. But don't be worried if you think that you speak our language indifferently. I remember I had a colleague, once, a genial character, rather rough and ready, to use your idiom, who had to receive a French football team. They arrived and the leader of the team said to my colleague, "Excuse, please, I don't speak English very well" and my colleague, with a flash of candour said, "Don't worry about that, old boy, neither do I!" (Laughter)

But all those things are passing phases. It is quite true that many of us had grandparents who came from what we call the "old country", from England, from Scotland, Wales, from Ireland, wherever it might be, and so there were none of these problems of language, although even there, there were some – some. And many of you have come from ancient countries in Europe and you have different tongues, different backgrounds, marvellous histories, marvellous literature, marvellous music. You carry with you an enormous store in the mind and in the heart. These are tremendous contributions to Australia. It was said a little while ago that migration has meant something tremendous to Australia in the post-war years and I want to repeat it. It is tremendously true.

I go around Australia a good deal in order to have the pleasure of having one man out of ten say "Good on you" – do you know that idiom? – And the other ten saying baa!" All this, of course, is the very proof of freedom in Australia. Prime Ministers here don't go around with a posse of police around them: they just go around. Sometimes people are friendly; and sometimes they are not. And the Prime Minister hopes for the best, being by nature and experience a good high-spirited fellow, you see.

But when I look around this country, for whose political leadership, rightly or wrongly, I have been responsible for a long, long time, I can't imagine that Australia would be as prosperous, as happy, as forward-looking, today, if it hadn't been for this remarkable inflow of good people into Australia. (Applause)

It has been a wonderful thing for us and I want every one of you who will be naturalised tonight to realise that this is not all one way. We are not just being nice to you: we are grateful to you. And you are not just to be grateful to us for having received you: I want you to feel a proper pride in what you find yourselves able to do in Australia. In some of the greatest industries that I know of in Australia the progress would have been a mere fraction of what it is today if it hadn't been for hundreds of thousands of people coming in willing to work, willing to contribute, willing to become good contributing citizens of Australia. Anybody who knows anything about our great industries will realise at once that what we call the great migration programme has been of immeasurable benefit.

So I just want to say to you: don't be nervous, as if you are in a strange land, because, as I explained to you before, your grandsons will be on the same footing as I am tonight. There is no occasion to feel nervous or strange. Don't feel that any man's hand is against you. Because the only really unpopular people in Australia are politicians and football umpires. (Laughter)

It is a great thing, a difficult thing for you, the parents, a difficult thing; a difficult thing for you who, having reached mature years have had to make this great change, I know, a tremendously difficult decision to make. But for your children, for your children, this is the land of opportunity. I am perfectly certain that nobody who looks at it along these lines will ever doubt that it was a great thing to come here. We are a friendly people. We are not stuffy. We are not consumed by snobberies of class, or some of this nonsense that has beset some of the older countries of the world. You are in an essentially democratic country where every man has a chance to stand on his own feet, and every woman, and to be taken at his or her own true value by other people. Nothing could be better than that: to be free, to feel that there is no shadow over you, to feel that there is none of the paraphernalia of dictatorship in this country, that we are, in the truest sense, a friendly community, a brotherhood, and a sisterhood of people.

And so we are, in Australia – where any boy or girl has a vista of opportunity which can be marched along provided there is ability and character and courage and determination – a country of freedom, of equality before the law, a country which governs itself at its own will, through the people it chooses, without compulsion of anybody else, to serve it in parliament or municipal life. This is, I am proud to say, in my opinion the freest country in the world.

And it is for all those reasons that I don't look down from a great height and say in a sort of patronising way. "Well, you all look rather new to me". Not a bit, not a bit. No newer than grandfather was. Make no mistake about that. And I will be surprised if, as this generation of people who have come to Australia from the old countries of the world we don't find Prime Ministers and Premiers and Judges, and Chief Justices, people of great distinction, serving Australia. I find that prospect very attractive. I hope you will find it very attractive. Therefore I say to you, "welcome". I am delighted that you have taken this decision. I am sure that it is good for you, and I am positively certain that it is good for Australia. (Applause)

Speech at Dover Castle, Dover, United Kingdom (20 July 1966)

Shortly before his retirement as Prime Minister in January 1966, Menzies was appointed by Elizabeth II to succeed Winston Churchill as Lord Warden of the Cinque Ports and Constable of Dover Castle. At his installation ceremony at Dover's Maison Dieu (Town Hall) on 20 July, Menzies famously appeared in his ceremonial Admiral's uniform complete with sword and cocked hat. At the conclusion of formalities, the former Prime Minister delivered this address at his installation ceremony. Whilst the occasion was one steeped in British pageantry and tradition, Menzies' speech exuded a distinctively Australian flavour with its evident affection for the nation's iconic and much-loved folksong, *Waltzing Matilda*. Although he regarded the song's lyrics as perhaps inappropriate for a national anthem, he praised its character as "superbly Australian". Turning to the historic significance of the ceremony, Menzies spoke of the importance of "historical continuity" for civilisations such as Britain and Australia. He emphasised that the defence of such civilisations was not merely a matter of employing military force but about the preservation of its received traditions and institutions, not least parliamentary democracy and the rule of law.

·····································

Sir, ladies and gentlemen ... I must say I am immensely grateful to the Recorder for the marvellous little speech, so false and so agreeable, that he has made about me. From now on remembering my Scots ancestry, if somebody says: "Quit yer havering" I'll say "No no, I want him to go on."

I must tell you something – do you mind a little personal remark? – but here I am masquerading as a species of Admiral – now stick to your desk and never go to sea, you'll be the ... – anyhow these things are called epaulettes[29], I am instructed by my ADC [aide-de-camp] and I want to let you into a secret. All admirals, genuine admirals, understand this – but I didn't until today – but you are sitting at the table and you

---

29 An epaulette is a type of ornamental shoulder-piece used as insignia of rank on a military uniform.

turn around to speak to your delightful neighbour and these things come to your eye and you say: "Yes what is it?" and I've been saying "Yes what is it?" to the epaulettes right through lunch. I don't know whether there is a moral in that story, there maybe not, but anyhow I give it to you for what it's worth.

The other thing I'd like to say is that I enjoyed hearing the songs of Australia and in particular "Waltzing Matilda". Now "Waltzing Matilda" is superbly Australian. In other words its immoral, it's all about a sheep stealer but it's musical. It has much in common with some Australians you know. I listen to it with great pleasure and I remember that about five years ago I paid an official visit on the French government. Now that's pretty heavy weather business although I did make "Le Grand Charles"[30] laugh twice – I must claim that immortal credit – but I had to go up to the Arc de Triomphe to lay a wreath to the Unknown Warrior and the band of the French Guard was playing; it was a great affair and as I came back along the Guard they played "Waltzing Matilda" and do you know that was the most moving thing in my life because the breeze blew down the Champs Elysees mildly and took with it "Waltzing Matilda" right to the heart of Paris. And so that made it a very pleasant event for me.

Now this morning we had these fierce lights; they're not as bad now, I'll probably get on rather better this afternoon and may speak a little longer as a result, but these dazzling lights are very devastating. My old friend Macaskie (Judge Official) stood side on to them so he was all right but I had to be glared at by them. But this afternoon I want to make a few remarks which I really intended to make this morning and one of them was this, and it's a platitude to say it to you. They were talking about Pitt and Wellington and Churchill and all the time I was hoping that my old friend Mr Macaskie wouldn't come out and say: "Well of course as London is to Paddington so Pitt is to Addington". This would indeed have been disastrous, but being a man of Gray's Inn he does the right thing always by me.

---

30 Reference to Charles de Gaulle (1890-1970), the President of France from 1958 to 1969.

Now I said something this morning about the historic significance of this post and this ceremony. This is true but now, quite briefly, I would like to remind you, if I need to remind you, that these occasions involve more than recalling the glories of the past. The moment we as a people – and we are one people, never forget it, one people, these are the immortal words of Pitt – begin to live on our past glories and have nothing but doubts for the future then we will be nearing the end of the road. These are not occasions for retrospectivity. In times of peace – and technically we are at peace in our various parts of the world – the hardest thing is to project into contemporary affairs the spirit of comradeship and sacrifice and patriotism at its best that we have accommodated ourselves to in times of war. This is terribly difficult. Men who, under the great heat and pressure of events in a war will perform miracles of self-sacrifice, will not have that feeling at all in time of peace and yet, without being too grandiloquent about it, this is what we need. I think there is no problem which is insoluble – and we all have problems, this ancient Kingdom has problems, we have problems which I have now bequeathed to somebody else – of course there are problems, but if we can remind ourselves on an occasion like this that the things which saw us through are the things which will see us through, then all these problems become soluble.

It would be a great pity, if historical continuity turned out to be intermittent or spasmodic so that we have a sense of continuity at a great time in history and then relapse into a form of lethargy and forget about it, and then come out of it again under the influence of some great man or some great challenge. What we really need is continuity in the truest sense because after all this part of England has been associated with the defence of the realm since before the beginning of history. We've been reminded of it today. We are tempted to think that the defence of the realm is something which occurs in terms of arms and nothing else. Arms, war, the defence of the realm. But the defence of the realm is a continuing thing. The defence of the realm includes the defence of its, to be quite homely, its economic structure, its prosperity, its social justice, its institutions, the rule of Parliamentary democracy, the rule of law, all of these things are matters which have to be defended. Don't take them for granted. They have been destroyed in many parts of the world overnight. We must not take them for granted. All these things are included in the defence of the realm and if we think of it in that way we will have less grumbles and more resolution. We will have less self-interest from time to time and more belief in the overwhelming interests of the country, of the nation and of the people. That's all I want to say.

When I began this morning and was buttoned up somewhat precariously into these garments by a very skilled man I said to myself: "By three o'clock this afternoon I'll be out of them in paradise." Now it's a quarter past four and I'm not in paradise, and I strongly suspect you are in the other place.

6

EDUCATION

The Place of a University in the Modern Community, Address delivered at the Annual Commencement of the Canberra University College (1939)

From his own rich educational experience as a distinguished law student at the University of Melbourne, Menzies came to appreciate the immense value of the university to the formation of a citizen's knowledge, character and professional expertise. Far from functioning merely as "degree factories" to equip students for the workforce, Menzies saw universities as citadels of civilisation that would serve to build the character of their students and encourage them to seek truth. In this 1939 lecture, Menzies outlined what he identified as the sevenfold rationale of the modern university to enrich both the individuals and the society to which they belonged. In an age when a university education was still the preserve of a small minority, his vision for the university in the 20th century was evidently broad and farsighted, yet informed by the scholastic traditions that had given birth to the academy in the Middle Ages. With the world on the brink of a second great conflict in the late 1930s, barely a generation after the Great War, Menzies saw Western civilisation as in dire need of education and its humanising influence as never before.

·······································

The question implied in the title of my address is an old one; it has frequently been discussed before. In every century since the Middle Ages it has provoked the speculation and the action of enlightened minds which perceive that, in the state of civilisation in which they found themselves, the homes of higher learning must be defended and the sons of those homes equipped for an intelligent life. But, ancient though the question may be, it was never more important than it is today, when all beliefs are being challenged and old values reassessed, and when barbaric philosophies of blood and iron are resurgent …

What then are we to look for in a true university? What causes should it serve? In the light of what ideals is it to discharge its great and magnificent responsibilities? My answers are seven in number.

First, the University must be a home of pure culture and learning. This was its original medieval function, and is still its first in order of real importance. Learning, "academic learning" as it is sometimes half-contemptuously designated, is one of those civilised and civilising things which the world needs as never before. And it is needed the more largely because we are so frequently unconscious of the need. The world is full of practical men. Their philosophy is utilitarian. They have weighed the classics, literature, and philosophy in their commercial balances and have found them wanting because unprofitable. They have put pure learning on the defensive.

Let me accept their challenge. Let me defend a so-called useless scholarship on the great grounds that it represents a sanity badly needed in an insane world; that it stands for a due proportion in life and living; that it develops the humane and imperishable elements in man; that it points the moral that the mere mechanics of life can never be the sole vocation of the human spirit …

Second, the University must serve as a training school for the professions. This is a great and relatively modern function. As time went on the notion of higher education as a qualification for life produced the notion of higher education as a qualification for a learned profession; a canalisation of knowledge was set up. The age of specialisation dawned. It brought its own dangers …

Third, the University must serve as a liaison between the academician and the good practical man …There must be a mutuality between the theory and the practice …

Fourth, the University must be the home of research. This is an impatient age. We want results. So urgently do we want them that we tend to resemble nothing so much as a small boy who, in a newfound zeal for gardening, pulls up his radishes every week to see how they are growing. The work of research requires infinite patience, precise observation, an objective mind, and unclouded honesty. Its publicity will, as a rule, be in inverse ratio to its merit …

Fifth, the University must be a trainer of character … It is not only wrong, but dangerous, to divide intelligence and character into watertight compartments. There are great temptations which arise from the acquisition of learning, temptations of self-sufficiency, of humanity, of cynicism. The man of learning who has resisted all these things will have a character strengthened and purified by his resistance. A man whose native impulses are good and whose instinctive standards are high will have his impulses touched to finer issues and the whole horizon of his life enlarged by the pursuit of a higher learning.

Sixth, the University must be a training ground for leaders. I am not so foolish as to underwrite the man who, if I may borrow a phrase once tellingly used in the Commonwealth Parliament, has "graduated with honours in the University of Life". Indeed, I regard any Parliament as incomplete which does not contain honest men of every walk of life, schooled and unschooled. But at the same time the complexity of the modern problems of government will inevitably require more and more trained and imaginative men. In other words, the public responsibilities of the universities must grow … Democracy demands leaders and leadership. It demands leaders who will not be afraid to tell the people that they are wrong and endeavour to persuade and guide them. I do not deny, on the contrary I uphold, the right of the people to censure freely, to criticise, to elect, to reject. But not one of these things, as Edmund Burke pointed out so clearly in Bristol, is inconsistent with resolute leadership, and a parliament of men who bring with them not only their votes but their character and their judgement.

Seventh, the University must be a custodian of mental liberty, and the unfettered search for truth. I could say much to you about liberty. Like most precious elements, it is intangible and almost indefinable. But of one thing I am sure, and that is that the motto of liberty is not "Each man for himself and the devil take the hindmost". Liberty and discipline, so far from being opposed, are complimentary; each is essential to the other. But, whatever the true limits of liberty may be, there can be no bounds set to the flight of thought. There is an infinite value in the individual human soul; there is something infinitely moving in the spectacle of the human soul struggling towards the light.

I have never been able to understand the notion of a heresy hunt at the University. It may be necessary under some circumstances in an organised society to set some limits to what a member of that society may say or do. But I am clear that he must never be prevented from coming at the truth. Indeed, without the truth how can our freedom ever be perfect? "And ye shall know the truth and the truth shall make you free".

I am so definite on this that to me a rugged honesty of mind that does not shrink from the truth when it comes upon it in its path has always seemed one of the noblest of virtues; a glib dishonesty of mind which argues to a predetermined conclusion, determined in the light of passion or prejudice or selfishness, has always seemed to me the most contemptible of vices. And so I had stated to you my seven answers. I might perhaps have taken as my text the words: "Wisdom hath builded her house; she hath hewn out her seven pillars".

The Future of Education, Broadcast, Melbourne (19 February 1943)

The expansion of Australian universities in the 1950s and 60s has often been cited as one of Menzies' keynote achievements, and his lofty vision for higher education surfaced in this 1943 speech. Even at a time when the percentage of Australians with a college or university qualification was still miniscule, Menzies recognised that the formal education of the future must extend beyond one's "school years". For Menzies, advancing the education of Australians was a priority because he believed that it was conducive to a more enlightened and successful self-government. The most important consideration, however, was not only the level of education but also the quality and essence of that education. In Menzies' eyes, the religious backdrop to education was critical because it helped furnish the emerging generation with a better understanding of their relationship to God and their fellow citizens. Accordingly, he placed a high value on financially supporting what he called the "church schools" to inculcate these values in their pupils. Indeed, the educational philosophy behind his government's historic 1963 decision to provide Commonwealth finance for science facilities in schools, whether government or independent, could be traced back to this speech.

....

Among the more pleasant illusions which some of us entertain is the belief that in matters of public education, Australia even if she does not lead the world, is at least in the vanguard of progress. This belief cannot be supported.

It is true that many years ago our grandfathers took the bold step of introducing free, secular and compulsory elementary education and a system of State schools. This step, which was seen to assure to every boy and girl the elements of education, was properly regarded as an enlightened substitute for the somewhat sporadic unregulated methods there before existing.

The results have, within sharp limits, been extraordinarily good. The State schools give an elementary or primary education which is extremely sound and most competently imparted. But if we regard a good system of primary education as the be all and end all of the public educational system we shall make a serious if not fatal blunder.

If we start off with the assumption that one of the greatest things that can happen to a community is that every man and woman in it should have been educated to the limit of his or her capacity to receive education, then we can never rest content with a system which provides an excellent primary education up to the age of fourteen and then says in effect to the fourteen year old boys and girls: "Now you are educated, go away and earn your livings". For the truth is that if education is to have any value to the individual it must represent a continuous process and not something which abruptly terminates when school days end. It is I think unfortunate but true that a widespread disposition among our people to regard a primary education in itself as adequate for the tasks of life has tended to produce in us a disregard for higher education, an undue addiction to the acceptance of superficial views without much criticism, a sort of general feeling that what is good enough will do.

One of the great functions of education is to produce a critical mind in the best sense. Anybody who understands Australia and concerns himself with her future must have long since realised that if we could only substitute on a large scale critical minds for merely critical tongues we would go a lot further in a lot less time.

Having in mind all these things, it is clear to me that one of our greatest post-war developments must be a real attack on the question of education. We must spend far more millions upon it than we have ever dreamed of spending.

Three problems in particular, though they are only three out of many, are worth some emphasis tonight:

The first is the problem of the preschool child: There can be no doubt that we are only at the beginnings of a true understanding of the significance of preschool training. It is true that we have in Australia, some conducted by the churches and some by outside bodies, a very valuable series of kindergarten schools. But a matter of major importance cannot be left to the patriotic but necessarily limited efforts of a few highly intelligent men and women, principally women, who direct their attention to the kindergarten problem. The time must come when the community acknowledges its obligation to take all the steps which may be needed to see that the child who enters upon his primary education at the age of six or seven has not had his mind distorted or impaired by conditions existing before he has reached the school age.

The second is the problem of post-school or adult education: How many men there must be who, having been dragooned through school and having learned as little as the law and the schoolmaster would permit, suddenly come to realise at the age of eighteen or nineteen or twenty how handicapped they are by want of education.

It is always unwise to engage in generalities, but I would not be a bit surprised if a careful series of studies revealed that the average boy of twelve is reluctant to absorb knowledge, while the average young man of nineteen has a real thirst for it. This inevitable growth in the human mind produces the great educational paradox, which is that at a time when most of us really have no desire to learn we are provided with facilities for learning, while at a time when we would give anything for learning, the work of the world has swallowed us up and facilities for instruction are both rare and difficult to reach.

The answer to this is not to be found merely in Workers' Educational Associations or University Extension Lectures, admirable though they are. We cannot satisfy the real cravings for knowledge of a young man or a young woman by giving to him or to her a mere superficial smattering. What we must try to devise is some way by which adult education of what we call an academic kind is given to hundreds of thousands of people side-by-side with the practical experience which they are having in whatever their life's work may be. We are well behind the rest of the world in our dealing with this problem of adult education. In a number of European countries, notably Germany and Denmark, very great attention has been paid to it. The fact that in Germany the whole business was put to deplorable political and national ends should not be allowed to obscure the fact that the greater the facilities for post-school education, and the more continuous the interest of the citizen in the cultivation of resources of his own mind, the more successful and intelligent will self-government become.

The third problem that I want to mention is the problem of the non-State school: Standing right outside the arena of the State system we have, for example, in Victoria, various great public schools which are run by School Councils and are in each case identified with the activities of some particular religious denomination, while there are many other church schools, both primary and secondary, the parents of whose pupils for the most part pay fees, and which in any event are not a charge upon the Public Revenues.

What, broadly, is to be the future of the church schools? It is impossible to contemplate that they are going to be abolished by a wave of the hand. It is true that mounting taxation and a possibly difficult economic future will make it extraordinarily difficult for people to send their children to church schools. But there will be great and proper hostility to their abolition, for they are the answer made by many thousands of people to the purely secular education provided by the State. There are very many thousands of people in this country who believe that education divorced from religion not only is incomplete but may actually be dangerous. It is to the eternal credit of these many thousands of people that they have been prepared, for the sake of that deeply held conviction, to pay twice – once as taxpayers for the maintenance of the State schools, and the second time as parents for the maintenance of their children at church schools. My own opinion is that it is unlikely that the church schools can in the post-war period efficiently survive unless there is some measure of State assistance to them. Such State assistance would naturally involve some change in the structure of these schools but it need not affect their essential character. After all, if these schools were not maintained by great Church communities the public as a whole would have to provide far more money for State schools and State instruction. In the past this problem has unhappily been somewhat clouded by a belief that some special case was being made out for the Catholic Church schools.

It is unfortunate for any discussion on a matter so important to go off into a merely sectarian dispute. My own belief is that the maintenance of the church schools, of whatever denomination, is so important – because a religious background for education is so important – that we must all be prepared to come together in the post-war world to devise ways and means of ensuring that those who are content with a purely secular education should be able to get it while those whom such an education will never satisfy should be able to get the kind of training they want for their children without absolutely bankrupting themselves in the process.

Each of these three problems is of great significance; each can be no more than stated in the time at my disposal. But I hope that we shall all be able to think about them and perhaps contribute something to their solution.

Speech to the House of Representatives, Motion on Education, Parliament House, Canberra (26 July 1945)

Casting his mind to the great task of post-war reconstruction, Menzies envisaged a critical role for educational institutions in the rebuilding of Australian society. To borrow an often repeated phrase of Menzies, the business of post-war reconstruction was much more than a mere matter of "pounds, shillings and pence", it was about investing in the moral and spiritual character of the next generation. As important as it was to stimulate economic growth through private enterprise and job creation, schools and universities would play a priceless part in cultivating the simple human virtues of integrity, compassion, understanding and religious faith. In this speech to the House of Representatives, the then Leader of the Opposition argued that all future education policy must be guided by the two grand objectives of educational institutions to produce good citizens and to produce proficient workers. In so doing, Australia could raise a new generation of men and women to bring both human understanding and precision to their chosen vocation.

....

My primary purpose is to direct the attention of the Parliament and the nation to the vital importance in post-war reconstruction of a revised and extended educational system in our country, and to suggest to the government that a commission should be set up in cooperation with the States in order to map out a plan for such reform. A good education, although it is not by any means indispensable to worldly success, is, or should be, I believe, one of the basic elements in the establishment of a citizen in life. This does not mean that everybody can receive usefully a higher education as we so describe it. It does not mean that the education of every citizen is to follow exactly the same lines as if all citizens were destined for exactly the same career. It does not mean that education must be so devised as to develop identical faculties in every human being whom it touches. The whole problem is one of infinite variety. But our experience, particularly in the last few years, has shown that we cannot combine progress with security unless the general level of the trained capacity of our people is very high indeed…

The broad problem ... is the problem of education for citizenship ... The greatest failure in the world in my lifetime, and I am sure that honorable members will agree with me, has not been the failure in technical capacity or manual capacity half as much as it has been the failure of the human spirit. War after war is the result of a failure of the human spirit, not of some superficial elements but of the fatal inability of man to adjust himself to other men in a social world. With all our scientific development of this century, it still remains true that "the proper study of mankind is man", and that the real "peace-maker" is human understanding. The closer the countries of the world have come to each other in point of time, the more they have tended, unhappily, to develop a narrow spirit of self-sufficiency. The more absorbed the people become in the technique of material living, the more they have neglected their social responsibilities, and the more, unhappily, they have neglected the problems of popular self-government. It is well to remember that for years, the greatest danger to democracy has been, not so much a danger from without, as a danger from within.

My own view is that there are two reasons for this decline – there may be scores of others – but these two deserve particular mention. The first is the increasingly pagan and materialistic quality of our education. I have no hesitation in saying, and I have said it many times before in the course of my life, that I believe that religion gives to people a sensitive understanding of their obligations, and that is something which the world sadly needs at the present time. For many years we have had in Australia the advantage of a system of church schools of all denominations, based upon the belief that education should always be conducted against a religious background. But our State schools are, by statute, purely secular in their teaching. What the answer may be to that problem, I do not undertake to say, because that is a matter which calls for consideration by a commission. But I should like again to direct the attention of honourable members to the British Education Act of 1944. Section 7 imposes on local education authorities a duty to contribute towards "the spiritual, moral, mental and physical development of the community". That is a very fine charter for education. Section 25 provides that the school day in every county school and voluntary school shall begin with collective worship on the part of all pupils in attendance at the school, with a proviso excusing a pupil from religious worship or religious instruction upon his parents' request. Section 26 provides for religious instruction in accordance with an agreed syllabus, but it shall not include any catechism or formulary distinct to any religious denomination. This matter is one of vast importance. Nobody can suppose that we are educating our children, except for disaster, by turning them out of purely secular establishments at the age of fourteen, fifteen or sixteen years, merely educated to a point at which they think that there is nothing left for them to learn, aggressively conscious of what they suppose to be their rights, and oblivious of that penetrating feeling of moral obligation to others, which alone can make a community of men successful. That is the first reason, I believe, for the decline to which I have referred.

The second particular reason is the unthinking contempt which has fallen upon what people are pleased to call "useless learning". The old classical conception of education has declined into disfavour. As parents, we clamour more and more that our sons and daughters shall be taught things at school which will enable them to earn money after they have left school, and nothing else. Again, I say plainly that that is a pitiful conception of education. The old classical notion of education may have had its limits. No doubt it did. It ignored far too many modem factors; but the study of humanities in the schools and universities can at least develop a sense of proportion – the balancing of all special knowledge against general knowledge of the world, of the men in it, and of its problems. "Useless learning", as it has been described, must, I believe, come back into its own in this world if we are to produce a really civilized point of view. The first function of education is to produce a good man and a good citizen. Its second function is to produce a good carpenter or a good lawyer, and the good carpenter and good lawyer will be all the better at their respective crafts if they have become aware of the problems of the world, have acquired some quality of intellectual criticism, and have developed that comparative sense which produces detachment of judgment and tends always to moderate passion and prejudice ...

Now I turn to the position of the Commonwealth with regard to education. There is an agitation in some quarters for the transfer to the Commonwealth of the constitutional power to make laws with respect to education. I do not propose to discuss that, because, in my view, the problem is urgent, and it should not be considered upon the basis of some more or less remote constitutional possibility. After all, education was not included among the subjects referred to the people at the recent referendum, and therefore the constitutional aspect does not at present arise. There is, however, no legal reason why the Commonwealth should not come to the rescue, of the States on the matters that I am discussing. Either by appropriations under section 81 of the Constitution, as to which I agree that there is some constitutional doubt, or by conditioned grants to the States under section 96, as to which there is no constitutional doubt, the Commonwealth could make available substantial sums in aid of educational reform and development. It is inevitable, I think, that that course should be followed, and, thinking so, I have put forward the proposal mentioned at the outset of my speech. I believe that the Commonwealth will, in all probability, be a substantial contributor to educational reform, and, if so, it is in the interests of the Commonwealth to establish forthwith, in collaboration with the States, a highly competent committee or commission to investigate the problem and submit recommendations. 1 believe that such a body should be composed of highly qualified persons completely detached from party politics, and reinforced by the inclusion of a member or members familiar with developments abroad. We should not be parochial on this matter. We have men and women in this country excellently equipped to sit on such a body, and I think that we could secure the services of somebody from Great Britain and another from the United States of America to reinforce the committee or commission.

I have said that the Commonwealth must, in my opinion, give aid to the States. Ever since the passage of uniform taxation laws, the States have not been masters in their own financial house. Whatever State Ministers of Education may say about what they would like to do, there is a sharp limit to their available resources. Yet in more States than one there is a burning desire to do something about this matter. I should like to say, in the presence of the honourable member for Denison (Dr Gaha), that no State has a better record with regard to education than Tasmania. The most dramatic and interesting educational experiment made for a long time in Australia has been carried out by the government of Tasmania in the establishment of area schools. These schools will not only bring immediate advantages to those who attend them, but will also provide a notable piece of educational research. Unless the Commonwealth, no matter which political party is in power, can aid the States financially, only limited objectives will be sought. I have profound distrust of limited objectives on the great and vital problem which we are now considering. If adequate resources are not available to the States, they will cut their coats according to their cloth, and that should not be allowed to happen. As a nation we cannot afford to do anything less than our best in a campaign the result of which will be to determine whether, in the new world, we are to be a nation of strong, self-reliant, trained and civilized people, or whether we are to be content with second-rate standards, and more devoted to the pursuits of material advantage than to the achievement of a genuine humane community spirit.

Speech by the Chancellor to Graduates at Degree Ceremony, University of Melbourne (26 April 1967)

Returning to his Alma Mater from which he had graduated in 1916 with First Class Honours in Law, Menzies addressed a graduation ceremony as the newly-appointed Chancellor of the University of Melbourne. In his speech to the graduates, the former Prime Minister sought to impart some of the lessons he had learned since his student days. He reminded the graduands that learning was a lifelong journey and something that did not simply end at the conclusion of formal education. Foreshadowing the increased number of students who would go on to pursue postgraduate study in the ensuing decades, Menzies expressed his hope that some in his audience would undertake postgraduate research work in the future. In the late 1960s, Menzies appreciated the importance of research endeavour to the future strength and prestige of Australian universities which he had done so much to develop with his higher education policies as Prime Minister. If Australia aspired to be a leader in higher education, it was essential for the country to invest in building "first-rate" universities to produce its own crop of eminently qualified researchers.

....

I just want to say that now the fun is all over, but, as you have to pay some price for it, the price today is that I am to address a few golden words to the new graduates, if they can stand it.

I just want to say to them, as one who has been through the mill, that I know that this is a great day in their lives. Not a great day because something has ended but in reality because something has begun. I occasionally encounter somebody who says to me in a rather smug way, "I finished my education in such and such a year". Well, obviously he didn't ever begin because, so far from having finished your education today, you have begun the next phase of it, which I am quite sure will be even better than the phase of the past. Because a university teaches us, I think, two things. First of all, it teaches us how to learn. This is very important – how to learn. And if it succeeds with us, it breeds into us a desire to learn. To know how to learn and to wish to learn are the two greatest equipments that graduates can take away with them from a great University. And I would add to that, that whether we are graduates with honours or not, whether we are doctors, or masters, or whatever it may be, one of the great things which the University seeks to contribute to the world through its graduates is a sense of imperfection – not a sense of omnipotence – but a sense of imperfection, which is the sense that drives men and women into enduring intellectual effort.

Now there are a number of people today who have taken a variety of degrees. Some may contemplate, having regard to the nature of their training, that they will involve themselves in due course in the great rumbling world of production, finance, and business, because in all those worlds graduates are needed. That has been very well understood in the United States of America for a long time, where the greatest of houses put a premium on having a university graduate recruited to their staff. It wasn't so well understood in my earlier days in Australia, but I think it is an aspect of the matter in which we are steadily improving. But I want to say to those who have graduated today, who may contemplate a life of this kind to which I have been referring, that if that is your destination, remember that you won't succeed because you are a graduate but because your faculties have been trained and sharpened so that you're quick to learn. In other words, the getting of a degree – great landmark as it is in the life of all of us – is not an end but a beginning.

And there are those of you – I have seen a large number today – who are graduates in my own Faculty of Law, and I have been delighted every now and then to find the name of somebody who was a contemporary of my own – the names do tend to go on, I'm happy to say, in the Law. Well, I say to them – don't fall into the error of thinking that you now know all about the law. Even the High Court doesn't profess to know all about the law. What you have had is a first class grounding in the law and a training in how to learn in the law. I very well remember that in my own time, if you will permit me to be a little autobiographical, I was what they call a terrific student – you know what I mean – examinations just come like that – wonderful! And when I was finally called to the

Bar, I was tempted for a while to think that I knew a good deal about it. I had had first-class final Honours, I had won the Supreme Court prize, and then I had a great stroke of fortune because I read with Owen Dixon at the Bar – the greatest lawyer this country ever had. And in three months' time, I was much more conscious of what I didn't know than I had ever been before, and therefore I was able to learn, and learn, and learn, not to the perfection he would have demanded but at any rate to some extent. What I had had was a beginning – an essential beginning – but incomplete in its nature. Now some of you today, I know, will be looking forward to teaching. There were a great number of graduates in Arts today and I think quite a few of them will be looking forward to teaching. And I am sure that if they had the fullest advantage of this place, they will be good teachers because they will have learned how to learn. You can't be a good teacher unless you know how to learn. Then you will understand the people you are teaching, and their minds, and their outlook.

There is one other thing that I would like to say. There are very many of you today who have taken first degrees. I hope that quite a few of you will go on to post-graduate work and research work, because if I may repeat in other words something that I said here only a few weeks ago, the whole future of university education will depend upon the people who from now on do postgraduate and research work. There is nothing more terrible than a second-rate university. There is nothing more inspiring than a first-rate university. And if this is to continue to be a first-rate university, then more and more we will have to produce our own teachers, our own experts in the field of research, because we have reached the stage in history where we can't import them with the ease with which they were available 40 years ago. We must produce our own good ones, and if we don't then the standards will fall. And therefore to me it is tremendously important that we should produce each year for postgraduate and research training a substantial percentage of the people who on occasions like this take first degrees. This I think is an imperative truth – that postgraduate and research work are of the essence, because without them the future of higher education in Australia will become dark. I hope, and indeed I believe, that it will be well understood by the whole community, a community that provides the great bulk of the cost and upon whose understanding of the importance of these matters so much will depend on the future; and that equally it will be understood by those who allocate and direct the funds provided by the public. Because, ladies and gentlemen, the past is fascinating. I hope it will always be fascinating to good minds, because the past has so much to teach us. But the future is more important than the past, and you who graduate today can contribute to that future. I am sure you will. But I'm sure that if you do the future will be a great future – good not only for this university; good not only for you in your personal occupations; but good for this State and good for this nation.

Now the only other thing I want to say to those to whom I have awarded officially degrees today is that I wish them well. I almost envy them – "bliss was it in that dawn to be alive", you know – I almost envy them to be at the beginning of something, though I have no complaints about my own venerable years. But knowing the chances of life, and attributing to them the honour that we do them today, I just want to say to them in the famous phrase in the Book of Common Prayer – "Good luck have thou with thine honour".

7

SOCIAL WELFARE AND SECURITY

Social Security after the War, Broadcast, Sydney (4 December 1942)

With Menzies using his time in the political wilderness during the early 1940s to develop a coherent liberal philosophy, he turned his attention to social security policy following the release of the influential Beveridge Report in November 1942. In this speech, he outlined some of the core principles that should underpin Australia's approach to social welfare after the War. The first of these was that any scheme of insurance providing citizens with necessary social security benefits should embody the "principle of contribution". According to Menzies, this would foster a healthy self-respect and serve to discourage a self-entitlement mentality. The second principle was that a robust private enterprise sector was the friend of social welfare and not its enemy. As the key generators of wealth and job creation for the nation, private industries and businesses would play a vital role in the elimination of poverty. The third and most important element for post-war social security was what Menzies termed the "human spirit". This essentially meant that the social security of each citizen would be advanced not merely by an increase in material prosperity but by the adoption of a selfless ethic of responsibility towards one's neighbour.

....

Yesterday's newspapers contained summarised accounts of the proposals made by Sir William Beveridge and his committee in a report on social security for Great Britain. According to the cables, the report recommends the establishment of the scheme of insurance on an all-round contributory basis which will provide all persons with retirement pensions, unemployment and disability allowances, free medical treatment and other benefits. The proposed payments are on a scale much more liberal than heretofore contemplated, the ultimate cost when the scheme reaches its full development has been estimated at £850 million, which is the equivalent of about £150 million for Australia. Until all the documents reach Australia it will be useless to offer any detailed views on this scheme. In the meantime, however, it is interesting to notice two outstanding features of it.

The first is the principle of contribution; a principle which was embodied in the ill-fated national insurance scheme in Australia just before the war. It is a very sound principle. I have never believed that a virile and independent and really liberty-loving community can be built up if the habit is developed of regarding social benefits as something handed out by the government and paid for by other people. "Contribution" means self-respect. It destroys any suggestion of charity; it means the citizen is paying his own premium towards his own insured protection.

The second feature is that the whole scheme appears to be built up on the framework of private enterprise.

I noticed that Mr Ward, who it must be said sticks to the main track of his mind very faithfully, has at once condemned it on this ground. He sees – as no doubt his colleagues see – the real hope of the improvement of the lot of mankind in socialism. If the State, he says, is the universal owner and employer, then the State will be in a position to protect the interests of its citizens and to shelter them from the icy blasts that blow in an unregulated world. But, so far as one can judge, Sir William Beveridge has assumed that the main structure of the business world will continue and that the real problem is to impose such burdens upon each member of that structure as will produce really reasonable security for the whole.

The additional comments should, I think, be made while I am discussing this great problem with you. The first is that the greatest fallacy that can be put into people's minds and indeed the greatest deception that can be practised upon them is to be found in the view that private enterprise can be destroyed and social conditions improved at one and the same time. It is common knowledge that if we in Australia were merely to redistribute the existing body of wealth, a certain number of individuals would be much worse off, but most people would be substantially no better off. If we are all to make some reasonable advance there must be not a mere redistribution of the world's goods but a marked increase in the world's goods. In other words, progress is essential to the elimination of poverty.

At this point you have only to ask yourselves whether such great industries and productive sources of individual income and national wealth as the iron and steel industry, the engineering industries, the textile industries and the wool industry would ever have been developed in the astonishingly rapid fashion that we have witnessed in Australia if there had been no private ownership, no incentive to earn a profit, but only regimented control by some government department.

There must be a few thinking people in Australia today who really believe that government by a vast mass of regulations is calculated to advance the material success and prosperity of a nation.

In any new order or, as I prefer to put it, in any improved order after the war, therefore, the initiative of the individual and the legitimate desire for reward must be encouraged and not throttled.

The second observation that I want to make is this. There is, I fear, too much concentration of thought on the notion that when the war ends we will at once enter into a material earthly paradise. It would be pleasant and I suppose politically profitable, to join in the chorus of those who appear to think that the losses and ravages of war need not be paid for or repaired, and who encourage citizens to believe that the main business of politicians when the war is over will be to enter into competitive bidding for the popular vote.

True, every humane citizen must be willing to devote his energies to the improvement of the human lot. For myself, I shall advocate and support the most drastic attacks upon the problems of steady employment, of better education, of better public health, of better housing, but when I remember how many hundreds of thousands of people in Australia are enjoying at this moment a false material prosperity occasioned by the vast expenditures of war, that is, by vast dispersals of capital, I cannot believe that there is something not quite real and not quite honest about encouraging those people to believe that when the war is over all these things will be automatically easier still, and that shortly after the armistice, we shall all be getting more money for doing less work. These popular doctrines ignore the biggest factor in a healthier human society – that is, the factor of the human spirit. Men will not necessarily be better because they are better-off; the Germany of 1938 and 1939 was a country in which educational facilities were much more extensive than they are here; in which public health facilities are amazingly advanced; in which the problem of housing had been resolutely attacked; in which there was virtually no unemployment; in which public credit was utilised to a far-reaching extent. But, in spite of all these things, Germany set about the conquest and ruination of Europe and aimed at a blood-stained conquest of the world.

If this proves anything, it proves that while there can never be any justification for a smug acceptance of poverty and bad health and unemployment as the inevitable fate of man, it is even more fatal to assume that man abandons his dark thoughts of hatred or revenge or greed just because he is, in a material sense, more secure.

Our democratic system has exhibited far too much evidence of social injustice and human insecurity; but its underlying disease, of which the other things are merely symptoms, is the disease of selfishness and irresponsibility. If the new material order or an improved material order is to serve the biggest needs of mankind, it must be accompanied by a moral revolution which will make every citizen feel that the well-being of his country is his own responsibility, that he is his brother's keeper, and that his stature as a citizen will depend far more upon what he gives than upon what he gets.

Social Security, Broadcast, Melbourne (17 September 1943)

During the 1943 election campaign which eventually saw the return of the Curtin Labor government, Menzies returned to the theme of social security. Dispelling any notion that social security was merely a Labor Party issue, he defended it as a necessary part of the State's obligations to its citizens. In this speech, however, he differentiated his "liberal democratic" approach to social welfare from that of his Labor opponents. According to his approach, the ultimate aim of social welfare was not simply to address the material needs of the less fortunate but to elevate the dignity of individuals in need and to give them a sense of independence. Menzies reiterated his belief that a contributory scheme of social betterment was the best means for helping the needy to gain a sense of self-respect and self-reliance. The contributory principle accorded with his philosophy that the citizens of a society each existed as "contributors" as well as "beneficiaries". Echoing the words of Sir William Beveridge, Menzies desired a social welfare system that would "not stifle incentive, opportunity and responsibility", but empower ordinary men and women to be their best selves.

....

In all probability, judging by what was said during the election campaign, one of the issues before the new federal parliament will be that of social security. It has already been made clear on behalf of the government that it stands for non-contributory benefits, that is, it believes that payments made to citizens for old age or sickness or unemployment should be made out of the general revenues of the country or if necessary out of bank credit, and should not be based upon the insurance principle of contribution. The opposition, on the other hand, stands for the contributory principle – for reasons to which I shall refer in a minute or two.

This is unquestionably a major issue, and if public opinion upon it is to be coherent and well informed it is necessary that more of us should begin to analyse the reasons that we have in us for the beliefs that we hold. It is so easy to take a superficial view of a question like this; it is so simple to say that if unemployment relief is to be paid, for example, it should be provided by the rich taxpayer. But the truth lies somewhat deeper than that. It is perhaps natural for Labour to be opposed to the contributory method, because the Australian Labour Party is a Socialist party and honestly believes that the ideal state of society will be reached when the State is a universal employer and therefore the universal provider.

If I were a Socialist, I would not attach any importance to a contributory scheme, because I would have a sort of idea in my mind that my socialism would work best if the spirit of independence in the community became less prominent. But those who are not Socialists believe that while the State has enormous functions to perform, and while the obligations of private industry – socially, industrially, and economically – must continue to grow, the essential driving force in human progress is to be found in the natural instinct to look for a reward for enterprise or skill or endurance.

This means that the essence of the non-socialist political philosophy or, as I would prefer to put it, a "liberal democratic philosophy", is that in a successful and happy community it is the individual who matters; that you cannot make a powerful State out of weak men; and that you cannot enjoy independence as a nation unless you have encouraged independence among your citizens. To the Liberal Democrat, therefore, one of the first tests to be applied to any scheme of social betterment is whether it pauperises the individual by making him dependent upon community charity or whether it elevates and dignifies the individual by giving him his social benefits as a matter of right, and as a result of it, among other things, his own efforts.

Last year in Great Britain the eminent economist, Sir William Beveridge, made a report on social insurance and allied services which has been widely read and greatly admired in many countries. I would like to quote to you one or two passages which seem to me to be of great importance. He says:

> Social Security must be achieved by cooperation between the State and the individual. The State should offer security for

service and contribution. The State in organising security should not stifle incentive, opportunity, responsibility; in establishing a national minimum, it should leave room and encouragement for voluntary action by each individual to provide more than that minimum for himself and his family.

Under the scheme of social insurance, which forms the main feature of his plan, every citizen of working age will contribute in his appropriate class according to the security that he needs, or as a married woman will have contributions made by the husband. Each will be covered for all his needs by a single weekly contribution on one insurance document. All the principal cash payments – for unemployment disability and retirement – will continue so long as the need lasts without means test, and will be paid from a social insurance fund built up by contributions from the insured persons, from their employers, if any, and from the State. This is in accord with two views as to the lines on which the problem of income maintenance should be approached. The first view is that benefit in return for contributions, rather than free allowances from the State, is what the people of Britain desire. This desire is shown both by the established popularity of compulsory insurance, and by the phenomenal growth of voluntary insurance against sickness, against death and for endowment, and most recently for hospital treatment. It is shown in another way by the strength of popular objection to any kind of means test. This objection springs not so much from a desire to get everything for nothing, as from resentment at a provision which appears to penalise what people have come to regard as the duty and pleasure of thrift, of putting pennies away for a rainy day. Management of one's income is an essential element of a citizen's freedom. Payment of the substantial part of the cost of benefit as a contribution irrespective of the means of the contributor is the firm basis of a claim to benefit irrespective of means.

I confess that until I had read this report I had never fully appreciated the significant association between the free pension and the means test. Take the Australian old-age pension which is a free, that is, non-contributory pension: It costs the country many millions a year. Its grant is subject to a means test, that is, every applicant for an old age pension must satisfy the authorities not only that he or she has reached the pensionable age but that he or she has no more than a limited amount of property or of income. In brief, you get an old age pension on conditions which include proof of poverty.

Every political party has supported this principle, and with good reason; for if the old age pension were universally payable, irrespective of means, the amount required to meet it would at once be trebled and the community would be assuming huge financial responsibilities not warranted by true social needs. We have therefore the principle that wherever the community pays benefits without contribution a means test is practically inevitable. But where you have a means test there is, however much we may smother it by words, some indignity, some loss of complete self-respect, some feeling that charity is being dispensed after proper investigation. Surely it is a far better thing, a far more democratic thing, a thing far more consistent with the full stature of all of us as independent citizens that we should, through the State, enter into a great contract, each of us with everyone else, under which we shall all be contributors and all, irrespective of means, beneficiaries.

If you insure your life under a policy which matures at the age of sixty, you collect your insurance monies on the due date with no feeling of obligation. You have carried out your part of it and you collect the benefit.

As those of you who have listened to me for many months past will realise, I have a deep-seated conviction that with all its faults the true strength of democracy lies in its elevation of the ordinary man and its recognition of the fact that there are amazing possibilities in every boy and girl. If we are to develop these possibilities, if we are to match with proper care our rights and duties as citizens, surely there can be no doubt that every measure of reform we take must have in mind, as Sir William Beveridge said – "that the State in organising security should not stifle incentive, opportunity, responsibility".

There are great dangers in some of the easy doctrines now current; doctrines which appear to assume that for the normal man the ideal state of life is one in which security is provided for him by others while his own efforts, being those of a mere unit among millions of units, are of comparatively minor importance.

No forward-looking Australian can afford to neglect these dangers. However much and however humanely parliaments and parties may labour for the elimination of poverty and disease and unemployment, it will always remain true that our greatest asset and our greatest security will be found in a virile and independent manhood.

The great feature of such plans as those of Sir William Beveridge is that they reconcile, with skill and understanding, the proper obligations of the State with the equally proper and in some ways more important responsibilities of the citizen.

Speech at the Opening of Legacy Week (5 September 1960)

As an Australian charity established to care for the dependents of deceased Australian service men and women, Legacy invited the Prime Minister to launch its annual week of community fundraising. In his address, Prime Minister Menzies touched upon two major themes, the important place of charities such as Legacy in the provision of social welfare and the need for Australia to act charitably towards its less fortunate neighbours in the Asia Pacific region. On social welfare policy, Menzies defended government spending on the provision of social services for needy citizens but singled out the indispensable role of private charities for their unique capacity to provide *personalised* care on a case-by-case basis. According to Menzies, organisations of generous, community-minded individuals such as Legacy were qualified to fulfil the human need for "loving-kindness" in a way that governments, for all their best intentions, were simply unable to match with their wholesale, bureaucratic approach. Citing the creation of the Colombo Plan, together with that of Legacy, Menzies credited this as evidence that Australia could show generosity towards others both within and beyond its own borders.

....

Mr President: I think it is a very remarkable honour to be invited by you to open "Legacy Week" – a great honour. But in one sense a very easy thing to do because I think most people now in Australia – I would have hoped all people in Australia – regard Legacy as one of the finest things in our modern history in Australia. It seems almost fantastic to me to look at the notice paper and to see that it was founded only in 1923 by your old friend and my old friend, Stan Savige – one of the finest Australians of our time – and in 37 years it has established itself as something, I think, quite unique.

We are all pretty good when we are in the right mood at explaining to other people what our rights are, what would be done for us if only justice were done. I must not make an exception of myself in that connection, because if justice were done to me, I probably wouldn't be here, at any rate in my present capacity; but it is true that most people who give service to their country create in their country very properly, a sense of obligation, and occasionally may be disposed to emphasise the nature of that obligation. That is inevitable, quite understandable, and indeed, in a great number of cases, most popular. But this organisation is unique – an organisation of people who have, on the basis of their service to their country, accepted and performed additional obligations which they regard as arising out of that service. That is a very remarkable thing, and all of us who have watched the work of Legacy through all these years never cease to be thankful that such a spirit should have found embodiment in so many people.

A legacy. When one talks of a legacy a little hopefully occasionally, it indicates an idea that we are going to get something in cash or in kind. We are going to be at the receiving end. Most people think of a legacy in that sense. There are not too many people who think of a legacy in another sense. It is a cant phrase to talk about certain evil things in the world being a legacy of war. It has been left to this body, almost alone in the world as far as I know, to regard this legacy of war as something which imposes upon it a great trust for other people, and an obligation to do things for other people. This is a brilliant use of this word, and it is a very fine thing for thousands and thousands of people that you should have thought of it in that way.

We live in a time when people look to governments more and more for almost everything and because people elect Members of Parliament, Members of Parliament are under an obligation to give effect broadly to what people want; and more and more over the course of recent years in Australia – the last 20 years in Australia – the position has been that governments are expected to perform more things, and do, in fact, perform more.

I was reminding another audience yesterday that when I was first Prime Minister, which, believe it or not, is over 20 years ago now, the total Social Services bill of the Commonwealth was £17 million and this year it is £330 million. Now this, of course, indicates how more and more governments are to make provisions for people in the country who need it. But the thing to remember is that governments can act only in the broad. They, so to speak, deal with human problems by wholesale; they establish a rate of pension; they establish statutory conditions for a man or woman getting that pension. These rules have to be hard rules, precise rules, because you can't have social services paid out by the government according to the whim of individuals at any point of distribution and, therefore, you have the broad sweep of the law. Injustices must happen in individual cases, but that is unavoidable if you are going to have a body of rules laid down which will, in the broad, do the highest common measure of justice that Parliament thinks appropriate.

You are not in the wholesale business. You are doing something which no government could do if it had all the goodwill in the world and all the money in the world. You are dealing with people, not as members of a group, not as one person out of the million who must be dealt with according to the rules that apply to the rest of the million: you are dealing with individual cases with humanity, with knowledge, with the capacity to select, with the capacity to understand how to deal with this individual widow or this individual child: how to do something which will help this particular boy or this particular girl to be educated, to be trained for something. This is a tremendously human task, and it can be dealt with only by looking at individuals and dealing with them on their merits so that you don't have to say, and you have no desire to say, "Well, there is a broad rule here and it doesn't fit this case, but it is just too bad. We have the broad rule and it is unalterable".

The great essence of Legacy, to my mind, as a man watching at work, has been its capacity for selecting the individual for individual treatment, and this is something that no government department can do.

I am not among those who criticise Civil Servants. There are an awful lot of them about, and no doubt a fair number of you here today are, or have been, Civil Servants. The Civil Service in this country consists of an honourable body of men, of a level of capacity not inferior to the level of capacity in other undertakings. Let us not be too quick on the draw when we are dealing with the Civil Service; but the Civil Service can't do what you are doing. It must act under the rule. It must act according to the book, and if it didn't act according to the book we would be in strife. But you are able to do the things that the Civil Service can't do.

We have many departments, if you will allow me to repeat something that I have said before today. There is no "Department of Loving Kindness", and there cannot be a "Minister of Loving Kindness". "Permanent Secretary to the Department of Loving Kindness". Dear me! The first thing that would happen would be that someone down the line would say: "But look, I must have the book of the words. What are the rules of Loving Kindness?" And you let us get to work defining the rules of loving kindness: we'll have a magnificent body of rules, but there won't be any loving kindness. This is something that no government can provide for you. As individuals we're really quite a soft-hearted lot. You'd be surprised. But we cannot dispense loving kindness as you dispense a pension or a benefit under some Act of Parliament. And therefore, Sir, I am a great believer in Legacy. I think it is quite unique. I hope that in this Appeal that is going out this week, you will raise at least twice as much as in your wildest dreams you hope to. And, indeed, if it becomes adequately known in Australia that this appeal is on, I want to tell you that I believe there will be a response in the hearts and minds of people that will astonish you. I wouldn't be too modest in what you are looking for; wouldn't be too modest in what you tell people about what your work is, because this is the greatest humane operation conducted by individual private citizens, most of whom might say quite well: "Well, I've done my share. I've done my tour of duty. Let somebody else look after this. Let the government look after this". This is a magnificent heart-warming thing …

It ought to be remembered here with some pride that just as Australia was the country that created Legacy, so Australia was the country that promoted the Colombo Plan, and we have at all times been active contributors to the Colombo Plan – not just to make good fellows of ourselves. You don't do your work in Legacy to make good fellows of yourselves: you do it with both eyes on the end result, the end result being the helping of somebody to live a fuller and free and better life. And similarly, when we give aid internationally we must be vastly careful to see we're not doing it to be just "good fellows", not doing it just to advertise some goods, but that we are doing it because we realise that a rise in the economic standards, a rise in the standard of living of these new countries that have come to political independence, is the one thing that will not only do justice to their people, but enable them to maintain their independence and to resist the onset of the strange, mad doctrines of communism. The best defence for them against communism, against any other form of what I will call disorder, is that they should develop their own strength, that their people should look forward to a rising standard of living, generation by generation ...

We must all do more and more: won't always be very popular. There's always somebody who is able to say: "Well, look at the money you spend on Colombo Aid. Look at the money you spend in relation to the other powers of [the] South-east Asian Treaty Organisation. Look at the money that you layout on the various agencies of the United Nations. Why, if we didn't spend that abroad, think of the houses we could put up in our own country: think of all the slum clearances that could be facilitated. Let us look after ourselves." If every nation in the world, which is now a free nation, decided that from now on it would look after itself – each for itself and the devil take the hindmost – the world would be tumbling into the most frightful catastrophe of history before we're 20 years older. The whole condition of survival is that the new nations should be made to feel that they have our sympathetic, individual interest, our desire to help, our desire to build them up. There's one aspect of that which I have mentioned once before publicly, but which I propose to mention wherever I have the opportunity, and it's this: it was pointed out rather graphically at the last Prime Ministers' Conference by Mr Nehru himself in a very thoughtful speech. After all, if there's one man in the world who can speak about countries achieving independence and about their problems, it is Nehru himself, with this enormous country of his own, full of economic problems, and, of course, now with international problems of a rather unforeseen kind: but he pointed this out, and it bit itself into my mind ...

You gentlemen don't honour the name of Legacy by doing as little as you can. You honour it by doing as much as you can. The whole of the Legacy movement is based upon doing something without technical obligation at all, doing something voluntarily, doing something because you realise the tremendous individual purposes to be served. And in the same way we, the nations of the free world who enjoy prosperity, who can see in front of us a long vista of dramatically improving standards – must turn aside from time to time and have a look at our neighbour, though the neighbour maybe five thousand miles away, and say: "What about him? Is he coming along too? Couldn't we take just a little less of the surplus of our own comparative wealth in order to enable him to develop those technical matters in particular in his own country, which will enable him to live in a century that is free, but not only self-governing, but self-supporting and proud and independent?"

Now, sir, that sounds suspiciously like a sermon, but if you invite me to come to Legacy you provide me with the text of the highest magnificence, and no Presbyterian can be presented with a text without instinctively getting up to preach a sermon.

8

THE LAW AND THE CONSTITUTION

The Machinery of Government (1928-1929)

In Menzies' liberal philosophy, the law and the judicial branch of government represented the supreme guarantor of an individual's rights and freedoms. In this 1928/1929[31] speech as a minister (without a designated portfolio) in Sir William McPherson's Victorian State government, Menzies stressed the importance for democracies such as Australia to preserve an independent and authoritative judiciary. This was essential to maintaining the due separation of powers between the judicial, executive and legislative arms of government. According to Menzies, the best protection an individual citizen could have against tyranny or government overreach was an independent judge capable of interpreting the law impartially. In the Australian judicial system, the key organ for protecting individual rights and liberties was of course the High Court of Australia, a court at which Menzies had appeared before in his earlier days as a barrister. As the highest court of appeal it served two primary functions; first, to operate as an appellate court in the ordinary judicial business of reviewing cases, and second, to determine whether any law of the Parliament, or any act of the Executive, was valid under the Australian Constitution.

....

What I really want to talk about to you is to consider with you some of the modern developments in the structure of government as we are all more or less familiar with it; government in a British community and, in particular, in a modern British community like this. Now, government in most English-speaking communities is a matter which depends upon

---

31 The transcript indicates that Menzies gave this speech either in 1928 or 1929; it does not specify a precise date.

an organisation, and that organisation in turn depends – as very many organisations do – upon a division of function between the various sections of government; and in the systems with which you and I are familiar, the division most familiar to all of us is the division into the functions of legislating, of carrying out the laws, and of judging – the division into the Legislature, the Executive and the Judiciary ...

The Judiciary is in my opinion the most important element in our institutions of liberty. Without an independent or authoritative judiciary liberty would become a mere name. I wish I could persuade everybody in Australia to understand how true that is. We have had as a nation experience of the tyranny of Kings. We are also quite capable of having experience – and in some parts of the British Empire we have – of the tyranny of parliaments, and the greatest guarantee we have against tyranny in any shape or form is the maintenance of a judiciary which is independent and authoritative.

What I find, and to a rather alarming extent, is this – that many people regard the judiciary as an ordinary branch of the Civil Service. Many people discuss the position of the judges as if they were discussing the position of highly paid civil servants. That involves a fundamental error. The Judiciary is not a branch of the Civil Service; the Judiciary is not a branch of the executive government of this country. The government of this country consists of the Legislature, the Executive, and the Judiciary, and the Judiciary is equal in rank and authority with either of the other two departments of State. It is not a branch of the Executive. It exists in a proper case to give orders to the Executive and to set bounds to the actions of the Executive.

Let us illustrate this by referring to the High Court. There are not wanting people in Australia who believe that the High Court ought to be an instrument for recording the political wishes of the people. The High Court, like the Parliament of the Commonwealth, is established by virtue of the Commonwealth Constitution. The source of its authority is just as high as the source from which the whole legislative authority of the Commonwealth Parliament proceeds. The greatest legal document we possess is the Constitution. When we understand that, we will realise that the High Court is not established to be the servant of anybody, and it is certainly not established to be a portion of the Executive Government of the Commonwealth.

Now, when it is established, and when members are appointed to it, it proceeds to exercise two great functions. Broadly speaking, one of them is the function of acting as a Court of Appeal in ordinary judicial business – and that, of course, is the bulk of the High Court's work – but it is also established to exercise a very particular function, the function of determining whether any law of Parliament, or any act of the Executive, is unconstitutional; and in a proper case it is not only the power but the duty of the High Court to say – "This act of the Executive is in excess of its power and it is annulled". This is a very great power to give anybody, and when we realise that the High Court has repeatedly exercised that power in respect to both legislative and judicial acts, we will begin to realise that when we deal with the Judiciary we deal not with an inferior body, but with a body which is of the highest independence and authority.

In the Constitution of Australia it is expressly provided that the salaries of the Judges of the High Court shall not be diminished during their term of office – another very wise, and if I may say so, essential provision, because as one judge in America said recently, "If parliament may reduce the salary of a judge for some reason that seems good to it, it may equally abolish his salary altogether if his judgments are not satisfactory to it". Suppose our High Court judges in Australia had salaries which depended upon the current role of Parliament, and suppose those judges, in the honest discharge of their duties, declared some Act of Parliament invalid – an act strongly advocated in Parliament and passed by Parliament. You can imagine the kind of dispute that would arise, and the kind of criticism that would be made; and if their salaries were within the control of Parliament, an unscrupulous Parliament could effectively remove every one of those judges from the bench by the simple process of removing his salary and rendering it necessary that he should get a job in order to keep himself. And with six judges out of the way, the path would be clear to have six more judges selected. Because of their honesty and fearlessness? It is not likely, but appointed to repair the evil that had been done by their predecessors by declaring the popular Act of Parliament invalid.

It is vital to the whole of the Judiciary that the Judiciary should in no sense depend on parliament, because the moment it becomes to any extent at all the servant of parliament its authority over what parliament is doing is in [the] process of being destroyed. The moment you allow these three functions to be aggregated in one set of hands, you are approaching to [sic] tyranny. The best protection that you and I have against tyranny is, as Alexander Hamilton said, an independent judge, and when we destroy his independence we take steps to destroy the protection that we have as citizens against an oppressive or illegal parliament or an oppressive executive. These, I venture to think, are things worth talking about.

You and I have become so accustomed to the ordinary orderly march of government that we regard most our historical problems as disposed of forever. But are they? Have we not had illustrations in the last year or two of the extent to which parliament may be responsible.

Have all these fears vanished forever? Can we afford to sit down complacently and say that it matters nothing to us that the Judiciary falls from its position of authority, or that parliament abdicates its responsibility, or that executives become irresponsible and tend in the direction of decay? We can't afford to regard those things complacently. If there is one thing that emerges from our whole constitutional history it is this – that the genius of our nation has been expressed in an elaborate system of checks and balances, of balancing one power against another power, in order that by a balance achieved by the whole of them tyranny on the part of any one of them may become impossible.

It is because I for one feel that it is important that we should have our eyes opened to the lessons of the past with a view to preventing error in the future, that I selected this subject I have been discussing with you, and that I have taken the opportunity you have very kindly afforded me, of pointing out some of the ways in modern times in which this old division of the machinery of government has been impaired, and possibly in some aspects threatened.

Constitutional Guarantees, Broadcast, Canberra (27 November 1942)

In the Australian context, the Commonwealth Constitution of 1901 represents the supreme body of law to which both the legislature and the judiciary are subject. Given Menzies' firm belief in the supremacy and continuity of the Constitution, he regarded government proposals to alter it as grave matters warranting the highest scrutiny. In this speech, he warned that the proposals of the wartime Curtin Labor government to amend two sections of the Constitution were fraught with danger. The first section in question referred to the existing "religious freedom guarantees" of s 116 which the government desired to extend from the Commonwealth to the States. The second referred to the insertion of a new section which would prohibit the Commonwealth and the States from making "any law abridging the freedom of speech or of the press". While Menzies unquestionably affirmed the principles of religious freedom and free speech, he argued that it was gratuitous for the Australian Constitution to either extend or enshrine freedoms that every free and reasonable person accepted as unwritten "givens". It appeared "astonishing" to Menzies that a self-governing society could so distrust itself that it had to make recourse to the Constitution to guarantee its own freedoms. This attitude essentially stemmed from Menzies' conviction that the spirit of freedom sprang from human hearts rather than codified laws.

....

The constitutional Amendments which we have been discussing this week at Canberra contain at least two provisions of a remarkable and unusual kind; and, as you may have gathered that I am opposed to them, it seems right that I should tell you why.

The first says this:

> Neither the Commonwealth nor a State may make any law for establishing any religion, or for imposing any religious observance, or for prohibiting the free exercise of any religion, and no religious test shall be required as a qualification for any office or public trust under the Commonwealth or a State.

217

The second is:

> Neither the Commonwealth nor a State may make any law
> abridging the freedom of speech or of the press.

Now, you may say to me at once: "Well, really, what is there to argue about here: don't you believe in religious freedom; don't you believe in freedom of speech and of the press?" The answer is that of course I do. The real question is whether these great vital principles of citizenship to which the overwhelming majority of people subscribe should be compressed into the four corners of the written formula, given, so to speak, an artificial form, and written into the Constitution as if we were afraid that unless they were in the bond we might forget them.

In modern times there has been a considerable passion, particularly on the part of some of my brethren of the law who have occupied high offices in various parts of the British world, for putting things into writing. This notion is, I believe, contrary to the whole genius of the people. We don't live under codified laws and we have always distrusted codified ideas. There is nothing truer than that "the letter killeth.

With that preliminary, let me say a little more about each of these two matters: first, the freedom of religion: Has there been any attack on religious freedom in Australia? Has any parliament been meditating bringing in some Bill to establish a religion or to prohibit the free exercise of a religion, or to impose religious tests? Of course not. Dr Evatt is defending us with sword and buckler against a non-existent enemy. If religious freedom were really beeing threatened in Australia I should hope to be among the first to act promptly to destroy that threat. But seriously to ask the people of Australia to have a referendum in time of war solemnly to put into a Constitution some written guarantee of the principle which every intelligent person accepts seems to be almost fantastic.

And then there is freedom of speech and of the press: This I suppose has been produced because there has been a good deal of curtailment of each during the war, and assurances are felt to be necessary. But there are several answers to the proposal that such an assurance should be written down in solemn words and put into the Constitution. The first is that

218

this Constitution is our constitution. We as a self-governing community made it. We are, without any subtraction, the makers of our own laws and the creators of our own executives. If free speech or a free press is to be destroyed, it can only be because we, through our Parliaments, have authorised or permitted it.

What an astonishing thing that a completely self-governing community should so distrust itself that it finds it necessary to write into its own constitution an admonition that it is not to make a law abridging the freedom of speech or of the press!

Now, somebody may say: "Look, they had this very provision in the American Constitution. If they found it necessary, why should not we? They are just as self-governing as we are".

True, the provision has been in the American Constitution for a hundred-and-fifty years. It was put in by the first Amendment and was one of the 10 amendments referred to in America as the "Bill of Rights". There was great argument as to whether they should be adopted or not. The great Alexander Hamilton opposed their inclusion, using the same argument which I have already glanced at, that self-government ensures a better recognition of popular rights than carefully written guarantees. He pointed out that –

> Bills of rights are in their origin stipulations between Kings and their subjects, abridgements of prerogative in favour of privilege, reservations of rights not surrendered to the prince.

That was a very just observation.

We are apt to forget that the great historic documents which are associated with our freedom, such as Magna Carta and the Declaration of Right, all represented stages by which men passed from being slaves and subordinates to free men and civic equals. At a time when Kings were absolute rulers the liberty of the subject had to be from time to time demanded and occasionally fought for. But in due course all these battles ended and, with the coming of modern democracy, the people became the source of power, the agency by which power was exercised, and the subject to which power was addressed. In other words, we are, again speaking in terms of substance, not only the ruled but the rulers.

The man who is, in fact, his own master will scarcely need to have on the wall a list drawn up by himself of things which he must not do.

And we must not deceive ourselves as to the value of this guarantee proposed to be put into the Constitution. Again to quote Alexander Hamilton:

> What is the liberty of the press; who can give it any definition which would not leave the upmost latitude for evasion? I hold it to be impracticable; and from this I infer, that its security, whatever fine declarations may be inserted in any Constitution respecting it, must altogether depend on public opinion, and on the general principle of the people and of the government.

That is a true saying.

As the Attorney-General himself said at the convention: "Liberty does not mean licence, but means ordered liberty"; and that means ordered by the community, acting through parliament.

In the last resort it will be found the only reassurance of freedom of speech or of the press will be a real spirit of freedom in the minds of the people. But if the people at any time become so carried away as to seek to destroy these freedoms, which are of our life blood, no pretty little form of words in the Constitution which they had themselves made would prevent them from doing it.

Any visitor from another planet making an examination of the character and habits of our people, and searching for the mainspring of that love of freedom which distinguishes us, would find it not in Acts of Parliament or blue books or dusty records, but in the hearts of the people themselves.

Civil and Political Rights, Recorded Speech for the Melbourne *Herald* (15 March 1974)

As an ex-prime minister, Sir Robert made it a principle of his to generally refrain from public commentary on Australian domestic politics, but he did see the attempt of the Whitlam Labor government in 1974 to introduce a Bill of Rights as a critical issue meriting a public warning about some of its far-reaching legal implications. In a recorded speech for publication in the Melbourne *Herald*, Menzies analysed key provisions of the legislation introduced by the Attorney-General, Lionel Murphy, and argued that a Bill of Rights would have undesirable repercussions for the civil rights and liberties of Australian citizens. His basic thesis was that Australia's existing common law already served to protect individuals against infringements of their personal rights, thereby rendering any Bill of Rights superfluous. Having evolved over many centuries, the common law was sufficiently comprehensive and broad in its capacity to guarantee the rights of the individual. Furthermore, Menzies was also concerned that a Bill of Rights would take Australia down the American path of a politically-motivated High Court. Whilst a great admirer of American democracy, Menzies understood that Australia and the United States differed considerably in their respective traditions of government and jurisprudence. Unlike the US, Australia enjoyed a system of "responsible government" under its Constitution which served as a working guarantor of human rights without the need for a statutory or constitutional Bill of Rights.

....

In November last [1973], Senator Murphy, the Attorney-General of the Commonwealth of Australia introduced into the Senate, a bill for an Act "to implement an international covenant on civil and political rights and for other purposes".

In the course of his speech, he indicated that he would desire to see in due course an amendment to the Commonwealth Constitution to give effect to these rights. For the present purpose, I want to make some observations on his bill and then some more observations as to whether the Commonwealth Constitution should be altered to include a "Bill of Rights" on the American model.

His present legislation seeks to give effect in one way or another to the international covenants which are fully set out as a schedule to this bill. Many of the "human rights" are commonplace enough to us and it may have some superficial appeal to people to feel that those rights will have been guaranteed by statute.

The bill introduced by the Senator has two comprehensive provisions which should be noted. The first is that this Act binds Australia and each State. The second is that approval is given to ratification by Australia of the International Covenant on Civil and Political Rights and the Convention on the Political Rights of Women.

The first thing to be remembered is that Australia is a common-law country and, as Mr Justice Dixon once said, that simple statement carries with it "prodigious consequences". (Common law is defined in the Oxford dictionary as "the unwritten law of England administered by the Queen's Courts based on ancient and universal usage and embodied in commentaries and reported cases". The term is used in distinction from statute law, because over the centuries it was evolved from the judgements of the courts producing ultimately a series of legal rules such as we find in the law of contract and the law of civil wrongs). The outlook of people nurtured in and living under the Roman law, as so many European countries do, can never be the same as that of the people whose conception of government, of liberty, of justice, and of right, have been moulded by the common law. Further, it must be recognised that the vast majority of the signatory nations to the present Covenants, are not protected by the Common Law, and may feel that specific guarantees are necessary.

When we, in Australia, come to discuss civil and political rights it is necessary to remember that one of the functions of the Common Law, devised over a course of centuries in England and adopted by us by inheritance, has been to protect the individual against infringement of his personal rights. In the result, I may proceed along my path in life knowing that my rights to think and to speak are recognised, that the rights of myself and other people to be protected against defamation are recognised, that my right to be at peace in my own house is recognised, that the inability, legally speaking, of my neighbours to commit nuisance against my property is recognised. Indeed, one could write a long essay on the value of the Common Law and its supreme function in protecting the rights of the individual.

The common law has been worked out over centuries. It is judge made, if you care to put it in that way, and it cannot be impaired, except by specific action on the part of a competent legislature. Having looked carefully at Senator Murphy's Bill, I doubt whether there is a solitary matter in it which has not been dealt with under our Common Law system to protect the rights of the individual.

I will not write a long essay on this matter because I am sure that most lawyers would recognise that to live in a Common Law country is, in itself, the very best guarantee of the rights of the individual. Why Senator Murphy should wish to substitute for the Common Law a long category of various rights as if they had no existence apart from his legislation, I will never understand. Looking through his Bill I find, for example – I will take just one example because time would not (and space would not) permit dealing with every clause – but in clause 11 of his bill, there are various provisions. "Everyone shall have the right to hold opinions without interference". Well, of course, he has today, unless some Act of Parliament deprives him of that right, and an Act of Parliament is an Act of the Parliament elected by him and his fellow citizens. "Everyone shall have the right of freedom of expression, including freedom to seek, receive and impart information and ideas of all kinds", and so on.

Realising then, that this is a very far-reaching provision, he says that the exercise of the rights referred to maybe subject only to such limitations as are prescribed by law (that's the present position) and are reasonably necessary for respect for the reputations of others. Now let me pause there. That is merely a rather crude summary of the present Common Law rights of the citizen to speak freely and the rights of other people not to have their reputations taken away from them by him without justification.

It seems to me to be a bold experiment to try to sum up the existing Common Law rules about defamation in one section of an Act of Parliament. The law of defamation occupies in its history and application, hundreds of pages, not only in textbooks but in the decisions of the courts of law. I am yet to believe that it needs to have any improvement by statute. I think that the law, as it stands, has achieved a rather nice balance between freedom of speech and the right of people not to be defamed in their community.

This is merely one example. There are dozens to be found in this Bill, each of them apparently trying to put into statutory form those Common Law rights which we have enjoyed in our lifetimes and which have been applied by an independent judiciary with great success.

I would like to go on to add that, apart altogether from the tremendous importance of our Common Law in the preservation of civil rights, there is a further point to be made.

The further truth is, of course, that the best guarantee of human rights in the future, is to be found in our system of responsible government, where Ministers sit in Parliament, can be questioned, and give answers, and the government itself maybe turned out if Parliament feels that it is doing things which violate the proper rights of individuals …

Senator Murphy has foreshadowed the introduction into our Constitution of a "Bill of Rights". What he has in mind, of course, is the Bill of Rights introduced into the American Constitution as among the earliest amendments made to that famous instrument. I will first quote one of the phrases.

"Congress shall make no law … abridging the freedom of speech, or of the press; or the right of the people peaceably to assemble, and to petition the government for redress of grievances."

I will then quote another one. "A well-regulated militia, being necessary to the security of a free state, the right of the people to keep and bear arms shall not be infringed."

(No doubt the founders of the American Constitution felt it necessary to validate retrospectively the action of the colonists in bearing arms against England. Yet the fact is that this right to bear arms has had some curious and indeed dangerous consequences in the United States. I found when I was there that in most towns there could be found somewhere on or off the main street a shop branded "Gun Shop". It is perhaps no wonder that the gun population in the United States exceeds that in any other civilised country.)

Now the first phrase is an expression of a very broad significance. Why was it written into the American Constitution? Well, I believe that the reasons for this are not far to seek. In America, there is a long history, and there was even then a short history of distrust of official people. These people were not directly answerable to Congress because they did not and do not sit in Congress or answer questions there; and, therefore, the American people at that time and since, have thought it necessary to impose constitutional limits upon them, with the Supreme Court of America as the interpreter of those limits.

These provisions in the Federal Constitution of America, the provisions which I refer to as the Bill of Rights, have been adopted by most, if not all, of the States of the United States. Some of them are more detailed in their provisions than the others but, for the most part, we may take it that State Congress is in each state, or most states, controlled by the "Bill of Rights". That means something quite curious to us. So political is the interpretation of the Bill of Rights – and I don't wonder at it since it is couched in by far from legal language – that some remarkable decisions have occurred. I need refer only to one.

One state was bold enough, or intelligent enough, to provide that the children and schools should (provided that their parents consented, because it was purely voluntary) have read to them each week a chapter of the Bible. And the Supreme Court of the United States, in spite of the vigorous dissenting judgement by one justice, found that this was an attempt to establish a religion in breach of the Bill of Rights.

Now I confess that that kind of decision baffles me. I can understand very well that anybody teaching English in school would think it advisable to introduce children to some of the finest English in the language, to wit the Authorised Version of the Bible. It should be part of an English education. Yet it is barred by the Supreme Court of America because it was an attempt to establish a religion. Well, wonders will never cease. Every time Federal Congress meets it is opened by prayer, and the prayer is delivered by a selected minister of religion. But nobody has thought fit to say that by performing this ceremony (which we perform in Australia, except that the prayer is read by the Speaker), Congress was introducing an established religion. Curiously enough, the Supreme Court has its proceedings opened with prayer!

I wonder if people in Australia would like to have their rights guaranteed not by the Common Law and Statute Law as interpreted by lawyers, but by somewhat vague phrases as interpreted by people, I am sorry to say, in the light largely of their own political convictions.

Modern experience in the United States has shown that broadly expressed guarantees of individual rights have recently been interpreted by the Supreme Court in the light of the political and social concepts of the judges whose judgements will, in very truth, be legislative.

We think in Australia, and the founders of the Constitution, who were no boobies, let me say (they were as remarkable a collection of men and lawyers and thinkers as this country has had), came to the conclusion that they would not write in to our Constitution a "Bill of Rights" and for these reasons. We are setting up in the Constitution a system of responsible government. No man can be a Member of the Executive unless he is a Member of Parliament. There is a trifling exception to that but it doesn't matter. And, therefore, ministers being Members of Parliament, sit in Parliament, introduce and debate their own Bills and are available almost daily for questioning or challenge.

In America, there is complete separation between the Legislature and the Executive. What we would call ministers, the holders of great offices of state in America, like the Secretary of State or the Secretary of the Treasury, are appointed by the President, do not sit in Congress and are not answerable in Congress for what they do.

We have an entirely different system. We believe that the members of the executive government ought to sit in Parliament. They ought to be answerable to Parliament. If the Prime Minister of the day loses the support of Parliament and is voted out by the Lower House, then there will be either an election or a change of government.

In the United States, on the other hand, the President is elected for four years. And for four years there he will remain, whether he loses the support of the Congress or not. True, he may resign. True, he may die. True, he may be impeached by Congress. That is a process which has not so far been accepted. It was tried once in the 19th century and it did not come off and therefore you don't have a responsible government in the sense that we have, where the Prime Minister is in Parliament and responsible to Parliament and may be voted out by Parliament.

In Australia, under our Constitution, the system of responsible government is established. We think that legislation is for a responsible legislature and, in my opinion, we are right. The thought of a High Court of Australia applying political consideration to what ought to be purely legal issues fills me with horror. I refer to this matter because I believe that we should stand for both the Parliamentary system and the independence and legal integrity of the Courts of Law.

Just let us look back on some of the words of the American Bill of Rights. "No law abridging the freedom of speech or of the press". Is this what we want in Australia? Do we desire that libel and slander maybe freely engaged in? Do we desire that the press is to be free to say what it likes at any time without let or hindrance? Take a simple example. Suppose we are at war and the government decides very properly that there ought to be censorship of news coming from the battlefront. This, to me, is most elementary common sense. And yet, in the United States of America, though the Courts have recognised that there may be censorship in time of war, it turns out that there is no such thing as a "war" unless Congress has authorised a Declaration of War. Now there was no Declaration of War in Vietnam but there was a tremendous amount of fighting. Casualties on a great scale were incurred and, yet, because there had been no Declaration of War, the United States found that its press representatives, its war correspondents, could be right up among the strategic and tactical exercises and could publish them to the world, including the enemy, with impunity.

This, to me, is the most dangerous nonsense. If the United States likes it, well and good, it is their business; but that it should come about in my own country seems to me to be an absurdity of the first order. My horror at the thought of a politically motivated High Court (and that is what it means if they are going to interpret vague political statements in the light of their own political conceptions) will be readily understood by all of you who have followed the events of recent months in the United States.

Suppose there is a vacancy on the Supreme Court. The president has power to nominate, but the actual appointment requires the advice and consent of the Senate. The Senate Judiciary Committee examines the nominee. Some glancing attention is paid to his qualifications as a lawyer but much of the questioning and discussion seems to centre about his political views. If he has been a judge of a lower court, has he given decisions against unions, or taken some particular view in a case involving race relations?

Now to an Australian lawyer of constitutional experience, this kind of thing is alarming. It is a procedure which is not calculated to produce a superior court of outstanding lawyers such as we have and have had for a long time in the High Court of Australia. For just as I believe that it is the function of the Members of Parliament who represent us to enact Statues which embody political ideas and policies in a legal instrument, so do I also believe that the interpretation and validity of the product must be determined not by another body of politicians but by Judges who will apply legal rules to what will then have become a purely legal task.

9

FAITH AND RELIGION

Communism and Christianity, Broadcast (1946)

For Menzies, the ideology of communism represented not simply a political menace, but a spiritual and moral problem that arose from the malaise of the human heart. The worldview of communism was deficient because its narrow, materialistic thesis of class warfare failed to appreciate the essential, spiritual impulses of the human heart. The Presbyterian Menzies conceived of these spiritual instincts in Christian terms where human beings under the fatherhood of God were called to the "obligations of mutual love and understanding" as brothers and sisters. In this 1946 broadcast, Menzies drew from both the *Communist Manifesto* itself and Nikolai Bukharin's influential book, *The ABC of Communism* (1919), to argue that its social doctrine of class envy and conflict ran directly counter to Christian principles. Returning to this theme in his 1951 election campaign speech, Menzies said that communism "derives from the darkest recesses of the human mind" and "has nothing in common with the Christian gospel of love and brotherhood". According to Menzies, communism's fostering of hatred between people was "no instrument of progress but merely a sign of decadence and despair".

....

There is nothing more astonishing then the success with which revolutionary communism in Australia has wooed and won the support of not a few ardent Christians and churchgoers, including some of the clergy.

I say "astonishing" because, while I am no theologian, it seems as clear as crystal to me that between Christianity and communism there is a great gulf. Indeed, the two conceptions of man and of life are as far apart as the Poles.

229

Once again let me beg of you not to confuse communism, which means and intends the revolutionary overthrow of the existing order, with reforming radicalism, or a Parliamentary socialism, or any other set of ideas intended to be applied under a self-governing democratic system.

To the Communist, democracy is a poor joke and communists will enter Parliament only to destroy it. But if to your revolutionary communist democracy is a joke, Christianity is anathema.

Apart from all dogmatic or doctrinal differences among Christian denominations, what is the essence of Christianity as a code of conduct for human beings?

Let me get my answer from its most perfect expression, the Sermon on the Mount: First, man is a spiritual animal and by his spirit, not by his body or his bodily circumstances, shall he be judged. Thus the Sermon on the Mount speaks all the time of the "meek", the "merciful", the "pure in heart", the "peacemakers", they "which do hunger and thirst after righteousness".

Second, the Christian faith is one of love, and rejects hatred of human beings as an instrument of true human progress. "Blessed are ye, when men shall revile you and persecute you, and shall say all manner of evil against you falsely for My sake". And again, "Love your enemies, bless them that curse you; and pray for them which despitefully use you". A counsel of perfection, you may say, and truly. But it is the Christian counsel.

Third, Christianity connotes a faith in a Divine Creator expressed by a willingness for sacrifice embodied by its highest symbol, the Cross of Crucifixion; not crucifixion of the enemy, which is the expression of hatred and revenge, but of ourselves, which is the expression of unselfishness and universal love. For all Christians the Cross, after nineteen hundred years, remains the symbol of the freely accepted sacrifice for others.

Now, how do these ideas compare with communism as proclaimed and intended by its founder and its prophets?

I turned for convenience and for accuracy to the *Communist Manifesto* of Marx and Engels, and the *ABC of Communism* by Bukharin.

The *Manifesto*, after resolving the struggle in the world into one between proletariat and bourgeois (the bourgeois being in brief the man who owns a home or property of any kind, great or small, or who in some way derives his living from what is called "capitalist enterprises", which may, of course, range from large manufacturing concerns to the small shop at the suburban street corner!) says:

> Law, morality, religion, are to the proletarian so many bourgeois prejudices behind which lurk in ambush just as many bourgeois interests.

The result of this concept is the doctrine of violent revolution. Again to quote the *Manifesto*:

> You must therefore confess that by "individual" you mean no other person than the bourgeois, than the middle-class owner of property. This person must indeed be swept out of the way and made impossible.

If you secure a copy of the *Manifesto* and look at chapter 2 you will see how it embraces the abolition of the family; the abolition of what is called "bourgeois marriage"; the abolition of country and nationality. The *Manifesto* concludes by saying:

> In short, the communists everywhere support every revolution-ary movement against the existing social and political order of things ... The Communists disdain to conceal their views and aims. They openly declare that their ends can be achieved only by the forcible overthrow of all existing social conditions.

In chapter 11 of the "ABC of Communism" there is a very frank declaration as to the relationship between communism and religion. Let me quote this passage:

> "Religion is the opium of the people" said Karl Marx: It is the task of the Communist Party to make this truth comprehensible to the widest possible circles of the labouring masses. It is the task of the party to impress firmly upon the minds of the

workers, even upon the most backward, that religion has been in the past and still is today one of the most powerful means at the disposal of the oppressors for the maintenance of inequality, exploitation, and slavish obedience on the part of the toilers. Many weak-kneed communists reason as follows: "Religion does not prevent my being a Communist. I believe both in God and in communism. My faith in God does not hinder me from fighting for the cause of the proletarian revolution. This train of thought is radically false. Religion and communism are incompatible, both theoretically and practically."

And again,

The same theory has demonstrated that the very idea of God and of supernatural powers arises at a definite stage in human history, and at another definite stage begins to disappear as a childish notion which finds no confirmation in practical life and in the struggle between man and nature.

Later, we are told that —

In practice, no less than in theory, Communism is incompatible with religious faith … One who, while calling himself a Communist, continues to cling to his religious faith, one who in the name of religious commandments infringes the prescriptions of the party, ceases thereby to be a Communist.

It may be objected to this that the word "revolutionary" is consistent with nonviolent action, as some recent apologists for communism would have us believe. But the founders and prophets of communism will have no truck with such evasions. Bukharin says (on page 189 of *The ABC of Communism*):

To think that the revolution can take place without civil war is equivalent to thinking that there can be a "peaceful" revolution. Anyone who believes this is turning away from Marx to those antediluvian Socialists who imagine that the factory owners can be talked over…Marx was an advocate of the civil war, that is to say, of the fight of the armed proletariat against the bourgeois.

Engels, Marx's famous collaborator, defined the word "revolution" in these words:

> A revolution is an act in which one part of the population imposes its will upon the other part by means of rifles, bayonets and artillery.

I need not, I imagine, labour my point. In whatever mild and attractive terms communism may choose to express itself before audiences which it seeks to capture, it is above all things the doctrine of sheer materialism and of armed revolution, and as such can have nothing but hostility towards religion, and in particular towards the Christian faith.

Speech on the Establishment of Israel as an Independent Jewish State (1948)

As a longstanding friend and supporter of Australia's Jewish community, Menzies applauded the proclamation of Israel as an Independent State. Australian support for the State of Israel had been bi-partisan with the Chifley Labor government's Minister for External Affairs, H V Evatt, recommending to the United Nations the establishment of an independent Jewish State in Palestine. The new State was officially proclaimed in Tel Aviv on 14 May 1948. Appreciating the oppression and discrimination that Jewish people around the world had suffered through the ages, Menzies welcomed the establishment of Israel as a new beginning for the world's Jews to once again thrive and prosper, not least within Australia itself. In this brief speech, he praised the historic contribution of the Jewish community to Australia and hoped that the establishment of Israel would embolden them to take renewed pride in their identity as both Jews and Australian citizens.

....

… The establishment of Israel as an independent Jewish State was vitally assisted by the Jewish national fund and swiftly acknowledged and encouraged by Australia. It had a world significance. [To quote] Scott[32]: "When Israel, of the Lord beloved, out of the land of bondage came, Her father's God before her moved an awful guide in smoke and flame". The disabilities and persecutions of centuries culminated in Hitler's Germany, and are not extinct elsewhere. But in spite of this, you have a great inheritance of talent. The civilised world saw in the establishment of Israel not only the providing of an independent home to many Jewish people but also a shining symbol of delivery from bondage, and (I believe) of world repentance. But I speak of the 70,000 Jews in Australia not only in Australia but of Australia. For here, you are not, and should not be, a race apart. In this free country, all are free; all are equal before the law; religious or sectional prejudices tend to "fade into the

---

32 Sir Walter Scott (1771-1832) was a Scottish historical novelist, playwright and poet who composed the hymn, "When Israel, of the Lord beloved", in 1817.

light of common day". True, you will continue to be clannish. (No man of Scots blood can deny you that privilege. e.g. Melbourne Scots!) The great Jewish contribution to Australia is not sectional or sectarian but a community contribution, neither discriminating nor being discriminated against. It is your historic function and destiny to enrich the Australian character by making your special contribution to the whole composite body. Isaacs[33] and Monash[34] – enduring and honoured names. Jews they were; but they are honoured as great Australians.

---

33 Sir Isaac Isaacs (1855-1948) was a prominent Jewish politician and judge who served as Chief Justice to the High Court of Australia (1930-1931) and as the first Australian-born Governor-General of Australia (1931-1936).

34 Sir John Monash (1865-1931) was a Jewish Australian civil engineer and military commander of the First World War.

Speech at the Opening of the Jewish War Memorial Hall, Waverley, Sydney (7 February 1960)

Invited to open a Jewish Memorial Hall in Sydney's eastern suburbs, the Prime Minister revealed his deep respect and admiration for Australia's Jewish community. While a professing Christian of the Presbyterian tradition, Menzies was in awe of the tenacious and sincere quality of their religious faith that had withstood centuries of opposition and persecution. He assured the Jewish community, many of whom had fled from violent persecution in Nazi Germany, that modern Australia was an open and tolerant society where they could freely exercise their religious traditions. Indeed, he not only regarded the Jewish community as a welcome presence but valued their sense of family responsibility and friendly, community-minded spirit as making an infinitely rich and enduring contribution to Australian life.

....

Mr President, Your Excellency, distinguished visitors and Ladies and Gentlemen:

I think that this is a very happy occasion for a very material reason and I also have two quite irrelevant reasons for being here this afternoon.

The first irrelevant reason – though perhaps it isn't irrelevant – is that I have observed with great interest that your President's name is Felix. I was going to say his Christian name but I suppose that wouldn't be right. (Laughter), But his name is Felix which, if I remember my Latin correctly, means "happy" – happy – (Applause). And I should think he ought to be.

The second irrelevant reason that I have in my mind is that the last time I had the honour of making a speech to a Jewish congregation in Melbourne I was a little troubled about having to wear my hat all the time. I look bad enough without a hat on, but when I have a hat on I look terrible (Laughter) and I made a little bargain with the Rabbi who is a most courteous and obliging man and he said: "'Well, if you start off with it on, you may then remove it and put it on again before you finish," and that's what I did. And this afternoon Felix – Happy here – said to me just before we came up: "It's all right; from now on it's hats off". Therefore I'm so speaking – cool, calm and collected.

Now, Sir, I'm not going to detain you but I just want to say two or three things about you and about this remarkable and interesting occasion.

There are three things that have always struck me about your community. I hope you won't mind a rank outsider like myself, who is an unblushing Presbyterian – you know what I mean – making a few observations about a community, so many members of which are very close personal friends of mine. But three things have always struck me and I think they're worth mentioning.

The first is your adherence to your faith. You've been persecuted for it in the course of the centuries; you've been attacked for it; you've almost been ordered to abandon it from time to time and you have adhered to it through thick and thin until it has been hammered into true steel. Now that's a wonderful thing, a wonderful thing – your deep, loyal and abiding religious faith. I admire that enormously. Everybody does. It produces in any community an element of sanity and balance and reliability which no community can afford to be without, I don't want you to think that people who are not of your particular religious faith necessarily, or frequently, or at all, object to you on that ground. Of course we don't. On the contrary. Any man, any woman, who has the flame burning and who keeps it alight is a great man and a great woman and the community is proud of him and proud of her.

That's the first thing that I've always liked and admired about the Jewish community. It's an enduring quality.

And the second thing that I've always admired is that I really think that you have a remarkable sense of family. I have met a few people in Australia – not too many, I hope, but some – who are a bit anxious to pass off the responsibility for their families to somebody else. I've never met a Jew who felt like that, I've never known a Jewish family in which the welfare of every member of the family wasn't the constant task of the lot. Now that's a marvellous thing because the family – a good family, a healthy family, a proud family, a family generous in itself – this is of the very essence of community life. There can be no great nations without great family feeling and I admire your community immensely because all through my life I have observed this extraordinary, devoted sense of family pride and family responsibility. I hope that will always continue.

Your community is not a separate body in a great nation. It's not a sort of colony. You have no intention that it should be. But your faith and your inherited instincts are a great contribution to the community in which you live.

And the third thing that's always excited my admiration – I've said something about faith, family – well the third is friendliness. I want to say a word to you about friendliness, if I may.

I know that recently there have been strange people putting up strange slogans. If you'll allow me to say so, I know a little bit about this kind of thing, because "Out with pig-iron Bob" or something (Laughter) (Applause) has been on every railway crossing, and every brick wall and of course, being a low-down politician I've never objected to it because I've felt that this was unpaid publicity (Laughter). But I think that we just want to have in our minds that there will always be a few people who intend mischief, who desire to defile the community, those who don't believe in that orderly system of government that we believe in, that there will always be a few people who want to make rude noises or put up offensive slogans. And if one could grab one of them that would be the day – never been able to get one myself (Laughter). They have no place in this country. They don't represent any opinion in this country but as usual they've traced around themselves what might be called the "lunatic fringe". Do you know what I mean? They are the silly – well to use a good wholesome Australian expression – the "ratbags" who say: "This is pretty good; this'll do me" and they will go around chalking up or painting up slogans.

I don't want to discuss that problem with you except to say this: that 99.8% of the people of Australia regard these manifestations with contempt. These things don't represent a great movement in this country. Nobody need ever fear in your community that, in the case of some of you, you have come out of great tribulation and persecution into a country in which you might still be persecuted. Forget about it (Applause). You have come into the freest country in the world (Applause). That's the great charm about Australia; that's why my friend Landa[35] and I can be up here instead of biting (each other's heads off) (Laughter) and find ourselves on common ground, you know, on common ground admiring this spectacular and devoted piece of work. But it's a free country; it will remain free.

You know I came down here to do this job and I came down yesterday and as I drove in from the Airport; the car stopped opposite a Hotel – there was a traffic light against us – and it was in one of those suburbs that vote for Landa and don't vote for Menzies – you know what I mean? – (Applause, laughter) and in the charming alfresco habit that people have in Sydney there were three fellows sitting on the doorstep of the Bar with their feet in the street having a drink and there was another one – a rather ill-conditioned sort of fellow, he didn't look entirely sober – and the first three fellows waved their beer mugs at me and said: "Good on yer Bob" (Laughter). Well, I thought that was rather nice. And the next fellow, sitting all hunched up by himself, he just looked at me and said: "Huh, yer big mug" (Laughter). Now Sir, I like that; I approve of that very warmly. You see I'm very proud to be the Prime Minister of a free country, liable to be dismissed by the free citizens one of these days, proud to be serving them and with no complaints of what their decision might be because we are free people. (Applause)

Every one of you who was born in Australia knows that; you don't need to be told by me. And those who have come into Australia, particularly since the war, out of the horrors of Europe, in particular, I know that you've breathed more freely since you came here and that you feel that you're in a free land where you have your own opportunity and where, by your great talents and immense industry,

---

35 The Hon Abram Landa (1902-1989) was a prominent member of Sydney's Jewish Community and a NSW State Labor MP who served as Minister for Housing from 1956 to 1965. He held the seat of Bondi in Sydney's eastern suburbs from 1930 to 1965.

you can make great places for yourself. And that being so, while I would willingly stamp my foot on one of the deplorable creatures who do these deplorable things, don't get that out of proportion. That doesn't represent anybody of intelligent, decent Australian opinion, and it never will. (Applause)

And so, Sir, I come back to where I began. I'm very proud to have been invited to come here. I think this is a marvellous development. Only people with vision and courage could have imagined this centre, with all its costliness, with all the hard work that had to go into it. Only people with vision and faith and imagination could have done it. And I want to say to you; "God speed". I think this is a great occasion, a great occasion in the history of your own religious community, a great occasion in the history of Sydney. I can well understand the Mayor's pride of this in Waverley and I, speaking on behalf of Australia, if I might, am proud to think that such a work could have come about through faith, a feeling for the family and a friendliness which is, I assure you, reciprocated all round this country.

And so, Sir, I say "Thank you" for having invited me. I offer to the whole of this immense audience or congregation, my warmest good wishes. I think it's a marvellous occasion. I'm proud to have been associated with it. (Applause)

Opening of National Memorial Bible House, Canberra
(13 February 1960)

Invited to address the British and Foreign Bible Society at the opening of their new headquarters in the national capital, the Prime Minister revealed his love for the sacred scriptures precious to both Jews and Christians. With Menzies imbibing the Scots Presbyterian faith of his family background, with its habits of regular scripture reading, the Bible had formed part of the "furniture of his mind" and represented a personal source of Christian faith. As an ever-admiring student of Western civilisation, he appreciated the pre-eminent place of the Bible in shaping the historic traditions, values and institutions of the Western world, not least the Judeo-Christian ethic. In addition to its spiritual and cultural significance, Menzies esteemed the Bible, particularly the Authorised Version, as something of a "gold standard" for English literature. This was a quality of the Bible he was keen to impress on his audience if they aspired to be exemplary practitioners of the English language.

....

Mr Chairman, Your Grace, Your Excellency, ladies and gentlemen.

This is a great occasion, and it is a wonderful thing for the Federal Capital that we should have a Bible House as the Australian headquarters of one of the most famous organisations in the world – the British and Foreign Bible Society. This is a great society which possesses perhaps a more truly international character than any other I can think of. And what is its business? Its business is to make the Bible, or portions of the Bible, available to as many millions, and hundreds of millions of people around the world as can be reached. And therefore, when you think of the Society, when you think of this building, you think of the Bible.

People occasionally say to me, "Oh yes, there are millions of Bibles in circulation, but people don't read them". You know, I take leave to doubt that! I would still think that the Bible is not only the best seller in the world, but certainly the most widely read of all books. I want to give you, for myself, one or two reasons for entertaining that belief.

Firstly, for all of us or almost all of us, the Bible is the most remarkable repository of religious history. Frankly, I don't think that any man could regard himself as educated unless he had become familiar with the great historic stories in the Bible.

In the second place, and of course in the greatest place, the Bible is the repository of our faith and our inspiration. Never out of date, always up-to-date, always difficult of application and therefore stimulating to thoughtful people. It is the great source of faith, and of course that is why we ought to read it. That is why so many of us who are credited with light minds, like myself, constantly do read it!

I remember many years ago I was reading in the Chambers of a very eminent constitutional lawyer. When a case for an opinion on the Constitution of the Commonwealth came in, he would always say, "Now, Menzies, the first thing we ought to do before we become too involved in the decision given by the courts is to read the Constitution again". We always sat down and read it from beginning to end so that we might not miss the elements of the problem by being led on to the side issues which occasionally do find their way into judicial interpretation.

Now of course all that was an illustration of an old Latin tag: "*melius est petere fontes quam sectarei rivulos*" – "it is better to seek the fountainheads than to divide up the little streams".

That is a perfect description, isn't it, for what our approach ought to be to this great and immortal book? Let's seek the fountainheads – it's all there! The story is there, the great history is there, the great gospel is there, the whole spirit of Christianity is there.

It is better for the ordinary layman at any rate, like most of us, to go to it than to be taken up too much with theological refinements. There is the heart of the matter. And it is a good thing that this building should be for the heart of the matter in all questions of personal faith and personal inspiration.

The only thing I want to say, I think could be said to anybody whether Christian or not. And it's this – that this is the greatest piece of literature in the history of man. Unbelievably great! I am an old-fashioned Tory reactionary myself, as everybody knows. And therefore I like the Authorised Version, and will undertake to say that anybody who wants to understand English at its best ought to read from the Authorised Version every week and if possible every day.

I remember a number of years ago attending a School speech night. I have attended a great number in my time, and I have always had the deepest sympathy with the boys and not with the parents.

On this occasion I decided to depart from the orthodox. You know – "the best days of your life are at school, boys, and I hope ..." – you know, all that! Very tedious! I remember it was tedious when I was a boy sitting listening to it, and so I said I'd say something off the beaten track. And so I took 100 words at random from a most competent speech delivered in recent times in the House of Representatives. And I took 100 words from the Bible. I read them both aloud, and the interesting thing was this – that in the 100 words from the current modern political speech there were only, I think, 15 words of one syllable and all the rest had two or three or four and of course, under the influence of the economists, five or six, And the 100 words from the Bible had 80 words with one syllable – 80!

In the Bible you have this noble simplicity, this illustration of the most complete command of English. Because you either have command of words, or words have a command over you. And that is the difference! And in the language of the Bible, its superb eloquence based upon superb simplicity, you have what I will always believe to be the greatest piece of literature in the world.

If I were, as I am not, an atheist or agnostic or some other such unhappy person I would still take the Bible with me to a desert island for two reasons. One, that I would have a noble piece of literature to accompany me and, two, because given ample opportunity to study it I might cease to be an atheist or agnostic.

This is a wonderful occasion. I am not going to keep you here indefinitely because you all know it is a wonderful occasion. It is a very great pleasure to me to have even the smallest thing to contribute to it, but so long as this building stands here in this city, as the city grows, it will be a constant reminder to us of what is after all the most important thing in the world.

10

STATUS AND ROLE OF WOMEN

Women for Canberra, Broadcast (29 January 1943)

Menzies entertained a keen interest in the advancement of women both inside and outside the Liberal Party. Progressive and farsighted for their time, his views on women were informed by his philosophy of liberalism and his personal experience of witnessing women make a distinguished contribution to the war effort in all manner of fields. In this speech, he made it clear that the possibilities for women in politics should be limitless and that their gender should pose no handicap whatsoever to their eligibility to stand for public office. As the founder of the Liberal Party, he sought to put his ideas into effect by encouraging the Australian Women's National League to mobilise women into the organisational wing of the Party to then create a talent pool of potential female candidates to enter the political arena. At the same time, however, he distanced himself from the views of affirmative action feminists who argued that women should be promoted merely by virtue of the fact that they were women. To Menzies, such an attitude was deficient because it overlooked the personal merits and talents of the individual female candidate.

....

There is a revived movement to send a woman or women to the Parliament of Canberra. Political good judgement requires that I should say nothing about it for fear of attracting one of the few candidates to Kooyong. But why not? It is a free country (to some extent at any rate) and anyone is free to stand for Kooyong and, in any event, the question of women in parliament is so important that it deserves an honest answer.

We have travelled a long way in our civic outlook upon women, and even if we were reluctant and struggling wayfarers, the events of this war in which women have been such workers and warriors, would surely have speeded us on our journey.

In the Middle Ages, we are told, Divines solemnly disputed as to whether women had souls. In the 20th century our intelligence has increased, and no career is closed and no faculty denied to her. In brief, the real equality of the sexes – though not their identity – was recognised long ago. True, I have met a few feminists whose chief ambition appeared to be to look, to sound and to act like men; but their obvious dissatisfaction with their own sex has left my views untouched.

Of course women are at least the equals of men. Of course there is no reason why a qualified woman should not sit in Parliament, or on the bench, or in a professional chair, or preach from the pulpit, or, if you like, command an army in the field. No educated man today denies a place or a career to a woman because she is a woman.

But there is a converse proposition which I state with all respect but with proper firmness. No woman can demand a place or a career just because she is a woman. It is outmoded and absurd to treat a woman's sex as a political disqualification; it seems to me equally absurd to claim it as a qualification in itself.

I know that it may be said in answer that there is, particularly on social problems, a special woman's point of view. But again, quite frankly, I am sceptical. When I am asked, for example, what men think about such and such my only reply is that I have no idea since almost all men have different experiences and different points of view.

Is this not equally true of women?

It is just on this point that I joined issue with one or two of the advocates of the "Women for Canberra" Movement. They appear to think that, irrespective of her party or her views or capacity for direction or administration, some woman should be elected to Canberra because she is a woman and has the woman's point of view. But how you would all laugh if Jones stood for Parliament and said: "I am a man; therefore elect me".

For myself, I declined to vote for any woman just because she is a woman; but I will vote for her with no prejudice and with great cheerfulness if I am satisfied that she is, in the homely phrase, "the better man of the two". For, like most electors, I am not half so interested in the sex or social position or worldly wealth of my representatives and rulers as I am in the quality of their minds, the soundness of their characters, the humanity of their experience, the sanity of their policy, and the strength of their wills.

When I read of a meeting at which women aspiring to be Labor candidates, UAP candidates, Country Party candidates, Independent candidates, have all foregathered to derive common electoral strength from their association, I confess to being completely puzzled.

Does the Labor lady really believe in the policy of the Australian Labor Party? Does she earnestly believe that it is the best thing for the country? Does she really want parliament to contain a majority of members pledged to carry it out? If she is a genuine Labor supporter – as no doubt she is – her answer must be yes. If it is, what does she mean by supporting women candidates who are not of her party? Will she support Mrs Smith, UAP, against the sitting Labor Member for X, who happens to be a man?

This is far too important a question to be obscured by sentimentality which is fundamentally more characteristic of the 19th century than of an age in which men have learned to respect and reverence women for their courage, strength and intelligence.

I had always understood the case of women in politics to be: "Away with prejudice; good government is more important than the sex of the governor".

But that case appears to me to be flatly contradicted by a case which apparently says: "That the candidate should have the right sex is more important than good government".

Bring the whole matter down to an instance: Take Kooyong, which I represent. It contains as many women as men. On my side of politics its women's political organisation is much larger, more continuous and more effective than the men's political organisation. There is no reason at all why a woman should not be elected by such a constituency. But if Kooyong elected some woman, irrespective of her political views and, indeed, with glorious indifference to them, then Kooyong would, for all practical purposes, disenfranchise itself. For it is on the quality of our political philosophy, the depth and continuity of our convictions, and our fidelity to our political faith that the future of our democratic Parliament depends.

There is just one additional point that should be mentioned: It is beyond question that, particularly on such important social problems as education, health, and child-welfare, women can and should make a powerful contribution to the future of Australia. This undoubted fact has led some people to conclude that it would be a good thing to have in Parliament a few women who are specialists in these matters. But this argument ignores the vital political fact that Parliament is really not the place for the person who specialises on two or three matters. Parliament has to make the general laws of the country and provide general political administrators of the country. As a Member of Parliament I must be prepared to have a view on all matters which come up for decision and I must therefore have a policy which goes very far beyond two or three specialised topics. True I may have some very special knowledge of some matter and once a year or thereabouts I may have the opportunity of talking to Parliament about it, but for the most part it will be necessary to deal with matters which are not my specialty but upon which I must acquire knowledge and exercise judgement.

These requirements apply to women as well as to men. The matter of real importance therefore is not that we should be agitating for some special representation of women in Parliament – as if women represent some circumscribed electorate in themselves – but that we should shake our minds clear of whatever prejudice may linger in them and honestly and sincerely acknowledge that there is just as much room in all our public bodies for public-spirited and intelligent women as there is for public-spirited and intelligent men.

"Women in the community – Present and Future", Address to the Conference of the Headmistresses' Association of Australia, Melbourne (1 September 1958)

In this address to the Headmistresses Association of Australia, Menzies articulated some of his views on the status and place of women in society. Consistent with the progressive views of women he had espoused in 1943 and 1944, he welcomed the development of more women taking part in higher education and affirmed that no woman should be inhibited from pursuing the career of her choice simply by virtue of her gender. If men and women were equally endowed with various intellectual and athletic faculties, then there was no reason why women should be precluded from exercising these to any lesser extent than men. In 1958, the percentage of students enrolled at Australian universities who were female was just 22%. While the actual *number* of female students had steadily increased since the late 1930s, the *proportion* had decreased from a high of 39.3% in 1944. With Menzies regretting that higher education had not been regarded as "entirely appropriate for women" sooner, it was a trend he desired to arrest. Indeed, by the time Menzies left office in 1966, the proportion of female students was once again on an upward trajectory at 27.4%. In the realm of public life and international affairs, he held that women had an equal stake to men and that the division between public and private life was essentially gender neutral. While Menzies was open to women excelling in public life and in the professions, he was well aware of the traditional family responsibilities that arose in the course of a typical woman's life and therefore proposed that education for marriage and family responsibilities remain one of the "great objects of schools". In favouring a feminism that was liberating and empowering yet not socially disruptive, Menzies appreciated that a healthy society must balance the freedom for women to contribute to public and professional life with the traditional pattern of family life.

....

Madam President, I think I ought to begin by admitting that I always thought I would be a little bit bogus here tonight, confronting what was so famously called a "monstrous regiment of women", but I am extra bogus (if that is the right expression) because, if some of the people I see here tonight are headmistresses, then I will be very much surprised! I even felt on the way out that I might begin by saying that I felt like Daniel in the Lionesses' den, but I cannot do that because there they are – I can see a gaggle of headmistresses here, and this disturbs me a great deal, because I am a simple minded character – I agree to make a speech somewhere, and it is only about a week before it happens that I suddenly demand to know what it is I am supposed to talk about, and then when I am told I get the horrors. And tonight – well, not tonight, but about four or five days ago – I discovered for the first time, clearly and consciously, that my topic was "women in the community – present and future".

I want to begin by saying that this is an impossible assignment, rendered all the more impossible because my wife said to me not only the other day but over the last thirty years that if there is anybody who understands nothing about women, it is myself! So, that is a little bit awkward.

But I suppose, Madam, that the topic is proposed for me in the context of educational training, because, after all, you are all the heads of schools and you have forgotten more about educating and training girls then I will ever learn. If it does arise in that context, then perhaps I ought to give you a little reminiscence of my own. Believe it or not, I am a graduate of a University myself, and when I went to the University of Melbourne, there were very few women there. I see one or two of them here tonight, but there were very few. It was considered, at the time, to be rather odd to be a woman undergraduate. People used to make rude remarks about their millinery and their hairdos, they were considered quite remarkable. Today I understand the university is the veritable home of glamour. But things have changed, and as time went along, I frequently thought that it was a very great pity that higher education in that sense had not been regarded rather sooner in Australia as entirely appropriate for women, because in America, where they are, in one or two respects, ahead of us, the higher education for women has been – if I may use so deplorable a term – quite fashionable for very many years. In other words, they are ahead of us in understanding that men are not the only people who ought to have their brains brushed up, and who ought to be introduced to the total body of knowledge as far as possible. Today, as I said, there are very many women students, and the whole thing has changed.

Well, that led me on, that reflection, to say to myself, now should I look up the *Yearbook*? Should I find out about women in the yearbook? (which as you know, is a great body of statistics.) But I did not. I thought, "No, it would be much safer to engage in a generalisation". Therefore, I make these generalisations to you. I suppose that most women marry. Is that a bold statement? Is that too bold? I would think that was probably right – that most women get married, and I suppose that, of those who get married, most of them have children. I think those might be two fairly safe generalisations. I do not mean by that to divide people unduly into classes, because I have known a great number of women who were never married – whose failure to marry was merely a reflection on the intelligence of men – but that, of course, is not uncommon – but most of them marry and most of them have children, and, therefore, Madam, I suppose that it would be a safe thing to conclude that education – that is your problem, that is your subject – education for marriage and family responsibilities must still remain one of the great objects of schools. If it were not, then I think we would be ignoring some of the greatest human factors in the nation and therefore, I begin by saying, "Very well, education for marriage, education for family responsibilities".

That does not answer the question, it merely begins it, because then we have to go on to consider what that involves, in the course of education. It cannot just mean teaching people to cook. Some of the best cooks I have ever known where never taught to cook at all, unfortunately, and some of the worst cooks I have ever known had their certificates, so it cannot just mean teaching them to cook, although I suppose most men here would agree that it might be an advantage, if included. What it does mean is education for life. I will say something a little later about education for a career, but it must mean education for life – a life regarded from a particular angle – the life of a woman, and in particular the life of a wife and a mother. An education for that purpose and from that point of view.

I venture to believe that our ideas have changed a great deal in modern times. I am perfectly certain that in the 18th century, which was a century of good taste but which had no undue belief in educating women, and even in the 19th century, where almost the same ideas prevailed, it was thought entirely appropriate that a woman should confine her studies and her mental training to matters which were actually unrelated to the matters that her husband might study. She was to understand music, she was to do a little delicate work in watercolours, only in watercolours, mind you, painting oils would have been regarded as a gravure touch, quite unfeminine in its qualities – she could read a little discreetly edited literature so long as it was genteel; she did tapestry work. In other words, she was trained to understand that her world and the world of her husband were utterly detached. Well, I think we have got over this because we now believe, don't we, that education of a girl is education for life and the life of an entirely different character from the life which obtained before this century.

Now, Madam President, before I pursue that, I might perhaps just turn aside remembering that my topic is – what was it? Today and in the future – to say something about my own avenue of life which is politics. Well, politically, I have done a good deal to do with the work of women, a good deal to think about what they do. And the oddity is this: that although this country let the world into the women's path and into the idea that women should be able to sit in Parliament, you can put a sharp rule between what is done by women in politics outside Parliament and what is done inside, because outside Parliament women, in my experience, take a very large part in political organisation; indeed, I don't mind confessing that if they did not exist I would not be here tonight, because I would have been out of office long ago. They have a sense of continuity of work in political organisation which is denied to men and perhaps that is because a women will not think it beneath her to attend to all kinds of continuing details, whereas her husband says, "Oh well, tell me when polling day is coming on and I will see what I can do about it". The result is that, in my experience, an enormous proportion of the continuous day-to-day work of organising in politics is done out of the goodness of their hearts, out of sheer enthusiasm, by women.

"A sense of continuity in endeavour." Now that may seem to you rather like a platitude but it is rather profoundly true. A sense of continuity in endeavour – this, you know, is part of the genius of women. What woman would, unless she had that sense, go through all the labours, the frustrations, the joys and the angers and the sudden rages and the much more sudden forgivenesses of dealing with little children and bringing them up and dealing with them day by day. Again I speak only for myself in this connection. I am very much inclined to deliver a cuff and leave it at that, or a pat on the head and leave it at that, and get out of the house and feel rather thankful to be away. I speak only for myself, not for you much more patient fathers who are listening to me tonight! But women have that sense of continuity in patience and in endeavour and that, in political organisation, has meant a great deal.

Yet it is equally true that over these many years women have played a small part in Parliament. We have had a few women in Parliament; not very many compared to the great body of Parliament. It has been a small part and you may say to me, "Why does that happen?" Some of you headmistresses accustomed to discipline will say to me, "That is the fault of the men. They won't have women in Parliament". To which I reply: "There are more women on the rolls than there are men in Australia, and if women are not in Parliament more than they are, it is because women don't vote for them!"

Now why? Well, I think it is explainable. I have myself, on more than one occasion, listened to a woman candidate for Parliament who stood up and made it her great policy speech to say, "I am a woman. The woman's point of view ought to be represented." If I were to stand up and say in Kooyong (which through sheer animadvertance does me the honour of returning me to Parliament), "I am a man and the man's point of view ought to be listened to", they would think I had become a little odd. I have frequently had to say to my female political friends, "Look, don't ask people to vote for you because you are a woman. Ask them to vote for you because you are the best man in the field. You are the one to

253

represent them. You are the one who will understand public problems". But to say, "I think the woman's point of view should be represented, the woman's point of view being, with infinite respect, as elusive as a man's point of view, since who knows it – there are thousands of different points of view. That kind of statement is not an expression of equality, because if equality ought to be expressed there would be no occasion to say either, "I am a man," or "I am a woman". It is rather an expression of nervousness and uncertainty.

Of course, that leads to the other observance I want to make: that politically the great problems of politics, the very great determining problems of politics, of international affairs, of high policy, of economics, of finance, of all the things that barely put their hand out and touch the ordinary lives of people – these problems have no sex at all. They must be understood equally by men or women if they are to be dealt with in the Parliament of the nation and in the government of the nation. Therefore the whole process of training, if it is to be designed in the case of some women to lead them into public affairs, must be to produce an equality of knowledge, of understanding of these problems, and not to be left to depend on a sort of condescension.

The whole point is that if women are to occupy themselves in careers in life, in any of the professions, in any other great activities, then they will be the first to concede that in that field they must be able to stand on their own feet, in that field they must measure in competence against the people who are their rivals. I wouldn't like to have you believe for one moment that I have any inhibitions about women in careers. I began by saying – perhaps you might think a little too abruptly – that most girls at school will someday marry. Well, some do marry, but there will always be, and there will increasingly be in the modern world, women of singular talent who will devote themselves to careers, not just because they want to earn a living but because they have something in them that they must express. So we will have, as we have had in the past, women of immense talents in various professions, and to them the whole world should be open.

I have occasionally thought that what people called "a feminist" was occasionally rather more masculine than that. Our grandfathers, our great-grandfathers, they had pretty primitive ideas about the place of women in society, but, at any rate, they did recognise that women and men were not the same – that they had, very frequently, different tasks in life and different functions in life. They overdid it by saying, "Well that puts them in a class apart". We must not overdo it in that sense, but when it comes to the point of a woman saying what I am interested in is pursuing some great trained service in life", then I believe that there should be no doors closed against her – that the whole world, on the contrary, should be open to her. That, I think, is a matter which goes beyond argument in the present day and generation.

But, let us put on one side those whose talents lead them into unusual courses, because there are men the same way. Most men really like to lead a routine life. They like to be in a well-organised business. They like to be in something which leads on, step-by-step, to some reasonably visible conclusion. It is only occasionally that there is a man who likes to be different, and who likes to do something different, and strike out in his own way. That is true of women also.

But, if I turn aside from them and just look at the problem of women in the community generally, in the context of education and training, then I would just like to have a quick glance at the future. What is going to happen in the future? In the days that I was talking to you about – the 18th and 19th centuries – attics and basements were full of domestic servants who lived under great difficulty in ill-ventilated rooms, and they did not have the best time in the world, but there were masses of them, and so, lady X or lady Y was able to attend to her embroidery and play on the spinnet and do her watercolours, and this was all very genteel and very pleasant, because somebody else did all the work.

Now, in the modern world, where we have been improved by modern civilisation to a point where nobody wants to do any domestic service and nobody can afford to engage it, the average young married woman may be regarded almost as a slave to her house. She has children to look after. She cannot get any help or, if she can, it is very scarce and very expensive; and she must frequently wonder about the future, and wonder about her children's future – particularly her daughter's future. Well, we will need to get something out of this scientific development of the 20th century – something other than bigger and better wars – and, of course, we will. Modern mechanisation in the home will reduce household chores – and it is vital that it should.

Do you know, I was speaking not so long ago to a very civilised man who said to me, "you know I think we ought to devote a lot more attention – it is really a great social reform – to improving the lot of a woman in the kitchen". I said I understood that was right, but they have electric stoves and washing machines and things that grind up things for you, and drying machines. He said, "Yes, but what I have in mind is that we ought really to try to design the kitchen-ware which possesses a kind of surface, which I suppose scientific gentlemen would call a coefficient restriction, so that all you need to do is to hold it like that, near the tap and everything disappears from the surface, leaving the vessel in its pristine beauty". I said, "It is a most attractive idea," and he said, "I am perfectly serious about it," and he was. All he was doing was putting into graphic form that, in these days when every young housewife must do her own work and look after her own children, unless we succeeded in reducing the sheer labour, the chores of her household duties, she will inevitably find herself cut off from art, from literature, from thought, from bright conversation, from all the things that make for a civilised existence. That is a very great problem in the modern world, and the electricians, the mechanics, the electronic gentlemen, must do their best to solve it.

Well, suppose they do, Madam President, suppose they solve it and suppose the day comes when by the mere turn of the hand or a flicking of the switch or something of that kind a lot of things which used to take mother a long time to do are done more quickly and more easily, and there is, therefore, more leisure. What is to be done with the leisure? This is really one of the great social problems of our time, because we have become obsessed by the idea of leisure. Every time somebody thinks of some industrial reform he thinks in terms of a reduced working week. This, of course, is a splendid idea until we begin to say to ourselves,

"What will we do with all this time"? I speak to you in a heartfelt way on this matter because I have never known very much, in my lifetime, about leisure, but when I have had it, I have enjoyed it, I have thought it was a wonderful thing. But what are people to do, if outside their sleeping hours, the bulk of their time is leisure time? It is a great problem, it is a great challenge to our country, and it is a great challenge to the schoolmasters and the schoolmistresses and the professors and lecturers and the whole body of educationalists in the world. What are we to do about it? Because if leisure is to be fruitfully spent, it will require higher and higher educational standards. A man who is given leisure and nothing else is a miserable person. I have frequently said to myself, looking at some man on the point of retirement who has never learned to read or to think, who has merely been – as they say in the modern jargon – an extrovert, "What will you do in your leisure?" I have seen dozens of people of that kind. The only way to enjoy leisure is to have either some occupation of a different kind which will stimulate the mind and imagination, or to have developed those reflective faculties which depend on the inner reserves of the mind. That is the time in life when people need inner reserves, when they need to have read and remembered, to have thought and considered. Therefore, if, as I hope, the mechanics will shorten the labours of the housewife's task, then it is all the more important that in a mass of schools and of universities, these prospective housewives should have been given the highest possible educational standards so that leisure to them will be a great adventure and a wonderful thing instead of a mere episode of boredom.

One other thing I would like to say about the future is this: that there is a new status of women – there is no doubt about that, that is almost the hallmark of the 20th century; but it is not necessarily to be expressed by competition in all fields. Perhaps we are a little disposed occasionally to think whatever a man does in this world ought to be done by a woman and that there ought to be a source of constant competition going on in these matters. I don't think that is true, and before I conclude I would like to give you a single reason why I don't think it is true. It is a very contentious reason and it relates to a matter of which my ignorance is even uncommonly abysmal, but this is the age of science, the modern accent is on science. Everywhere I turn, particularly at Canberra outside Parliament House, I encounter a scientist, some of the most eminent in the world. I am even one myself, because they recently honoured me by making me a Fellow of the Academy of Science, strictly *honoris causa* – I want to make this abundantly clear. At any rate, in that somewhat remote sense I am a scientist and I have the greatest respect for scientists. They speak a language I have never understood, they use phrases which are completely beyond my comprehension; but I usually make up my own mind for some dubious reason of my own whether they know their business or not and, if I think they know their business, I listen to them and get them to put it into plain English, and if they can I think they are pretty good. There it is. It is the age of science and wherever we turn, we find more and more don't we, that people must study science. People produce statistics to show you we are not producing enough scientists, and no doubt we are not; though I would hate to be a compulsory scientist. That, of course, is something in our nature, but undoubtedly, as this century proceeds, the accent on science will be more and more acute.

Does that mean that all our daughters, or a heavy proportion of them, must become scientists? Without wishing to make any improper distinction, and realising as I do that many superb scientists in this country have been women, I don't think I want my grand-daughter to be a nuclear physicist. I hope you won't regard that as old-fashioned and prejudiced, because I have a feeling myself – going back to my beginning – that most of the girls in your schools are going to be wives and mothers and they are not likely to become eminent nuclear physicists.

Coming back to that, I would like to say that the more this accent comes on science the more that men – and more and more men in the world – are coming to believe that, as scientists, they understand the mysteries of life, whereas in fact they understand the mysteries of matter, which is a different thing.

But the more and more people there are of that kind, I believe, the more important it is that we should be able to look increasingly to the women in the community and to the women in the home for the humanising influence which alone can prevent science from destroying us. I beg of you to remember that in this 20th century, this clever century where we have learnt and put into operation more about science than all our predecessors in recorded times, this 20th century has been the most barbarous century, full of hatred, full of malice, full of cruelty, full of man's misunderstanding of man. What we need in this country is not only more science – which, of course, we must have – but more humanity, more understanding, more reflective minds, more cultivated minds, and therefore I am hoping and believing that in the second half of this century the educated woman is going to find more and more balance, not only for herself but for her man, in poetry, in art, in philosophy, in all the things that in the long run distinguish the civilised man and, therefore, Madam President, I say that our educational ideas, much as they have changed in this century, much as they have changed in my lifetime, must continue to change so that we begin to see the function in the community of an educated woman in a proper, in a more comprehensive, in a more civilised way.

11

SPEECH, LANGUAGE AND CHARACTER

Speech to Camberwell Grammar School on the Importance of Speech and Language, Melbourne (1938)

In his frequent addresses to school students, one of the key messages he was keen to impress on his young audiences was the need to cultivate good English. In this address to Camberwell Grammar School in his electorate of Kooyong, Menzies reminded his young audience that the beauty of English lay in its simplicity and directness. While Menzies was all in favour of acquiring a broad vocabulary as part of one's education in the language, he frowned upon English speech and prose that was more complicated than what was necessary to convey a point. Like the great 20th century writers C S Lewis and George Orwell, Menzies generally observed the rule of never using a long word where a short one would do. As such, he encouraged school students to aim for simple and unaffected speech, uncluttered by convoluted sentences, unwieldy phrases or technical jargon. In so doing, they would become not only better communicators but more proficient practitioners of the English language.

······································

In an age of specialisation and science it is old-fashioned but necessary to go back to first principles.

It will not really be a proof of the success of our education if we become wireless or air-minded and forget the resources of our own language, resources which will contribute more to our real enjoyment and understanding of life than all the laboratories in the world.

There is a struggle going on in our language and I want the school-boys of 1938 to be on the right side. The struggle is between simplicity and directness of speech and writing, on the one hand, and pretentiousness and obscurity on the other.

Thus:

> We do not finish things, we "finalise" them.

> We do not keep our promises, we "implement" them.

> We do not make an agreement with Tom Jones, we make a "bilateral" agreement with him.

> We are no longer busy, we are "preoccupied".

> We do not clean out the drains, we engage in "decontamination", or sometimes I believe, "re-decontamination" of the drains.

> We do not get hold of Smith, we "contact" him.

> The manager of a business has become a "big executive".

> The land agent at the corner of the street is beginning to call himself a "realtor".

In Parliament, in church, on the platform, the man who can express in plain language just what he means is thought to be commonplace, while the glib and partly illiterate speaker who never uses a short word where a long one (or wrong one) can be found, and who wanders in a mist of his own creation, is all too frequently thought to be a contemporary orator.

English is, of course, not a dead language, but a living one. It must grow. It must put out new branches and twigs. But if it is to grow in strength and beauty it must be from time to time pruned by the pruning knife of good taste and educated judgement.

Education and Moral Character, "Australia Today – Man to Man" Broadcast (17 March 1954)

Returning to the familiar theme of education, Prime Minister Menzies discussed the profound bearing that education has on the formation of an individual's moral character. He regarded a sound education in the humanities, in disciplines such as history, English literature and anthropology, as particularly fundamental to building a civilised society of ethical citizens. Given the barbarous conflicts that had disfigured much of the 20th century to date, Menzies saw the moral objectives of education as more pressing than ever in this post-war period. To illustrate his point, Menzies alluded to the contentious foreign policy issue of Australia-Japan relations that were a source of consternation for many Australians in the shadows of the Second World War. While acknowledging the justifiable pain that Australians had suffered at the hands of a cruel wartime enemy, he reminded his listeners that it would ultimately be to Australia's detriment if it were to prolong bitterness and enmity towards a country that was now emerging as a peaceful power with which Australia could happily do business. Education thus served the purpose of not only building good citizens but laying the foundation for a warm-hearted and constructive statesmanship in world affairs. Indeed, Menzies' forward-looking attitude towards Japan in this broadcast foreshadowed the historic commerce agreement with Japan that he and his Trade Minister, John ("Jack") McEwen, would sign in 1957.

....

Good evening ladies and gentlemen:

On some desk calendars, the publishers have the pleasing habit of printing the daily text. Here is one I have just been reading, from the Chinese writer Wu Ting-Fang:

> The more a man is educated, the more is it necessary, for the welfare of the State, to instruct him how to make proper use of his talents. Education is like a double-edged sword. It may be turned into dangerous uses if it is not properly handled.

When he was at Canberra, the Duke of Edinburgh opened a great building for the Australian National University. His speech was similar. Let us by all means have scientists, and the best we can find. But let us also have people of humane letters, who can remind us that the most important thing in the world is not the machine, but man.

The most important thing in the world, may I say for myself, is man's relation to his maker: his relation to the divine and spiritual law. The second most important thing is man's relation to man, with all that it implies of brotherhood and understanding and fair play and responsibility. The third is man's scientific and mechanical skill, and the extension of the boundaries of knowledge. To this third one the 20th century has devoted most of its genius with results sometimes magnificent, as in medicine and industrial production and transport, and living standards; and sometimes disastrous, is in the mass destruction of modern war. But it cannot truly be said that the 20th century is the century of true religion; for in sheer paganism we have occasionally put the Dark Ages to shame. Nor can it be said that humanity has got to know itself and its duties better, for international hatreds have seldom been more acute. At home, the old and superb spirit of charity and goodwill has tended to become the compulsory product, spiritually valueless, of the powerful laws of taxation and government control.

This is, in my long-considered opinion, substantially due to a failure of true education. We have, so we claim, made education universal. But what do we mean by education? I have known men with university degrees who remained basically stupid, and unperceptive and selfish. I have known men who had no schooling after they were thirteen, who spoke what we would call bad English, but who had character, wisdom, reflection, and a warm understanding of their fellow-men.

Education does not simply mean the compulsory getting of a stock of knowledge. Knowledge is good; but wisdom is better. It is the way a man's mind works that matters. To be educated is to have learned how to think; to have acquired self-discipline; to have understood duty and the rights of others.

These tasks are not merely scientific or mechanical. A man may be a great scientist and be uncivilised. He may have mastered the technique of the law but had no real understanding of that spirit. Education must produce a sense of values and ethical standards, and the spirit of tolerance, or it fails.

Now, please don't tell me that all this is obvious. Because it isn't. You know as well as I do that the easiest and quickest way to score in a political argument is to appeal to intolerance, hatred and prejudice. Such appeals are, perhaps, good politics; but they are detestable statesmanship. And in the long run we need statesmanship, don't we?

Let me take a current example. We have had a bitter war with the Japanese. They were a treacherous enemy, as our American friends discovered at Pearl Harbor. They were a cruel enemy as many thousands of prisoners of war learned in death or misery. We have no reason to love them and Christ's great injunction, "love your enemies," is, as yet, beyond our reach. Indeed, even some professing Christians go so far as to say that it is bad politics.

But the war is over. We are at peace with Japan. The United States of America, which lost so many thousands of young lives in the bloody wars of the South-West Pacific, has just made a defensive agreement with Japan under which Japan is, up to a point, to re-arm. The American reasoning is clear enough. They say – "If Japan is not to fall, with all her industrial strength, into the hands of Communist Russia and China, she must be able to be defended. Who is to defend her? Are we, and the Australians to defend Japan, or is she to defend herself?"

This is the conduct of a grown-up nation, which knows that the greatest stumbling-block to peace is the perpetuation of enmities. The conduct of foreign affairs is not a job for children.

Come back home on this matter – are we to trade with Japan? Well, in fact, we are. Last year we sold Japan £80m in worth of goods, notably wool; and we bought no more than £5m in worth from Japan. This, of course, cannot go on forever. No trader can buy unless he can sell. If Japan stopped buying Australian products tomorrow, our income and our standards of living would fall. Yet to talk sensibly of Japanese trade is to expose yourself to the offensive and silly charge of being pro-Japanese.

Would you like a short answer to that poisonous allegation? Here it is. I have the honour to be supported in the Commonwealth Parliament by about 100 Members. Of these, 69 are ex-members of the armed services. Their love of Australia is proved in action. Of these, no fewer than 32 served against the Japanese in the recent war. Of these, five were prisoners of war in Japanese hands. Are these members pro-Japanese? Or have they realised that the happiness of the future depends upon the future, and not upon nursing the bitterness of the past for cheap political gain?

Servant Leadership, Speech at the CTA Annual Association Smoke Social, Club Rooms, Melbourne (9 August 1958)

As guest speaker at the annual social function organised by the Commercial Travellers Association (CTA) in Melbourne, Menzies speaks warmly of the Association's enterprise before making some general comments on servant leadership. Viewing commercial enterprise as a force for good in the community, Menzies praised the Association's members as "servants of commerce and industry". The Prime Minister then compared their service to the public with that of elected representatives and the ministers of a government. He reminded his audience that such leaders, by definition, are servants of their constituencies and the country at large. The other point he made about leaders in public office was that their chief objective was to not do what was "popular", but what was right for the country. For Menzies, the mark of true statesmanship was to have the courage for leaders to make decisions for the betterment of the country, even if it meant their personal approval would be at stake.

....

... I always feel at home with commercial travellers, because in a sense I'm one myself. What is a commercial traveller? Is that something you thought about adequately? A commercial traveller is a servant of commerce and industry, and without him it can't go on. He is the man who charms the customer, who sells the goods, who tells at least one story when times are bad and a good three when times are good. (Laughter) And that describes me to perfection. Because, as I said, you are the servants of commerce and industry; I am a Minister and those many of you who maintain your early scholarship will remember that a minister is a servant, and the minister in a country is a servant of the country. All that can be said about the Prime Minister is that he is the prime servant of his country. If he forgets that he becomes a menace, but if he remembers all the time that he is a servant of the country and is bound to produce what he believes is right for his own country, then people may vote for him (people have been known to do that!) or they may vote against him – quite a lot of people have been known to do that. (Laughter) But he must, at all times, understand that he is Prime Minister, chief servant, because that's what it means: the chief servant of the country.

Therefore, Sir, I am not on some strange ground tonight. I am among my brethren – they, the servants of industry and commerce, and I, for the time being – and the time being seems to have gone on for quite a long time – the servant of the people ...

I should say just one thing to you that I'd like to say – there was a time when people thought and perhaps some people still do – that the political man and the business man live in a state of conflict. I think it may even be true to say that there are those who try to continue to promote this idea. But in reality, in this modern world, the businessman and the political man ought not to be in conflict. They ought, more and more, to discover that they're on the same side because, after all, we have the same interests to serve.

What is my job? Some people think that my job consists of making "airy-fairy" speeches – as if anybody can make a good speech about anything unless he had something to say; as if any speech that was worth listening to lacked thought behind it and ideas behind it. But there are people who think that's it.

I recently had occasion to think and to write a few words about one of the greatest men we ever had in Australia – Alfred Deakin. I can remember, as a boy in Ballarat, hearing people say that Deakin was the "silver-tongued" orator, meaning by that he was the voice and nothing else. Yet I have lived long enough, and learned enough about the history of my own country to know that that great man made a greater constructive contribution to the development of Australia than – if you'll allow me to say so – any other man in its history. (Applause)

You go to Mildura – some of you no doubt do – and receive magnificent orders, I trust – you go to the irrigation settlements and more and more people will talk about them as if they came just like that, by the inevitable circumstance; they don't know that the young Deakin, as a young Victorian minister, was the first man in the political field to begin to think about irrigation, to go to India to look at it on the spot, to go to America to look at it on the spot. But he came back and battled in the political field to establish irrigation on the Murray in our own State. It's a great pity that people looking back on him found themselves saying, "Oh yes, they tell me that he was a great speaker". He was a great creator; he did the most wonderful things in relation to irrigation. When I look back further on the political and social history of Australia as a Commonwealth I see the arbitration system, the protective system, all these matters which lie at the base of Australian development, and every time I see them I will see the name of Deakin and the deeds of Deakin.

I mention that to you not only because I think we ought occasionally to revive our recollections of truly great men, but because I firmly believe that any man in public life who thinks that politics to him is just a job that will provide him with an income, is making the most rash of all errors; the truth is that we must be the servants of the people. But in order to be the servant of the people, we are not to be servile, we are not to look at every problem and then say, "Will this be popular?" or "Will this not be popular?" Because if that's the kind of leadership you're going to get, it will lead the country into disaster. It is not a matter of saying, "Will this please somebody?", It's a matter of saying, "Is this the right thing to do if Australia is going to grow, if the country is to become richer and more powerful, if employment is to rise, if living standards are to rise?" And, Sir, that presents a problem which is a great challenge to any man of character and honesty and imagination. I'm not apologising for anything that I have done, though no doubt I've frequently been wrong; nor am I apologising in advance for anything I may do for such time as is left to me by the free and intelligent electors (Laughter), but I do want to emphasise one point to all of you: when you go out to sell goods, when you go out to maintain the vivacity of the business with which you are connected, your great idea is – I think that this is right, I think that these things are good, I think they ought to be bought, I am prepared to sell them and to come back next month or next quarter next year and sell them again …

It is true, you know, that the more you can get around, the more these things happen, the more people are disposed to treat you with an almost embarrassing respect. You're something they haven't seen before. Yet they are terribly kind about it, terribly courteous. But the danger of it is that I might begin to think that I'm different, whereas the truth, the lovely human truth is that I'm the same and that's why I like to come here.

I'm ashamed to think that it's six years since I was here last – I like to come here because I can look around a few hundred men and say, "Well, well, just the same, the same line of country, and same interests, the same characters, the same belief in Australia, the same interests are served". That's what I want to say to you. Don't begin separating ourselves – let us begin uniting ourselves, because, thank God, we are the same people, and with honesty, and good horse sense, and good hard work, and fidelity to our friends around the world, our great-grandchildren will be able to meet here and say still that they're the same people. Thank you very much.

Language and Character, Speech at Cranbrook School, Sydney (10 December 1960)

Delivering the end of year address at Sydney's Church of England Cranbrook School, the Prime Minister returned to the familiar themes of "good moral character" and "proper language". Interestingly, one of the virtues he cited as evidence of sound moral character was that of "pride", in which he sought to dispel the common misconception of equating it with conceit. Properly understood, pride provided the basis for a life of healthy self-respect and independence. This, for Menzies, was complemented by the virtue of courage which he saw as critical to effective statesmanship. In an age where Menzies began to perceive a decline in chivalrous conduct, he also appealed to the importance of "good manners" as the mark of a civilised society. Hailing the English language as one of the great traditions bequeathed to the younger generation, Menzies believed that his young audience owed a debt to its forbears by maintaining the art of speaking the King's (or Queen's) English. As Menzies had always believed, "good English" was defined by its simplicity and clarity.

....

… What are the great things, the great virtues that we ought to achieve when we are at school? Because if we don't achieve them, then our prospect of achieving them thereafter are not as good as they might be.

I think one of the virtues is what I will call "pride". I know, Headmaster, pride is supposed to be one of the deadly sins. But pride in the sense of a proper self-respect, a determination to do your own work, and to play your own play, and to stand on your own feet – this is one of the great qualities in mankind. Nobody knows it better than a man who has been engaged, fairly responsibly most of the time, in public affairs.

So many people in the world don't start with their self-respect, or their self-help, but make their first port of call the government, which is only another way of saying that they want other people, through the government, to do their work for them.

This is a great point with me. It is a great quality to be independent, for a man to have a proper pride, and to say, "If I can do this myself I am going to do it myself. And it is only if I can't do it myself that I must call on other people, if I have a chance, to help me to do it".

Pride is not to be confused with vanity. There is nothing sillier than vanity; and vanity brings about its own downfall every day of the week, or, as we say, every tick of the clock. But pride, in the true sense is a great virtue. I say, get it, and stick to it.

Then, of course you, most of you – I would have hoped all of you – have read J M Barrie's famous rectoral address at St Andrew's University – a remarkable speech which ought to be read by every thoughtful person at least once a year.

The theme of Barrie's address was courage. I had the great privilege, years afterwards, of walking up and down in a garden in the west of England for an hour with J M Barrie discussing this speech, and how he had gone about making it.

His theme was courage, the lovely virtue as he called it, the virtue without which other virtues can be broken into the dust.

Now we can think about courage in many ways. The rarest form of courage, I think, in the world, is moral courage. The courage that a man has when he is prepared to form his view of the truth and to pursue it, when he is not running around the corner every five minutes to say, "Is this going to be popular?" Not like the traditional old politician of fiction who said, "Find out what the people want, and that is my policy."

Courage is very important, all important. But of course it is no use becoming addicted to sticking to your own view unless you have taken all the preliminary steps to do your own best to see that it is the right view. Courage without work, courage without thought, courage without judgement will not be worth so much. It might ultimately amount to mere obstinacy. But properly considered and properly set, it is one of the great virtues.

There are two things – I could talk about a dozen – which perhaps are not very much respected nowadays. They are at the other end of the scale, I grant you.

One is to have good manners, courtesy. One becomes dejected occasionally at the decline in good manners. Why is it thought by so many people that to be strong, you must be rude? That to demonstrate that you have a mind of your own you must engage in the most brutal discourtesy to other people? "Manners maketh man" is one of the oldest of the old school mottos.[36] And although, of course, it goes deep into the character of the boy, and of the man, it also has its superficial aspect, the courtesy which human beings owe, one to the other.

Life becomes a rough, tough thing; public life is a rough, tough life. There are many aspects in the world which appear superficially to be rough and tough, in which victory goes to the strongest, and the most enduring. No man was ever less strong, no man was ever less tough by treating with courtesy what other people think or say, or do.

Since everybody has been here now for some time I just want to mention my fourth which you will think quite absurd, I'm sure. Because this is not one of the great virtues at all. This is something that I think is gravely misunderstood. I'm all in favour of boys when they are at school learning to speak their own language with respect and with justice.

I'm staggered, ladies and gentlemen, at the number of times I can listen to a man talking, not getting up and making a speech, but just talking, conversationally, turns out to have two or three degrees – but no degree at all in the English language! Speaking in a shoddy, snuffling fashion, murdering the King's English – or the Queen's English as I suppose it is now. This is no good. This is not a sign of intelligence. It is a sign of quite the opposite.

I don't know enough about Cranbrook to know to what extent you are an exception to a deplorable rule, but I'm bound to tell you quite frankly that in my experience the average Girls' school is more concerned at speech than the average Boys' school.

It is very easy, you know, when you are a boy at school to disregard that, because if a boy at school finds himself the exception in a little

---

36 The maxim first appeared in the *Vulgaria,* a Latin grammar textbook published by the Tudor-era Headmaster of Eton, William Homan (c1440-1535).

group, and has been in the habit of speaking his language with precision and correctness, and pleasantly, somebody may say that he is a bit "sissy"; somebody imitates him, you know.

I say don't worry about that. This English language of ours – I speak with the valour of partial ignorance – is one of the greatest and most flexible tongues that God ever put into the mind and mouth of man to speak. It is a marvellous language. (Applause)

It has produced more poetry, I venture to say, of the highest order than any other language in the history of man. It is a beautiful, adjustable, flexible language with, contained inside itself, all the subtleties in the world. And, like all other great languages, those who know it is best, will speak it most simply.

Don't fall into the error of thinking it is a proof of education to use long words with Latin endings. (Laughter) The people I have known who loved long words most, who were polysyllabic marvels, were those who understood the language least.

The great object of knowing your own language is to speak with justice and weight and simplicity. You read a speech by Winston Churchill, you go back and read a speech by the Younger Pitt 100 years before, and you will find the lovely simplicity of language.

Because after all, it is only a man who is a master of his language who can eliminate these rather foolish long words and settle for that simple, direct speech which is the ultimate proof of scholarship and of knowledge of the language.

Now I say that to the boys because I think this is tremendously important, that we should have in our own country – don't worry about other people's arguments over whether so-and-so has an accent of the home counties or whether he's got an English or Somerset accent, or Victorian accent – which of course is very good (Laughter) – or a Sydney accent, which has its moments. (Laughter) Don't worry about that.

What we ought to worry about is the quality, the justice, the conciseness, the effect of the words you use.

Now, Sir, I've given you a mixed grill really: two very great virtues at the beginning; a third, a considerable virtue; and the fourth you may not think a virtue at all. But since speech is the universal means of communication, and since in these days no man can lead in anything unless he can communicate his ideas to other people, never neglect speech. In the long run it is one of the great instruments that you will have to use all your life.

Now that is all I want to say. There have been people standing up around the back, including, I say with regret, as a Presbyterian, the Dean of Sydney. Normally I don't mind a Church of England fellow standing up and listening to me. But I do feel that I have made it a little bit hot this afternoon, both literally and otherwise.

I'm delighted to be here. On the last two occasions I couldn't be here for reasons that were beyond my control. On this occasion I made up my mind that I must be here whatever came or went. It only just happened because Parliament sat a week longer than anybody supposed, and it sat up till 4 o'clock on Friday morning. But this being Saturday, I've arrived, I have spoken, I apologise – but I'm delighted. (Applause)

INDEX

ACKNOWLEDGEMENTS

I wish to acknowledge the following people for their invaluable assistance in the composition of this volume, *Menzies: The Forgotten Speeches*.

First, I wish to recognise my supervisor and Executive Director of the Menzies Research Centre (MRC), Nick Cater, for providing me with the inspiration to embark on the timely project of researching and publishing a series of noteworthy speeches by Australia's longest serving Prime Minister. With this publication brought to fruition, these "forgotten speeches" of Sir Robert Menzies can be once again read and remembered by a new generation. Nick's encouragement and guidance throughout this project has been invaluable and much appreciated.

I would also like to thank my wonderful colleagues at the MRC, Kay Gilchrist and Michelle Ko for their encouragement and abiding interest in this publication.

In the collation of the speeches and other primary source materials for this volume, I also give thanks to the library staff from the National Library of Australia for their professional assistance in navigating the labyrinth of documents within the Menzies collection.

With the joy of personally knowing a living link to Sir Robert himself, I am grateful for the friendship and encouragement of Heather Henderson (née Menzies) who has expressed her great interest and support for this project.

I am very grateful to Professor Geoffrey Blainey AC for his Foreword. Written by a fellow Menzies admirer and one of Australia's pre-eminent historians and public intellectuals, this foreword provides a fitting adornment to the volume.

In bringing this volume to print, I am grateful to Dr Anthony Cappello and the team at Connor Court for overseeing the process of publication with their professionalism and expertise. I would also like to thank Prof John Nethercote for his valuable proofreading of the final manuscript.

I conclude by offering my profound appreciation to my family and friends who have supported me through this endeavour with their love, good humour, interest and encouragement.

David Furse-Roberts
Canberra
January 2017